NEW DIRECTIONS IN THEATRE

General Editor   JULIAN HILTON

NEW DIRECTIONS IN THEATRE

Published titles

FEMINISM AND THEATRE
Sue-Ellen Case

IMPROVISATION IN DRAMA
Anthony Frost and Ralph Yarrow

PERFORMANCE
Julian Hilton

TRANSPOSING DRAMA
Egil Törnqvist

Forthcoming titles

GENDER AND THEATRE
Susan Bassnett

NEW DIRECTIONS IN THEATRE
Julian Hilton (*editor*)

POSTMODERNISM AND PERFORMANCE
Nick Kaye

REPRESENTATION AND THE ACTOR
Gerry McCarthy

SEMIOTICS OF THE DRAMATIC TEXT
Susan Melrose

Transposing Drama

Studies in Representation

EGIL TÖRNQVIST

MACMILLAN

First edition 1991

Published by
MACMILLAN EDUCATION LTD
Houndmills, Basingstoke, Hampshire RG21 2XS
and London
Companies and representatives
throughout the world

Typeset by Wessex Typesetters
(Division of The Eastern Press Ltd)
Frome, Somerset

Printed in Hong Kong

British Library Cataloguing in Publication Data
Törnqvist, Egil
Transposing drama: studies in representation.
1. Drama in European languages. Translation
I. Title   II. Series
809.2
ISBN 0–333–44062–5 (hc)
ISBN 0–333–44063–3 (pbk)

Contents

To Kerstin

General Editor's Preface

In the past ten years, Theatre Studies has experienced remarkable international growth, students seeing in its marriage of the practical and the intellectual a creative and rewarding discipline. Some countries are now opening school and degree programmes in Theatre Studies for the first time; others are having to accommodate to the fact that a popular subject attracting large numbers of highly motivated students has to be given greater attention than hitherto. The professional theatre itself is changing, as graduates of degree and diploma programmes make their way through the 'fringe' into established theatre companies, film and television.

Two changes in attitudes have occurred as a result: first, that the relationship between teachers and practitioners has significantly improved, not least because many more people now have experience of both; secondly, that the widespread academic suspicion about theatre as a subject for study has at least been squarely faced, if not fully discredited. Yet there is still much to be done to translate the practical and educational achievements of the past decade into coherent theory, and this series is intended as a contribution to that task. Its contributors are chosen for their combination of professional and didactic skills, and are drawn from a wide range of countries, languages and styles in order to give some impression of the subject in its international perspective.

This series offers no single programme or ideology; yet all its authors have in common the sense of being in a period of transition and debate out of which the theory and practice of theatre cannot but emerge in a new form.

University of East Anglia   JULIAN HILTON

Acknowledgements

Without the assistance of several persons and institutions, this book, relying as much on audiovisual as on published material, could not have been written. For invaluable help in this area I wish to thank the staff of the National Archive of Recorded Sound and Moving Images in Stockholm, the Audiovisual Centres at the University of East Anglia and the University of Amsterdam, the Netherlands Theatre Institute in Amsterdam, Swedish Radio and Television, the Audiovisual Division of the Gothenburg University Library, and the Library of the Royal Dramatic Theatre in Stockholm.

I am obliged to colleagues and students at the University of Amsterdam for stimulating discussions, and to the staff members of the Skandinavisch Seminarium for bearing with me at times when I have been dealing more with media than with Scandinavia.

In addition to the general editor of this series, Professor Julian Hilton, whose suggestions have been very helpful, one person, already mentioned, has offered very inspiring and constructive criticism. I should also like to thank Graham Eyre for his very helpful editorial work on the typescript.

E. T.

Abbreviations

Stage/screen areas

L	left
R	right
C	centre
BG	background
FG	foreground

Shots

ELO	extreme long shot (human figure very small)
LS	long shot (human figure nearly height of screen)
MS	medium shot (human figure from waist up)
MCU	medium close-up (human figure from chest up)
CU	close-up (head from neck up)
ECU	extreme close-up (part of head)

Angles

HA	high angle (looking down)
LA	low angle (looking up)

Chapter 1

Textual, Aural, Audiovisual

Reading a play is almost like reading a musical score: it is difficult, and I do not know many who can do it, although a lot of people say they can. The very arrangement of the text, where the eyes have to wander from the name of the speaker to his speech, demands close attention; the seemingly uninteresting exposition has to be got through and carefully recorded in one's memory, since it contains the warp, by means of which the whole weaving is set up. The action noted within the parentheses delays and distracts one, too. Even to this day when I read Shakespeare I have to pencil in notes to keep the characters and particularly the numerous minor speaking characters straight, and I have to go back constantly to the list of characters and to . . . the first act to take a look at what the characters said then. A person has to read a play at least twice to have it clearly in mind . . . .   (Strindberg[1])

Reading a play may be difficult – even for playwrights. Which does not mean that *watching* a play is easy. Watching a play is in many respects more difficult for the recipient than reading it, since the spectator is faced with such a richness of *simultaneous* impressions that he is only able to grasp part of what he sees and hears. In live performance 'the [spectator's] eye will wander' – to paraphrase Strindberg – from the speaker to the listener(s) and the scenery or properties, and perhaps even to the audience. The same is true for television and film productions, where many shots will contain a wealth of visual and aural information. Radio drama elicits a similar response, since the lack of visual information means that the listener must mobilise his imagination and become a very active co-operator in the performance.

Text and performance

What then is the difference, more precisely, between experiencing a drama as text and experiencing it as performance? The distinction between the *drama text*, experienced by a reader, and the *performance text*, experienced by a spectator (or listener), is the subject of this work.[2]

There is still a tendency in literary criticism to regard the drama text as sacrosanct and hence to disapprove of any significant deviation from it in performance. As a counter-reaction to this, theatre practitioners tend to go to the other extreme and declare the drama text to be one element of many in the performance. This is certainly true, but on the other hand the drama text is unique in that it is the only common denominator for all productions of the play in question. Moreover, as Anne Ubersfeld puts it, 'the performance is something instantaneous, perishable; only the text is perdurable'.[3]

Since drama to the reader is textual, while performance to the spectator is audiovisual, they represent different semiotic systems. While much is added to the drama text in any performance, the polysemic range of the dramatic dialogue becomes narrower in performance simply by being spoken. As readers, we may think of numerous ways of phrasing a speech. As spectators we partake of one of these ways, chosen by the actor. In another sense, however, the performance text has a much wider polysemic range than the drama text, by virtue of its constant interaction between verbal and non-verbal elements.

Despite these differences, there is obviously a considerable overlap between the two types of text. This explains why we can partake of two radically different productions – even within different media or in different languages – and yet recognise that we are confronted with the same underlying play text. With Ubersfeld,[4] we may graphically indicate the relationship between drama text (T) and performance text (P) as follows:

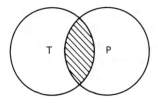

Naturally, the central, overlapping area will vary a great deal from one performance to another. And, as Ubersfeld points out,[5] a comparison between 'the different types of text–performance relationships' might yield interesting results.

When it comes to an examination of how a drama has been presented in different media, such a comparison seems, in fact, unavoidable, since the drama text, as already mentioned, is the only thing that provides a *tertium quid*, by means of which different productions can be compared with one another.

This does not, of course, mean that the drama text need be regarded as sacrosanct. When, in the following chapters, one production is found to be more faithful to the original text than another, this should be seen as a factual observation, in line with the distinction between literal and free translation, not as a statement of quality. Obviously, both faithful and less faithful productions may be either good or bad.

The old controversy about whether the drama text or the performance text should have priority can best be settled simply by recognising that a play has a double or hybrid existence. On the one hand, readers of drama must admit that plays are usually written to be performed. On the other, playgoers must acknowledge that different productions of the same play are based on the same text. Besides, whenever we complain that a play has been misrepresented in performance, we certain imply 'that a play is *there* and has its integrity before the interpreters touch it'.[6]

Far from being an academic question, the controversy mirrors two different attitudes to the relationship between text and performance, which have far-reaching practical consequences. Defenders of the priority of the drama text tend to protest against significant changes of it in the performance text, arguing that such changes can only spoil what has been designed as an autonomous work, in which the various parts interrelate. Defenders of the priority of the performance text argue that, since the play text is merely a blueprint and since the transposition from book to stage means a transference from one semiotic system to another, the difference is so great that the performance text can better be considered an autonomous work. Hence, the director must be allowed to make whatever changes in the drama text he thinks fit. In support of this latter view, defenders of the performance text also point out (i) that old plays need to be updated or the audience will not respond, and (ii) that directors should not compromise with their vision.

This is not the place to discuss at any length a dispute that has gone on for centuries and will no doubt continue as long as there are playwrights and directors, readers and spectators. Let us simply note that this discussion is today rather different from the one, say, fifty years ago, since 'the advent of film and television has shifted the base of our culture from a textual to an audio-visual one'.[7] With the arrival of new media this old discussion about priority has put the defenders of the drama text in a difficult position. After all, while it could earlier be maintained that a play should be presented complete on the stage, we now know that adapting a play for radio, television or film usually entails shortening the printed text considerably.

Uncompromising defenders of the play text might dismiss such versions simply on intentional grounds. Like those who claim that Bach's *Goldberg Variations* should be played on a harpsichord, for which they were written, and not on a piano, defenders of the play text might argue that plays written for the stage should exclusively be done there. Even those who do not share this historicist view may still find that, just as we do not shorten Bach's compositions, so we should leave those of competent dramatists intact.

Since, however, the majority of plays are performed in an abridged form – particularly on radio and television and, especially, in the cinema – this argument has been considerably undermined by stark reality. To defenders of the performance text it appears anachronistic. Their answer would be: had artist X (composer, playwright) been familiar with the new instrument (piano, television), he would have composed for it or adjusted his own composition to suit the new medium.

Instead of pursuing this speculation on the relationship between past, present and future, let us pinpoint the general differences between the drama text and the performance text (the latter term used as inclusive of stage, radio, TV and film productions):

1 While there is usually only one drama text, the number of performances is potentially infinite.
2 While the drama text is experienced directly by a reader, it is experienced indirectly by a spectator, the performance text serving as intermediary.
3 While the drama text is experienced verbally (by means of linguistic signs), the performance text is experienced audiovisually (or aurally).
4 While the drama text can be experienced as we like it—in small or big portions, forwards or backwards—we experience the performance text as a fixed linear continuum.
5 While the drama text is open—each prop, character, speech can be imagined in many ways—the performance text is closed: it selects *one* type of prop, specifies *one* type of character, settles for *one* kind of diction.
6 While the drama text is consecutive in the sense that at every instance attention is paid only to a few of the on-stage characters (usually the speaking parts), the performance text reveals a complex pattern of simultaneity.[8] Thus, while silent characters tend to be absent to the recipient of the drama text, they are visually present to the recipient of the performance text.

Irrespective of whether a play is experienced by a reader or a spectator, it is *received*: we are concerned, therefore, with either a *recipient* or a *re-recipient* of a play – the latter category knowing how the play will continue and how it will end. Re-recipients will necessarily experience various elements differently from those who partake of the play for the first time. Generally speaking, what Peter Pütz calls *what-tension* (what will happen?) will prevail for the recipients, while *how-tension* (how will it happen?) will prevail for the re-recipients.[9]

Fundamental for all the dramatic/theatrical modes is the distinction between *story* (what is presented) on the one hand and *plot* or *discourse* (how it is presented) on the other. Accordingly, we may distinguish between *story time* (the chronological time of the text/performance) and *discourse time* (the time as presented in the text or the performance).[10] The story time may be shorter, longer or the same as the discourse time. We may further distinguish between *scenic* (visualised) time and *pre-scenic/post-scenic* (non-visualised) time, and between *reading, stage, screen* and *air* time, the time it takes to read, watch or listen to a play/performance. Spatially, *scenic* (visualised) action may be set off against *off-scenic* action, an umbrella term for *off-stage* (theatre), *off-screen* (TV and film) and *off-air* (radio) events.

A matter of great importance is the relationship between verbal and non-verbal information, between dialogue on the one hand and stage- and acting-directions on the other. As Manfred Pfister has shown, there are here three possibilities: (i) *identity*, (ii) *complement*, and (iii) *discrepancy*.[11] A character may do what he says he is doing – a rare, because redundant, situation. He may do something in addition to what he says; this is the usual case. Or he may do quite the opposite of what he says – as at the end of *Waiting for Godot*, where the characters decide to 'go' and yet '*do not move*'. The discrepancy, which was probably introduced in drama texts by the absurdists, has now become standard fare in performance texts. Time and again actors nowadays play against the manifest version of the drama text in an endeavour to bring out (what they take to be) the latent text or *subtext*. Love scenes are turned into scenes of hatred and vice versa, so much so that we may here speak of a cliché characteristic of our psychotherapeutic era.

Transposing drama

What happens when a play is transposed from one medium or mode of presentation to another? What occurs when a drama, intended for readers of one language, is transposed (translated) into another language? Or when a play, composed for the stage, is transposed into a radio play, a TV play or a film? To what extent do differences between these various modes influence the transpositions? And to what extent do the interpretations of directors, responsible for the various productions – the directorial vision – play a part?

Despite the vast number of books that are being published about the mass media, despite the fact that radio plays, not to speak of TV plays, attract an audience which far outnumbers those of the hits on the London, Paris or New York stage, and despite the fact that the bulk of plays presented on radio and television are still transposed stage plays, remarkably little attention has been paid to the questions I have just posed.[12]

What we loosely refer to as radio plays, teleplays and films fall into two distinct categories: (i) texts written especially for these media, and (ii) texts transposed from other modes of presentation. Within category (ii) we may further distinguish between those transformations which are based on plays and those which are based on novels.[13] The latter do not concern us here.

The purpose of this book is to examine what happens when a drama is transposed (1) from one language to another, and (2) from one medium (drama text) to another (performance text). The study of transposition may be seen as a modern offshoot of an old stem: comparative literature. Just as the comparison of, say, Shakespeare's *Macbeth* to its historical or literary sources is undertaken primarily in order to illuminate the Shakespearian text, so the comparison of a film version of *Macbeth* to the original text will be undertaken chiefly in order to throw light on the transposed version. But the comparison certainly works both ways. Much more than 'pure' radio, TV or film drama, transposed versions invite comparison with the 'source texts'. They thus provide excellent material for an examination of media differences.

The verb *transpose* and its corresponding noun *transposition* are here used as umbrella terms for the two types of systematic shifts just mentioned. The terms also cover other types of shifts, such as the one (3) from draft to final version (rewriting) and the one (4) from original text to authorised or revised text (editing). These last-mentioned types, which are not only intertextual but also intralingual, will be dealt with only in passing, (3) in connection with Ibsen, (4) in connection with Shakespeare. In line with common usage, I shall refer to type (1) as *translation*, whereas I shall call type (2) *transformation*; the latter term will thus be used in a technical sense, as meaning 'transposing a play from a verbal semiotic system to an aural, visual or audiovisual one'; it does not necessarily imply that major textual changes have been undertaken. Transposing drama thus includes the following activities:

transposing from draft to final text (rewriting);
transposing from original to authorised text (editing);
transposing from source text to target text (translating);
transposing from one medium to another (transforming).

The last category, be it noted, includes the normal transposition 'drama text – stage performance'. In our terminology every production of a play is a transformation. There are faithful and less faithful transformations – just as there are literal and free translations. When a translation/transformation involves significant voluntary deviations from the source text, I shall, in conformance with common usage, resort to the term *adaptation*.

A simple example, borrowed from Erika Fischer-Lichte,[14] may help to clarify the nature of translating and transforming. Let us suppose that a stage-direction in a play reads, *It begins to rain*. To the reader this is a factual piece of information, which he can 'translate' in various ways in his imagination. One reader may be mostly aware of the linguistic aspect and link the *word* 'rain' with other (similar) words in the play text. (A reader of a target text may well relate the corresponding word – the French *pluie*, for example – to other words than those picked by the reader of the source text.) Another reader may be more aware of the visual aspect of the rain, while a third will be sensitive to the aural one. A fourth may think of the effect of the rain – the fact that you get wet.

Once the rain is transposed to an exclusively aural medium (radio) or to an audiovisual one (stage, TV, film), the rain is concretised in one way or another. Thus in a radio version we expect the sound of falling raindrops or, possibly, someone saying 'It's raining.' In the three audiovisual media we have, in addition, other possibilities. The rain can be visualised directly in the form of falling drops or indirectly by way of a change of lighting. A character can enter with a wet coat or with a newspaper above his head. He can fold an umbrella when entering the front door or put out an umbrella before disappearing through it. In the stylised, pantomimic oriental theatre a simple gesture might be enough.

We note that in some of these cases the textual stage-direction remains a *stage-direction* (i.e. referring to scenery and props) also in its transposed form, while in other cases it becomes an *acting-direction* (i.e. referring to the *dramatis personae*) or a verbalised reference; in the latter case we deal with an example of *transcodification*.[15] The question is now: what makes a director choose one way of presenting the rain rather than another? Clearly, a number of determining factors are here involved, such as (i) the chosen medium (applies especially to radio); (ii) the presentational style (illusionistic versus non-illusionistic theatre); (iii) directorial preferences (the contextual function of the rain, the significance ascribed to it); (iv) technical possibilities of realisation (this may be closely related to the choice of medium; it is, for example, much easier to visualise rain in a TV or film version than in a stage version).

Before tackling the actual subject, a brief characterisation of the examined presentational modes seems appropriate.

The drama text

Some fifty years ago Roman Ingarden launched his important distinction, with regard to drama, between *Haupttext* (primary text) and *Nebentext* (secondary text).[16] By *primary text* Ingarden means everything in a play that is verbalised in the performance text, i.e. the dialogue; by *secondary text* that which is verbalised only in the drama text, i.e. the stage- and acting-directions.

To the reader, the secondary text usually covers a fairly small amount of the total play text; Bernard Shaw and Eugene O'Neill are the exceptions to the rule. To the spectator, the situation is the reverse. In Fischer-Lichte's classification scheme, the verbalised (spoken) elements in the performance text constitute merely one semiotic code out of a total of fourteen.[17] The reader's primary text here, in fact, becomes the spectator's 'secondary' one; in this sense the term 'secondary text' may seem a misnomer. But this terminological inaccuracy is easily outbalanced by the need to retain the same terms for related phenomena, so as to make drama text and performance text comparable.

Whereas to Ingarden the secondary text seems to comprise primarily the stage- and acting-directions – he does not distinguish between the two – I shall here use this term in a wider sense, as inclusive not only of this category but of many others as well. In this way the term will comprise everything in a drama text that is not enunciated on the stage. In this wider sense, the secondary text comprises the following:

1 Name of author/pseudonym.
2 Year and place of publication.
3 Play title.
4 Subtitle/genre indication.
5 Motto.
6 Preface/postscript.
7 List of *dramatis personae*.
8 Divisional markers (act, scene, etc.).
9 Cue designations.
10 Indication of historical and/or geographical setting.
11 Stage-directions.
12 Acting-directions.

Only in the second half of this list do we deal with verbal signs that in the performance text are transposed into visual – and possibly also aural – signs. The divisions between acts/scenes (8) may be marked by the curtain, a blackout or lighting; cue designations (9) are marked by a change of speaker.

Since categories 1–7 would appear, if at all, only in the theatre programme, it is meaningful to distinguish between four kinds of recipients: (i) the reader; (ii) the spectator with a theatre programme (or some other kind of prior knowledge about the play text); (iii) the spectator without a theatre programme or prior knowledge; (iv) the listener.

The distinction between primary text and secondary text has a certain affinity to the one between author- and character-related point of view in narrative texts. The secondary text would then correspond to the objective, omniscient author–narrator, the primary text to the subjective *dramatis personae*. This means that the secondary text, unlike the primary one, is in principle reliable.

Patrice Pavis has expressed the opinion that, while the dialogue of a play is more or less obligatory for a director, the stage- and acting-directions are merely advisory, comparable to a recipe for baking a cake. 'As with the cake, some will prefer to scrupulously follow the recipe and others will add a "pinch of salt" or will substitute their own culinary technique.'[18]

It is true, of course, that a literal adherence to the playwright's stage- and acting-directions would normally be a sign of the director's lack of imagination and as such something to be blamed rather than praised. On the other hand, Pavis's discriminating view of the stage- and acting-directions in a drama text is in several ways problematic. First, it goes against the idea that primary and secondary texts are intimately interwoven and that changing the latter inevitably means that a new and perhaps less meaningful relationship is established. Second, it does not take account of the fact that precisely the non-verbal elements in many modern plays are of the greatest significance. Third, it is a sweeping generalisation, disregarding the fact that some stage- and acting-directions are of vital importance, whereas others are merely ad libs. To mention but one example: in Ibsen's *A Doll's House*, the '*piano*' in the Helmer living-room can hardly be left out, since it is needed for the tarantella, which in turn is central to the drama; we can thus assume that it will figure in almost every production of the play. The '*small bookcase*', by contrast, can easily be dispensed with, since its significance in the play is merely peripheral.

Drama in translation

The double status of drama as verbal text (for the reader) and audiovisual experience (for the spectator) means that the translator of plays, unlike someone translating novels or poetry, deals not only with two languages, but also with two audiences. Under such circumstances, the central question for him must be: how can the needs of *both* receptor groups (readers/spectators) be combined with a relatively faithful rendering of the source text?

Considered as a text for a *reader*, a play does not fundamentally differ from a novel. Hence the *textual* translation of a drama is in principle comparable to the rendering of any piece of fiction in another language. Considered as a score for a production, on the other hand, a play radically differs from a novel. Hence the translation intended for the *spectator* – the *audiovisual* translation, so to speak – has to take very special problems into account. In illusionistic (realistic) drama, where verisimilitude plays an important role, these problems are especially relevant.

Fidelity to the original text is certainly important. But since play translations are usually undertaken with a production in mind, it is equally important that the lines in translation should be idiomatic, actable and meaningfully related to the visual environment (the stage-directions). The target text must also be easy to grasp, since in the theatre we have little time to ponder. Generally speaking the target language plays a more important role in drama translations than in translations of novels. It is obvious that the criteria just mentioned compete with one another to a certain extent and that the balance between them must be settled from case to case.

Ethnic differences present a problem to all translators, but, whereas the reader of a play can be helped out of his ignorance by an informative 'translator's note', the spectator is at a loss, unless the translator or, preferably, the director somehow manages to incorporate the needed information in the performance.

Almost completely disregarded by translation theoreticians is the question of whether the subtext that can be deduced from the source text can also be deduced from the target texts.[19] Insensitivity to the subtext is presumably a major reason why many 'correct' drama translations seem so devoid of tension, of life.

While theatre critics devote much attention to such things as direction, stage design and acting, they tend to say very little about translation. This is of course especially true when they are confronted with a play translated from a minor or exotic language. Like most spectators, they must then simply assume that the translation is a faithful rendering of the original. This is another way of saying that those who translate from such languages find themselves in a situation different from that of translators from English, French and German. Unlike the latter, they can take liberties with the text without being found out. In this sense, an Ibsen or a Strindberg is more vulnerable than a Shakespeare, a Racine or a Schiller.

Stage drama

The chief characteristic of stage performance is that, unlike other modes of presentation discussed in this book, it is *live*. This has several consequences.

1   Unlike the situation in the other modes, where communication is one-way, the actors in a stage performance may respond to reactions from the audience. There is, in other words, two-way communication. The actors receive feedback.

2   Like a visit to the cinema, but to an even greater extent, a theatre visit is a social event: the reactions are those of a mass audience, and in the interval(s) – usually lacking in the cinema –

the theatregoers can exchange views on the performance.
3 Unlike performances in the other modes, every stage performance is unique, unrepeatable.
4 Unlike performances in the other modes, a stage performance
is in part determined by the spatial facilities available at the
time of staging. Does the theatre have an end stage, a thrust
stage or an arena stage? How is the audience located in relation
to the actors?[20] How large are the stage and the auditorium?
5 The distance from stage to auditorium necessitates larger-than-
life kinesics (mimicry, gestures) and paralinguistics (diction).
The spatial limitation necessitates abundant use of proxemics
(regrouping of characters).
6 Owing to its plurimedial and unrepeatable nature, it is
extremely difficult to notate a stage performance in a satisfac-
tory way.

Apart from the reasons mentioned in this list, stage performances
will differ from one another for innumerable other reasons, most
of which will apply also to the other modes. Important in this
respect are such things as the time and place of the performance,
the attitude of the authorities (censorship), the policy of the theatre
company, the interpretation of the director, the skill of the stage-
designer, the ability of the cast, the co-operative spirit of the
production team.

'No matter how detailed the instructions a playwright may give,'
Stanley Wells notes, 'he remains a participant in an essentially
collaborative act. The hints that he gives have to be transmitted
to the audience by people other than himself.'[21] And these people,
we may add, will even within one and the same production be of
varying quality: as the post-performance statement may run, '*She*
[the actress] was good but I didn't care much for *him* [the actor]' –
a statement that is meaningless when applied to the textual
characters. The fact that the performed drama, unlike the drama
text, is a *collective* undertaking by people skilled in different areas –
acting, directing, stage-design, costumes, lighting, sound-effects,
music, choreography, and so on – makes it unusually complex and
(if we except opera) uniquely plurimedial.

Radio drama

Martin Esslin has drawn attention to the similarity between reading a play and listening to a radio play:

> by having to provide the visual component, which is undeniably present in any true dramatic experience transmitted by radio, [the listener] is an active collaborator with the producer. In this respect he is in exactly the same position as the reader of a book who has to imagine the action in his mind's eye. The difference, however, is that the voices, music, and sounds of the radio play are of a far greater immediacy, have an infinitely more powerful emotional and sensuous impact in themselves, than the abstract symbols of print on the page.[22]

Characteristic of radio drama is the relatively short playing-time; few plays exceed an hour and a half. Transforming stage plays into radio plays therefore usually entails a considerable shortening of the text. It also means that very long plays are not considered suitable for radio presentation.

Act and scene division in radio drama is usually less explicit than in other presentational forms. Changes of time and place, which may be indicated by musical interludes, often occur rapidly and almost imperceptibly.

Without access to the visual code, the listener will often find it difficult to keep track of the various characters and to distinguish their voices from one another. To meet these problems, radio favours plays with few roles, such as duologues. In plays with a long list of *dramatis personae*, minor characters may be left out. A special problem is created by silent characters; usually either they or their speaking partners are given some lines to make the listener aware of their presence.

The scenery that is physically present on the stage must somehow be made mentally present for the listener, so that he becomes familiar with the environment surrounding the characters. This can be done (i) via a narrator, or (ii) by incorporating the stage directions in the dialogue – much as in Elizabethan drama. Sound-effects can also help to provide an equivalent of the cinematic establishing-shot.

Radio drama is an intimate form of drama. Deprived of any

visual correlative, the listener, like a blind person, will be very sensitive to aural nuance. The actor close to the microphone may be compared to the actor close to the camera in a TV or film production. The listener constantly partakes, so to speak, of aural close-ups.

One of the great assets of radio drama is that there is a free flow between outward and inward events, with a marked emphasis on the latter. Radio plays, like many novels, favour inner processes; we learn more about what the characters are thinking and feeling than about what they are doing. With the development of modern editing-techniques inner conflicts can be dramatised by, for example, having the actors record one part of their speech in one tone of voice, another in a different one. In these areas a radio performance provides more possibilities than a stage production.

The total reliance on an aural code favours the adaptation of ideological drama. In recognition of this, radio drama has some-times been called the 'drama of the mind'. Even more it favours the adaptation of poetical drama; in this area the radio play may be said to have mapped out an area of its own.

Sound-effects naturally play an important part in radio drama. These must be easy to decode by the listener; many sounds resemble one another too much to be really useful. A sound may also be undecipherable at one point and fully intelligible at another; many sound-effects 'come to dramatic life *after* the listener has been *told* what they represent'.[23] Next to the ordinary objective sounds, radio drama frequently employs subjective ones, mirroring the way a character experiences a sound. 'If we were ending a play with the sound of an iron door clanging shut on a young man who has been condemned to life imprisonment,' William Ash writes, 'no ordinary spot effect of a closing door would work. What is required is a sound like the slamming shut of the gates of Paradise behind our guilty first parents reverberating on and on down the ages.'[24] Although this may result in a rather melodramatic sound-effect, Ash's example certainly draws attention to the phenomenon of subjective sound as an important ingredient in radio drama.

Television drama

Like radio drama, but unlike stage and film presentations, TV plays are experienced in a domestic environment in relative privacy. In most discussions of television the audience, John Fiske and John Hartley point out, 'is characterized . . . either as the individual viewer or as the many millions of viewers for any one programme. But the audience normally experiences *itself* in neither of these ways.' It experiences itself as 'part of a family audience'.[25]

Like radio drama, TV drama is 'embedded in a continuous flow of largely non-fictional items'.[26] As a result, the recipient runs the risk of being more easily distracted – the phone may ring; the preceding programme may still be on his mind – than his counterpart in the theatre or in the cinema.

Of all the different presentational modes, the TV play is the most difficult to characterise – partly because it holds a somewhat unclear position between theatre and film, partly because the medium has developed so rapidly that the term *television play* (or *teleplay*), as the Waldmanns have clarified,[27] in fact covers four different types: (i) a pure documentation of a stage performance, (ii) a pseudo-cinematic adaptation of a play recorded in an electronic studio, (iii) a cinematic adaptation with interior and exterior scenes, and (iv) a purely non-realistic electronic production. Naturally, combinations of these four types may also occur.

The rapidity of development has meant that 'yesterday's confident assertions about what is and what is not televisual have turned out to be merely interim statements'.[28] Consider, for example, pronouncements such as the following:

Scenes between twos and threes are what television wants: quiet, intimate stuff which the camera can get right into. Five people on the set for any length of time is a producer's headache, meaning constant regrouping and cutting from shot to shot in order to show viewers what the characters look like in close-up.[29]

The isolated close-up of some object, or subtlety of facial expression which would look overdone if magnified on a cinema screen, or would be lost in a welter of other detail if shown there in a more reasonable size, becomes perfectly natural on television.[30]

Statements such as these remind one, by analogy, of the obsession with sound-effects in the early days of radio or of the stubborn defence of silent or black-and-white film in the face of sound and colour – all symptoms of the need of a new medium to map out its own territory.

While TV plays were formerly shot live in a studio – a situation approaching that of a stage performance – they are now almost always taped and edited: that is, produced in a manner closer to that of a cinema film. It is, then, no wonder if earlier statements about what is televisual no longer, or at least only partly, apply.

Certain differences between TV and cinema drama are undeniable. Thus the visual quality of cinema film is still better than that of film on television. Environmental descriptions remain more suited to the large screen than to the small one, which favours 'drawing-room shots' (medium to close-up). The dialogue of the original text is left more intact in teleplays than in versions for cinema.

But the technical variations within one and the same medium are considerable and each medium is constantly subject to new developments which may affect the intermedial relationship.

In addition, there are differences in transmission policy, Thus, when dealing with translations or target texts, some countries use subtitles, i.e. add a visible target text to the aural source dialogue, whereas others prefer to dub the dialogue, i.e. replace the source voices by target ones. In the Netherlands it is common to have a break in the middle of a film to promote the sale of chocolate and ice cream, a practice similar to the commercial breaks at strategic moments in British and American TV programmes.

Film drama

While TV adaptations will tend to retain both the stage area and the dialogue, as suggested by the playwright, cinema versions will tend to show more of the surrounding environment and at the same time transpose much of the dialogue into visual images.

Yet, as the points below demonstrate, the two media have much in common.

1   The film *shot* is the basic formal unit. By means of the shot
    the film-maker decides how the filmic image is framed, from
    what distance and angle it is photographed and how long the
    image lasts.
2   The combination of shots is of paramount importance. This
    can be studied graphically (relationship with regard to shape
    and colour), rhythmically, spatially and temporally. The funda-
    mental question is: are the shots *continuous* (similar) or
    discontinuous (dissimilar)?
3   Concerning the sound, we may ask whether it is faithful or
    not to its perceived source, whether it belongs naturally
    (realistically) to the story (*diegetic sound*) or is added to it
    (*non-diegetic sound*), e.g. to create atmosphere; whether it is
    on screen or off screen; and whether it occurs simultaneously
    with, before or after the filmed events.
4   Corresponding roughly to the theatrical term *mise-en-scène*,
    the filmic *mise-en-scène* comprises 'all the elements placed in
    front of the camera to be photographed: the settings and props,
    lighting, costumes and make-up, and figure behavior'. To a
    much greater extent than in a stage production, the *mise-en-
    scène* in a film 'is patterned in space and time to attract and
    guide the viewer's attention . . . and to create suspense or
    surprise'.[31]

Historically, film drama falls into three different categories: (i)
silent + black-and-white, (ii) sound + black-and-white, and (iii)
sound + colour. This triad calls for further distinctive descriptions
with regard to film drama.[32]

    Finally, with regard to directing drama, S. A. Elghazali reminds
us that a TV or film director, because of the 'editing' camera, is
by definition more powerful than a stage director, who has no
such selecting instrument at his disposal.[33]

Stage versus screen

Ever since the emergence of film, theorists have been discussing
the ways in which stage and screen – both audiovisual media –
differ from one another. Most of them seem to agree that the
difference is considerable and that the cinematic 'genre' is, in fact,
in some respects closer to the epic than to the dramatic genre.

In this perennial discussion, the following points are especially relevant:

1 'The human being is all-important in the theater. The drama on the screen can exist without actors.' In the theatre, 'drama proceeds from the actor, in the cinema it goes from the decor to man'.[34] Thematically, this means that, whereas stage drama traditionally emphasises the conflict between (i) man and man, or (ii) man and God, screen drama will emphasise the conflict between (iii) man and his environment, since the environment is precisely what the film camera can superbly and almost limitlessly describe. And as interest in inner processes has grown, fostered by psychoanalysis, a fourth conflict has strongly come to the fore, that between (iv) man's conscious will and his unconscious drives. This development, which, as Peter Szondi has shown,[35] has led to the crisis of modern drama, has favoured the screen media (as well as radio). Like the novel, they are well qualified to deal with inner processes, simply because they can bring us close to the human face and because the camera, functioning as an omniscient narrator, can create inner worlds by means of various cinematic techniques.

2 Whereas stage drama makes use of *continuous* space, screen drama relies on *discontinuous* space. That is, within each act/scene we remain visually within the same space in stage drama, whereas each film shot may take us to a new environment. The consequences of this are immense.

3 Similarly, whereas stage time is continuous, screen time may well be discontinuous: that is, move back and forth between different times – as is the case in the novel.

4 More dubious is Bazin's claim that in the theatre we tend to oppose the protagonist, while in the cinema we tend to identify with him.[36] This is certainly an exaggeration. But it is likely that we empathise more with the protagonist on the screen simply because we literally, via the close-ups, come closer to him. In this context, Brecht's epic theatre with its demand for distance between audience and actors can be seen as a reaction to the screen media, which have taken over the theatre's Aristotelian prerogative of empathy.

Four dramas

A comparison between different modes can in principle be carried
out in two ways. One can select a number of plays written *specially*
for, respectively, the reader ('closet drama'), the spectator of a
live performance (stage), the TV spectator, the cinema spectator
and the listener (radio). This approach has the advantage that it
is very democratic: it gives equal chances to all the media, showing
what opportunities they offer and their inherent limitations. But
at the same time it has the disadvantage that the examined
productions, being textually different, are not easily comparable.

Mainly for this reason I have preferred the more hierarchical
method of examining how a few dramas written for the stage have
been presented as radio, TV and film dramas. To make the
comparison even more revealing, I have selected a few passages
in each play text and, via transcriptions of the corresponding
passages in the various modes, attempted to show in detail where,
how and, at times, also why differences occur. Only in this way is
it possible to investigate in any depth what unites and separates
the various media and the various directorial approaches. The
plays discussed are Shakespeare's *Macbeth* (c. 1606), Ibsen's *Et
Dukkehjem* (*A Doll's House*, 1879), Strindberg's *Spöksonaten*
(*The Ghost Sonata*, 1907) and Pinter's *The Homecoming* (1965).

There are several reasons why these four plays have been
selected. Besides being significant dramas in their own right, they
belong – as the dates of publication indicate – to four distinct
periods in the history of drama, each period having its own
ideological, stylistic and theatrical characteristics. This enables us
to inquire whether plays of different periods/styles present different
transpositional problems.

The productions

A primary guiding factor was, of course, the need to select plays
which had been transposed for the media in question. Since this
criterion of selection would still have left me with a great number
of plays to consider, the ultimate choice was determined by the
accessibility of taped material. Radio, TV and film *scripts* may
certainly be helpful, but being blueprints they cannot, as Borup
Jensen notes, replace the finished products.[37]

In subsequent chapters emphasis is placed on two main categories of transposition today: for TV and for the cinema. The reason for this is twofold.

Commenting on the theatrical discourse, Keir Elam remarks that 'the text's density poses for the would-be analyst the problem of where to focus his attention, presenting him with an embarrassment of informational riches'.[38] While the richness will pertain to all the media, the problem of focus especially pertains to stage drama. Moreover, unlike radio, TV and film drama, stage drama cannot 'be interrupted or frozen for purposes of study'.[39] All this means that the notation of stage performances is a much more problematic task than that of radio, TV and film productions.

The second reason is, again, the accessibility of suitable material. Only in one case – Ingmar Bergman's 1973 production of *The Ghost Sonata*, which I followed closely – was I able to examine a stage performance in similar detail to a screen production. Although I have had access to another video recording of a stage performance – of *A Doll's House* – the quality of the recording is such that I have deemed it wise to refer only briefly to this production.

However, a more substantial principal objection may be raised against video documentation of stage performances. As Pavis has pointed out, a video recording 'imposes by its own particular framing a limited and partial vision'.[40] Besides, video recordings are hardly ever shot from the point of view of the spectator at a stage performance – that is, from one fixed point. Also in this sense, watching a video recording of a stage performance means partaking of a partial vision.

Videotaped films present fewer problems, though undoubtedly we lose something when we view them on the small, qualitatively imperfect TV screen rather than on the cinema screen for which the films are intended.

Clearly, the only material that more or less re-creates the intended situation of reception is audiotapes of radio plays and videotapes of TV plays.

Subsequent chapters

In the subsequent chapters, the initial synopsis is followed by brief
general characterisations of the various play adaptations. After
this, a few passages in the play text are compared in detail with
the corresponding passages in the examined productions. Ideally,
a book of this kind ought to be supplemented with audio- and
videotapes of the examined productions. But, even if this were
possible, it would be necessary to transcribe the audiovisual
elements of the productions into verbal stage- and acting-directions
comparable to the ones found in the play texts. I have therefore
at times considered it desirable to give a shot-by-shot notation of
the TV/film passages before proceeding to analysis of these
passages. In this way, my interpretations can at least to some
extent be verified.

Pavis is of course right when he states that to notate a performance 'inevitably means to interpret, to make a more or less
conscious choice among the multitude of signs of the performance
deemed *noteworthy*'.[41] But this is true also of a semiotic notation
of the drama text; on closer inspection even such a meticulous
notation as Elam's of the first seventy-nine lines of *Hamlet* proves
to be rather subjective – despite all the 'objective' symbols
employed.[42] Pavis's observation should therefore not make us
conclude that we must abstain from notation. Rather, the conclusion should be that we must improve our tools in this area.

In order not to burden the reader with a lot of names, I shall
refer to the *dramatis personae* in the plays rather than to the actors
incarnating them. For the same reason, I shall merely mention the
directors of the productions. This does not, of course, imply any
lack of appreciation of the contributions by all those taking part
in a performance. Readers interested in production data are
referred to the section 'Productions' at the back of the book.

When analysing passages of a play, one is immediately confronted with the question of how these passages are demarcated. For
drama texts, stage and radio versions the *sequence* will here be
considered the basic unit. By 'sequence' is meant a section
whose beginning and end, from the recipient's point of view, are
determined by (i) one or more entrances/exits (change of character
constellation), (ii) change of place, and/or (iii) change of time,
marked by curtain, blackout or, in the case of radio drama, musical

interlude.

For TV and cinema versions the *shot*, defined as 'one uninterrupted image from a single static or mobile framing',[43] is the basic unit. When the kind of shot employed (medium shot, close-up, etc.) is considered important and/or is not implied by the context, this is indicated; for a list of abbreviations used, see p. ix.

In the quotations from the play texts as well as in the transcriptions of the performances, I use roman type for the primary text (dialogue), italic for the secondary text (stage- and acting-directions/audiovisual elements).

There is, finally, the problem of tense with regard to the various presentational modes. The principle adhered to is that, for durative (repeatable) modes, the present tense is used, while the past tense is used for non-durative modes. Thus Macbeth '*enters*' in the play text and in radio, TV and film versions of it, but '*entered*' in stage presentations. The incidental presence nowadays of durative recordings of stage productions – in the form of records, audio- and videocassettes – cannot change the fundamental fact that the intended situation of reception in these cases has been that of a live performance – that is, a non-repeatable theatrical event.

As for the passages translated into English, the renderings, unless otherwise indicated, are my own.

Chapter 2

Variations on the Audiovisual: Shakespeare's *Macbeth* (c. 1606)

Of all Shakespeare's plays, *Macbeth* is perhaps the one that has been most frequently transposed to media other than the stage. The reason for this is not only that the play is one of Shakespeare's very best – some would say the best – but also that it is fairly short and full of (violent) action.

Familiar though the play is, a plot summary may nevertheless be helpful as a background for the ensuing discussion.

Synopsis

Act I. The play opens with the appearance of three witches on a heath. In the next scene Duncan, King of Scotland, learns that Macbeth, one of his captains, has led the royal forces to victory. Macbeth and Banquo, another captain, are confronted by the witches, who announce that Macbeth will become king but that Banquo will be father to a line of kings. Macbeth is displeased to hear Duncan proclaim his son, Malcolm, the next king of Scotland. Lady Macbeth receives his letter telling her about the witches' prophecy. When Macbeth returns, she is determined that her husband shall become king and begins to influence him to this effect. During the feast in Duncan's honour, Macbeth, assisted by his wife, plans to murder him.

Act II. After a brief meeting with Banquo, Macbeth imagines a dagger pointing the way to Duncan's chamber. He leaves to murder the king while Lady Macbeth waits in agony. Having done the deed, he returns bloodstained and remorseful. Lady Macbeth firmly leads him off while a knocking at the gate is heard. Macduff has come to rouse the king. The murder is discovered. Macbeth attempts to divert suspicions but is not altogether successful. Duncan's sons decide to flee.

Act III. Distrusting Banquo, Macbeth decides to get rid of him. Banquo is slain by hired murderers. At a banquet Macbeth learns that Banquo has been killed but that his son Fleance has escaped the murderers. Banquo's ghost appears to him and the banquet is disrupted.

Act IV. Macbeth again visits the witches and hears further prophecies. Learning that Macduff has joined forces with Duncan's son Malcolm, he has Macduff's family killed. Malcolm and Macduff assemble an army in England and prepare to overthrow Macbeth.

Act V. Harassed by guilt-feelings, Lady Macbeth has lost her reason and taken to sleepwalking. She eventually dies. Malcolm's and Macduff's army appears with boughs cut from Birnam Wood in fulfilment of one of the witches' prophecies. The remaining prophecy – that Macbeth is invulnerable to anyone born of woman – is vindicated when Macduff reveals that he was untimely ripped from his mother's womb. Macbeth is slain and Malcolm hailed as the new king.

Source text

Of all the plays discussed in this book, *Macbeth* is the only one for which we do not have an authorised text – that is, we cannot be certain that the original First Folio text, published in 1623, some seventeen years after the play was first performed, is identical to the one penned by Shakespeare. Most scholars in fact assume

that it is not and that alterations – cuts and/or interpolations – had
already been made in Shakespeare's time in connection with
various productions. Thus Kenneth Muir, whose edition will be
followed here, mentions in his introduction that earlier editors
have branded at least ten passages or scenes as spurious – according
to him, 'on insufficient grounds'.[1] He regards only iii.v (the Hecate
scene) and two passages in iv.i (referring to Hecate and the First
Witch respectively) as spurious, and the director Peter Hall defends
the authenticity even of these.[2] We must of course be aware of
the fact that, as in the case of other Shakespearian plays, the stage-
and acting-directions in text versions of *Macbeth* are frequently
additions by later editors 'not only to help the reader but also to
meet the production requirements of the only stage known in the
eighteenth century, the painted picture-frame stage'.[3]

Macbeth and Lady Macbeth

With his foul deeds Macbeth is a problematic protagonist. Seldom,
if ever, has a villain come so close to being a hero. What does he
look like? How old is he? In these respects the text, as often with
Shakespeare, gives little indication. Naturally, he has a certain
grandeur. But is he handsome, attractive? And what about his
collaborator, Lady Macbeth?

Granted that physical attractiveness is to some extent a question
of individual taste, most people would probably agree that the
couple in Roman Polanski's film, the film version examined here,
are more attractive than the pair in the teleplay versions by Trevor
Nunn and Jack Gold. One reason for this may be that film, for
economic reasons, must literally attract its audience to a greater
extent than TV – by means of handsome or beautiful faces in
close-up. But, putting aside this (trivial) extratextual explanation,
'a couple beautiful and sympathetic in looks but ugly beneath suits
a play in which "fair is foul" ',[4] and in which it is stated that
'There's no art / To find the mind's construction in the face' (i.iv.12–
13). Characteristically, in the film the attractive faces belong not
only to Macbeth and his wife but also to Ross, who is here the
true villain, while Macduff, the principal goody of the play, looks
decidedly villainous.

As for the age of Macbeth and his wife, most directors have
settled for a middle-aged couple, presumably because this seems

most in agreement with Macbeth's status as a thane and his concomitant ambition to be king. But sometimes, as in Polanski's film, the two have been played by young actors. 'It's much better to have them played young. There's some sex between them which I want to be understood', Polanski once remarked. And his collaborator on the film script, Kenneth Tynan, has pointed out that it would be completely unrealistic 'to have Macbeth and Lady Macbeth performed by 60-year-olds and menopausals. It's too late for them to be ambitious.'[5] However, one might just as well argue that, precisely at the age when sexual potency is diminishing, there is a growing need to feel potent in another sense and that ambition, therefore, lends itself extremely well to menopausals.

The opening

Text

The opening scene, Coleridge has said, strikes 'the keynote . . . of the whole play'.[6] The scene reads:

> *An open place. Thunder and lightning. Enter three* WITCHES.

I WITCH.	When shall we three meet again?
	In thunder, lightning, or in rain?
2 WITCH.	When the hurlyburly's done,
	When the battle's lost and won.
3 WITCH.	That will be ere the set of sun.
I WITCH.	Where the place?
2 WITCH.	Upon the heath.
3 WITCH.	There to meet with Macbeth.
I WITCH.	I come, Graymalkin!
2 WITCH.	Paddock calls.
3 WITCH.	Anon!
ALL.	Fair is foul, and foul is fair:
	Hover through the fog and filthy air.

> *Exeunt.*

(I.i)

The witches – or Weird Sisters – are mysterious figures, related

somehow to the thunder and lightning. Shakespeare gives them
no names and indicates neither their age nor their appearance at
this point, although the word 'witch' certainly suggests old age and
grim looks. From the dialogue of their later scenes, we may,
however, draw some conclusions as to what the Weird Sisters look
like. Banquo's manner of addressing them is revealing in this
respect:

> What are these,
> So wither'd and so wild in their attire,
> That look not like th'inhabitants o'th'earth
> And yet are on't? Live you? or are you aught
> That man may question? You seem to understand me,
> By each at once her choppy finger laying
> Upon her skinny lips: you should be women,
> And yet your beards forbid me to interpret
> That you are so.
>
> (I.iii)

Wild attire, choppy fingers, skinny lips, beards – these are the
characteristics a director who wants to stick closely to the text
would take into account when visualising their appearance. Note
that Banquo questions not only their human nature but also their
gender and that Shakespeare does not differentiate between the
three: there is no indication that they do not look alike.

The Weird Sisters have been interpreted and visualised in
many different ways. In his extensive discussion of their stage
appearances, Rosenberg distinguishes between the following
interpretations/visualisations: (i) women, (ii) witches, (iii) satanic
agents, (iv) fates, (v) projections of the mind, and (vi) symbols.[7]

Stage

In his 1948 Gothenburg stage production of *Macbeth*, Ingmar
Bergman highlighted two lines in the opening scene; as recorded
by Fridén,[8] his version, translated back into English, was as
follows:

3 WITCH. Fair is foul, and foul is fair:
2 WITCH. Hover through the fog and filthy air.
1 WITCH. When shall we three meet again?
3 WITCH. Fair is foul, and foul is fair.
1 WITCH. In thunder, lightning, or in rain?
3 WITCH. Fair is foul, and foul is fair.
2 WITCH. When the hurlyburly's done.
    When the battle's lost and won.
3 WITCH. That will be ere the set of sun.
1 WITCH. Fair is foul, and foul is fair:
2 WITCH. Hover through the fog and filthy air.
1 WITCH. Where the place?
2 WITCH.   Upon the heath.
3 WITCH. There to meet with Macbeth.
ALL.   Fair is foul, and foul is fair:
    Hover through the fog and filthy air.

The Swedish counterpart of this 'edited' passage was a compilation
of two different translations.

To Bergman, in 1948 – and to many others in that period –
Macbeth was an evil protagonist, akin to a recently dead dictator.
As the prime movers behind his actions, the witches were depicted
accordingly:

The first witch, a cripple . . ., was to be on the ground, and
spent the whole performance on her knees, an enormous grey-
green skirt hiding her legs; her witch was hunchbacked and had
an ugly nose. The second witch . . . was to have an elevated
position, spending much time in the [staged] tree with her arms
resting high up. . . . She made herself up to look as if drowned,
and was dressed in black rags, her face greenish yellow and her
wig partly bald, with wet wisps of hair. . . . the third witch had
a more normal position on the stage floor. She was dressed as a
whore, in a tight, red dress that left one shoulder bare. She was
adorned with heavy chains and carried a skull in her hand.
These chains and the cross-garters on her legs resembled
Macbeth's costume. [She] also wore a red wig and her mask,
with green eye shadow, was a copy of Lady Macbeth's face. . . .[9]

A cripple, a madwoman, a whore were thus visually suggestive of the Macbeths. Rather than emphasise the mythic nature of the witches, Bergman was suggesting that their outward deformity corresponded to the 'foul' souls that the 'butcher, and his fiend-like Queen' (v.ix.35) were hiding under a 'fair' veneer. From another point of view, these witches could be seen as 'three types of ill-treated out-casts'[10] and as such incarnating the protagonists' feelings after the murder of Duncan, feelings of being rejected by their own consciences.

In Trevor Nunn's 1976 stage production the witches were also differentiated. While 'the commitment to evil of the older two was total . . ., it was the young one, strangely possessed, who had the gift upon which they depended. . . . she was an innocent who gazed aloft like an ecstatic saint.'[11] The young witch actually seemed to bridge the contrast between the evil of the older ones and the saintliness of Duncan.

Television

Since Nunn's 1978 TV version was based on his stage production, the difference between the media can profitably be studied by comparing the two productions. In the stage production, Nunn adopted the now common practice of having the players sit around the playing area – marked by a white chalk circle – 'watching those parts of the action that did not involve them and springing into illusion when their cue arrived'.[12]

Such a Brechtian approach is hardly possible in a TV production. Yet Nunn retains something of this illusion-breaking effect also in his TV version by opening it with an overhead shot showing how dark figures, throwing long shadows before them, approach the stools surrounding the circular playing-area. Low organ tones immediately create a religious atmosphere. A saintly old man (Duncan), all in white, strikingly contrasts with the rest. The camera pans along the faces of the figures. The re-recipient wonders, who is Macbeth? Lady Macbeth? Where are the good people, where the bad? Who can tell from outward appearance?

The camera stops its panning by one of the witches. Then a shot of two of the witches in blue light. High organ notes. The witches are seen in their nineteenth-century, gaudy rags, strongly contrasting with Duncan's simple, white, timeless gown. The *hands* of the witches are brought into focus. A man (Macduff) approaches

Duncan. They seize each others' *hands*. Close-up of Duncan, praying with closed *hands*, while beastly sounds from the witches are heard. Duncan kisses the cross hanging on his breast. A shot of the three witches; beastly sounds; saliva is dripping from the mouth of the youngest one. Duncan is again seen praying. The three witches say their lines, accompanied by thunder and lightning. Duncan, still praying, beats his bosom and says, *'Mea culpa!'* ('I am to blame').

From the very beginning, Nunn contrasts white (magic) with black, what is human with what is beastly, good with evil. The circle may be seen as a magic circle, as a symbol of the world (the globe) or as a symbol of the ego. Significantly, the dark figures surrounding it throw their shadows inside it – just as the people surrounding us constantly have their imprints upon our lives.

Despite – or rather just because of – the strong contrast between Duncan and the witches, both parties relate to Macbeth and Lady Macbeth: to their primitive drives on the one hand and to their more 'cultivated' qualities on the other. Psychoanalytically, Duncan may be seen as the condemning superego and the witches as the amoral id within the double protagonist. The focusing upon their (strongly constrasting) hands initiates the hand motif that looms so large in *Macbeth*. The special place taken by the youngest witch in the stage production – that of an ecstatic visionary – is retained in the TV version. While this figure seems especially linked with Macbeth – her frothing preparing for Macbeth's 'epileptic' fit in the banquet scene – the oldest witch reminds one of Lady Macbeth: both wear a turban-like headdress.

While Bergman and Nunn chose to depict the witches as differing from one another – in make-up, costume and positions – Jack Gold preferred to emphasise their conformity in his 1982 TV version (figures left indicate shots):

1   *Trumpets and eerie music. Establishing-shot of a heath, in the middle of which is a huge horizontal slab resting on three raised stones. On top of the slab three 'bundles'. In the background some erected stones. Everything in brown tints changing into bluish grey. Thunder and lightning.*

2   *Zoom-in on 'bundles', i.e. the three* WITCHES *crouching, all of them dressed in bulky, ragged long dresses.* I WITCH C

raises herself slowly to standing position, followed by 2 WITCH
R and 3 WITCH *L.*

    1 WITCH *looking at* 3 WITCH.
       When shall we three meet again?
       Looking at 2 WITCH.
       In thunder, lightning, or in rain?
    2 WITCH.   When the hurlyburly's done,
       When the battle's lost and won.
    3 WITCH *turning head L, then R, looking at* 1 WITCH.
       That will be ere the set of sun.
    1 WITCH *looking at* 3 WITCH.
       Where the place?
    2 WITCH.   Upon the heath.
    3 WITCH.   There to meet with Macbeth.
    1 WITCH *looking upwards.*
       I come, Graymalkin!
    2 WITCH *turning head, looking R.*
       Paddock calls.
    3 WITCH *looking upwards.*
       Anon!
    1 WITCH *raising L hand.*
       Fair is foul . . .
    2 WITCH *raising R hand.*
       . . . and foul is fair:
       They join hands.
    3 WITCH *raising L hand.*
       Hover through the fog and filthy air.
       Her hand joins those of the other two.
       As they pull their hands apart, dissolve to next scene:

KING DUNCAN *and* ATTENDANTS *approaching.*

The initial establishing-shot, which may lead our thoughts to
Stonehenge, provides a ritual atmosphere for the play, linking the
witches with ancient, pagan times. The brown tints have the same
indication, since old photographs are often brown rather than
black-and-white. In line with this, the change from brown to grey
may be seen as a time-shift from ancient to present time. But
the more obvious change does not take place until the almost

monochrome initial scene, so removed from everyday reality, is replaced by the subsequent polychrome one, mirroring a recognisable situation.

The change from brown to grey, reminiscent of a fade-out, has its counterpart at the end of the teleplay, where there is a colour change reminiscent of a fade-in. By framing the play in this way, the director seems to suggest that life is constantly changing, that nothing remains the same, and that the play we are going to witness or have witnessed is merely a slice of ever-changing life.

While the witches in the text enter onto the stage, on the screen they are present from the very beginning – even if they first look merely like three slabs of stone. Only after a few moments are we confronted with the thunder and lightning – as though the change from brown to bluish grey, indicating a change of weather, was initiated by the three crouching (praying?) witches. As in the text, their physical similarity is stressed – they all look like middle-aged matrons — and there is a certain symmetry in their joining hands, as though swearing an oath, allowing us to see their 'choppy fingers' in close-up. Hands, as we have already noted, are later to function as an important *Leitmotiv*. Rather than have all the witches in unison speak the final lines ('Fair is foul', etc.), Gold divides the lines up between them. The effect, however, is much the same as with Bergman. In either case the idea is conveyed that this is a proverbial sentence they all know by heart. The ritual joining of the hands as these lines are spoken further indicates that we are concerned with one of the main themes of the play: the reversal of values.

Highly suggestive is the dissolve from this scene to the next. It is as though Duncan and his men approach us from inside the ragged grey dresses of the witches, who suddenly appear gigantic. In this way, the idea is underscored that the Weird Sisters are indeed supernatural beings – Fates, Norns, Parcae – deciding or at least influencing man's life.

Film

The opening scene in Polanski's film version is quite different:

1 *Establishing-shot of a slightly inundated sand beach, a dark mountain ridge in the distance. Twilight. Eerie, high-pitched music. As it changes to daylight, the mountain ridge disappears. Cries of seagulls, panting and coughing.*

2 *A crooked stick enters frame FG R. The hand of* 1 WITCH, *with hairy skin, wrapped in black, draws a circle with the stick in the sand.*

3 *The back of a blonde young woman [2* WITCH] *on her knees, a grey shawl over her shoulders, enters frame FG R. She is digging a hole in the sand within the circle. An older woman [3* WITCH] *with a white barbette and a black robe enters frame FG L, she too digging. Behind these two an old woman [1* WITCH] *in a black long robe with a black hood. Cry of seagull.*

4 *LA shot of flying, crying seagull, white against a light-grey sky.*

5 *Hands of 2* WITCH, *handling a noose, putting it into the hole. Cry of seagull.*

6 2 WITCH *takes a parcel out of a basket.*

7 2 WITCH, *appearing between 3* WITCH *and* 1 WITCH, *gives parcel to* 1 WITCH, *who unwraps it, revealing an arm cut off below the elbow.*

8 2 WITCH. *Sigh.*

9 3 WITCH.

10 *Cut-off arm in hole. Hand of* 1 WITCH *puts a dagger in its hand.*

11 1 WITCH, *in profile. Her eyes are bunged up. Cry of seagull.*

12 *Hands of 2 and 3* WITCH *sprinkling something from a bowl over the cut-off arm. Cry of seagull.*

13   3 WITCH.

14   *Hands of 2 and* 3 WITCH *covering cut-off arm with sand and filling up hole.*

15   2 WITCH *looking R to hand of* 1 WITCH, *carrying a flask. Flask is uncorked and red liquid is poured from it onto the 'grave'.*

16   2 WITCH *looking at red spot in sand.* 1 *and* 3 WITCH.
       Fair is foul, and foul is fair:

17   3 WITCH *L,* 2 WITCH *C,* 1 WITCH *R.*
       Hover through the fog and filthy air.
       All spit.

18   3 WITCH *looking at* 1 WITCH. *Cry of seagull.*
       When shall we three meet again?
       In thunder, lightning . . .

19   2 WITCH *supporting* 1 WITCH, *both moving slowly L.*
       3 WITCH *off-screen.*   . . . or in rain?

20   1 WITCH. When the hurlyburly's done,
            When the battle's lost and won.
       3 WITCH. That will be ere the set of sun.
       1 WITCH. Where the place?
       3 WITCH. Upon the heath. 1 WITCH *nods.*
       1 WITCH. There to meet with . . . Macbeth.

21   *All three move away,* 1 WITCH *and* 2 WITCH, *who drags a cart, L,* 3 WITCH *R. Grating of cart-wheel, squeak of violin, then cry of seagull.* 1 *and* 2 WITCH *out of frame L. Sustained shot of black figure of* 3 WITCH, *her shadow reflected in tidal water behind her, walking towards bluish ridge in distance. She vanishes in the white mist. Eerie, high-pitched sounds. Dissolve to*

22   *Credits. Sounds of battle in crescendo: shouting, clanging of swords, neighing.*

The opening shot establishes the equivocal nature of the play. Is it sunrise? Is it sunset? Soon we know it is sunrise, for – through time-lapse photography – the desolate beach is immediately seen in full daylight. Shortly after this we learn that the witches are to meet 'ere the set of sun'. We are thus given the impression that the whole film will be acted out within the span of one day. And in a sense it will: at the end of the film, when the enemy is closing in on Macbeth, it is sunset. Clearly, the rising and setting of the sun parallel Macbeth's rise and fall.

Unlike Gold, Polanski handles the opening scene very freely; the greater, pantomimic part consists of directorial additions. Three lines have been cut, while the central two ('Fair is foul . . .') have been moved so that they become the first words uttered in the film – as in Bergman's stage version. By this rearrangement, they not only gain in weight; they also seem like a satanic prayer following upon the cruel ritual that has just been enacted. Polanski further stresses the thematic significance of these words and of the whole opening scene by inserting the credits after it – that is, by separating it from the rest of the film. Thereby his opening scene even more than Shakespeare's, becomes a kind of prologue.

As Jack Jorgens has observed, this prologue provides a number of thematic clues to the main part of the film.[13] But it has also another significance. When Macbeth and Banquo first meet the witches (in I.iii), they are confronted with a number of verbal riddles. In this way Shakespeare provides his play with what-tension: will the prophecies come true? Besides, he creates a sense of identity between the recipient and the protagonist: *we* know as little as *he* does. In the course of the play the enigmatic prophecies are fulfilled: that is, they become intelligible both to Macbeth and to us.

With his initial pantomimic ritual, Polanski does something similar. When we first witness it, we do not understand what the ritual signifies. As in the play text, we are confronted with a series of (visual rather than verbal) riddles. The difference is that, whereas the prophecies offered to Macbeth and Banquo seem promising, the ritual in the film seems ominous.

Retrospectively, we can see its significance. The circle drawn in the sand, apart from being a magic circle and perhaps a symbol of man's limited vision, refers to the royal crown, representing the power relished by everyone. Not only do we see the crown on three different heads in the course of the film; it is also given visual prominence on two crucial occasions: when it falls from Duncan's head as he is murdered by Macbeth, and when it is taken from Macbeth's severed head and handed over to Malcolm.

Just as the crown obliquely comes to signify ambition and is, therefore, closely linked with Macbeth, so the buried dagger anticipates the dagger which Macbeth hallucinates in II.i and which guides him to murder Duncan. The significance of the circle-*cum*-crown hiding a dagger could thus be spelt out: murder of the king secures kingship. Yet the fact that the hand holding the dagger is severed ominously prepares us for the murderer's final fate: the severing of Macbeth's head from his body. The noose clearly refers to the hanging of the old thane of Cawdor, whose rebellion against King Duncan is merely related by Shakespeare but dramatised at some length in the film. Of the execution of Cawdor, Malcolm reports,

> very frankly he confessed his treasons,
> Implored your Highness' pardon, and set forth
> A deep repentance. Nothing in his life
> Became him like the leaving of it: he died
> As one that had been studied in his death,
> To throw away the dearest thing he ow'd,
> As 'twere a careless trifle.
>
> (I.iv)

Cawdor's death anticipates that of Macbeth; the last sentence applies as much to him as to Cawdor. It is an open question, however, whether also the first sentence applies to him. Audiences have witnessed both repenting and unrepenting Macbeths.

In the film, Macbeth remains unrepenting to the bitter end. Characteristically, Polanski cut the lines referring to Cawdor's repentance. Shakespeare does not tell us how Cawdor was executed. Polanski, by contrast, has him jump to his death by hanging after having uttered an enigmatic – repenting or provocative – 'Hail the King.' In a revealing two-shot shortly after this we see Macbeth, the new thane of Cawdor, in the foreground glancing at his predecessor, dangling in his noose. The noose reminds us of the one buried by the witches along with the arm and the dagger. We now realise that their burying of the noose ritualises the fate of Cawdor – and of Macbeth.

Polanski's witches differ markedly from one another. We see a young, blonde, rather pretty witch, dressed in grey; a possibly middle-aged one, dressed in black and white; and an old one in a black hooded robe with a skull-like, eyeless face. Taken together they seem to represent the ages of man (cf. the three stages of the sun) or, psychologically, Macbeth's change from youthful innocence – as we have seen, Polanski settled for an unusually young Macbeth – to middle-aged ambition and finally the guilty life-weariness associated with old age. The three witches could also be seen as incarnations of different aspects of Lady Macbeth. The resemblance to Bergman's approach is obvious.

The young witch, in Polanski's version, has no speaking part and gives the impression of being a trainee. As in Nunn's production, she is the most vivid, the most human of the three. The old witch, by contrast, who seems in charge of the ritual burial, is an almost allegorical figure: we may think of the 'blind' figure of Justice, or we may think of Death – as re-created in, for example, Bergman's film *The Seventh Seal.*

At the end of the sequence, special attention is given to the middle-aged witch. The sustained shot of her may be combined with two passages toward the end of the play. On the one hand it renders visually Macbeth's statement in v.v that 'life's but a walking shadow'; this explains why we see this figure for so long, walking alone towards we-know-not-what in the distance, then disappearing – a pregnant image of man's life. On the other hand, it offers an image of Macbeth's fate, for what we see is actually a walking black figure without a head, the white barbette mingling with the white fog to create this mirage.

Polanski makes use both of diegetic (seagull, cart) and non-diegetic sounds (eerie music). the dominant sound is the melancholy cry of the seagull, which is seen once, hovering over the witches – another symbol of man's desolate existence and his longing for freedom and purity. This shot can be compared with the contrasting one towards the end, showing Macbeth perched like a raven – he wears a black fur coat – on top of his castle.

It is a good imaginative touch to let the battle that is mentioned in the play take place while the credits are shown. The sound-effects are both suggestive and functional in that they transfer us from the opening scene, with its large metaphysical perspective, to the world of human emotion and ambition. When II.ii opens, the battle is over and, on the same beach where we saw the witches, we now see dying or dead soldiers. The juxtaposition suggests that the witches are Valkyries, determining the outcome of the battle.

The murder of Duncan

In the play text the murder of Duncan takes place off-stage. This is the way it usually happens in the theatre. In their teleplays, Nunn and Gold take the same approach. The advantage of this solution, harking back to ancient Greek drama, is (i) that emphasis is placed not so much on the violent act itself as on its repercussions, and (ii) that the murder becomes more suggestive since we are free to imagine exactly how it is effectuated.

It has rightly been remarked that what is especially fearful in Macbeth's deed is that he murders Duncan while the king is asleep. 'The wrong has been done, as it were, not only to Duncan, but also to the sacred nature of sleep. And "wronged sleep" rises in the conscience of the murderer like a real power. . . . *Sleep* runs like a keyword throughout the whole play and is the occasion of many metaphors.'[14] Yet the killing of someone who is asleep is hardly as arresting as that of someone who can defend himself; it can better take place off-stage.

While Shakespeare settles for an off-stage murder of a sleeping king, Polanski shows us the murder of one who is awake. In the film we see Macbeth enter the room where Duncan, his guest, is asleep. We see him hesitate to do the deed. Suddenly Duncan wakes up and now, in a sustained shot, Macbeth stabs him.

Polanski's Macbeth is not a callous murderer. He is rather a man who kills impulsively, desperately, out of fear. The impression we get is that he would not have mustered courage to kill the king, had Duncan not woken up and seen the dagger in Macbeth's hand. The crown falling off Duncan's head to the ground prepares us for the end, where the crown, still joined symbolically to Macbeth's severed head, falls to the ground. The contrast between the two killings is significant: while the crown sits loosely on Duncan's head, it is fastened to Macbeth's. In his concern to bring out this telling contrast, Polanski is plainly contradicting plausibility in the latter scene.

By enabling us to see the murder of Duncan, Polanski shows us an immediate reason for it: fear – a reason that does not naturally suggest itself to us when the killing is done off-stage. He also confronts us with the brutality of his protagonist, which 'violates Shakespeare's design of masking, hence minimizing, Macbeth's physical violences until much later'.[15]

In short, on the one hand Polanski increases our empathy for the protagonist; on the other he diminishes it, completely in line with his general tendency to confront the spectator directly with the acts of his protagonist, however 'foul' they may be.

The banquet scene

Text

In the banquet scene, suspense arises from the fact that we, unlike the guests, are in collusion with Macbeth in knowing that Banquo has been murdered. As a result of Macbeth's strange behaviour, the guests gradually begin to suspect something of the kind. The beginning of the scene reads,

MACBETH.   Here had we now our country's honour roof'd,
        Were the grac'd person of our Banquo present;
   The GHOST OF BANQUO *enters, and sits in* MACBETH'*s place.*
        Who may I rather challenge for unkindness,
        Than pity for mischance!
ROSS.   His absence, Sir,
        Lays blame upon his promise. Please't your Highness
        To grace us with your royal company?
MACBETH.   The table's full.
LENNOX.   Here is a place reserv'd, Sir.
MACBETH.   Where?
LENNOX.   Here, my good Lord. What is't that moves your
        Highness?
MACBETH.   Which of you have done this?
LORDS.   What, my good Lord?
MACBETH.   Thou canst not say, I did it: never shake
        Thy gory locks at me.

                                                    (III.iv)

When Macbeth mentions Banquo, he has just received news that Banquo has been murdered (at Macbeth's instigation). It is to cover up his own responsibility for this deed that Macbeth opens the dinner with feigned sadness at Banquo's absence.

The acting-direction '*sits in* MACBETH'*s place*' combined with Macbeth's statement that 'The table's full' tells us that there is only one vacant seat (Macbeth's) when the scene opens and that, when the Ghost of Banquo takes this seat, the table is indeed full. From this we may conclude that Macbeth has informed the servants that Banquo will not attend the dinner, so that no chair need be reserved for him. Already by this arrangement Macbeth is giving himself away. His mind is obviously confused already at the start of the banquet.

This interpretation is based on the assumption that the acting-direction '*sits in* MACBETH'*s place*', if not by Shakespeare, is at least in his spirit. Yet would it not have been more natural if Macbeth, anxious to cover up his killing of Banquo, had kept two chairs at the table vacant, one for himself and the other for Banquo? Is not the acting-direction merely an editor's interpretation of the situation? Another case in point is the Ghost's entrance. As Muir observes, there are different opinions among the editors as to when exactly the Ghost makes his first entrance.[16] As these examples indicate, even seemingly harmless stage- and acting-directions may have far-reaching consequences. With Shakespeare, the interpretative problems begin in a very literal way with the play text. Sticking to the Muir edition, we may state that Macbeth's obsession with his victim is indicated (i) by the fact that the Ghost appears as soon as Macbeth mentions his name, and (ii) by the Ghost's taking Macbeth's seat, an act symbolising how Banquo, in line with the witches' prophecy ('Thou shalt get kings, though thou be none'), *replaces* Macbeth.

Ross's invitation, characteristic of his ingratiating nature, serves to clarify the fact that Macbeth's vision differs from that of the others. From Lennox's reaction ('What is't that moves your Highness?') we understand that Macbeth at this point sees the Ghost of Banquo, whom Shakespeare brings onto the stage.

Stage

In stage productions of *Macbeth* the Ghost has sometimes been a
visible presence, sometimes not. Bradley, who sees this as marking
the difference between accepting the Ghost as real and treating it
as an hallucination, gives the following reasons in support of the
latter interpretation: (i) Macbeth has already had one hallucination, that of the 'air-drawn dagger'; (ii) his words about the Ghost
echo what the murderer has just told him about Banquo's bruised
head; (iii) the Ghost vanishes the second time on Macbeth's
assertion of its unreality – 'Hence, horrible shadow!'; (iv) at the
end of the scene Macbeth himself seems to regard it as illusory;
(v) the Ghost is mute; and (vi) it is visible only to Macbeth.[17] In
short, everything suggests that the Ghost is not real but a figment
of Macbeth's imagination.

Why then, Bradley asks, did Shakespeare allow for the Ghost
to be represented on the stage? His answer is that Shakespeare
meant 'the judicious to take the Ghost for an hallucination, but
knew that the bulk of the audience would take it for a reality'.
The critic seems here to be referring to Shakespeare's two
audiences: the groundlings and the more sophisticated spectators
on the balconies. Naturally, it is always possible to divide an
audience up into such categories; but the question posed by
Bradley can be answered in a different and more relevant way.

Granted that Shakespeare wanted his audience to share, as
much as it was able, Macbeth's guilt-feelings at this point, what
else could he do but re-create the dead Banquo on the stage, so
that not only Macbeth but we too can see him? Theatre is an art
of the senses. What we see is real to us; what we do not see is
not. Presenting Banquo's Ghost on stage is therefore a way of (i)
increasing the emotional impact of the scene, and (ii) making us
share Macbeth's agitated feelings – rather than the neutral ones
of the guests.

On the other hand, not presenting the Ghost – Nunn's choice –
besides seeming more attuned to the views of modern psychoanalysis on interiorisation, has the advantage that, in a scene with
multiple foci, the spectator's attention is concentrated on Macbeth.
By keeping him close to Lady Macbeth on the stage and by letting
him face the audience, Nunn further increased the focus upon the
guilt-laden king.[18]

Television

In Trevor Nunn's teleplay, almost devoid of stage properties, the banquet scene opens with a shot of Macbeth's and Lady Macbeth's thrones in the background and the court's semi-circular 'table' (in fact merely stools) in the foreground. All the characters are dressed in early-nineteenth-century fashion. Macbeth, in uniform, looks more like a commander-in-chief than a king. Seyton, acting as cupbearer, treats the king and his guests to a ceremonial toast. Both he and one of the murderers strikingly resemble the king – an indication of how Macbeth constantly sees himself in others, how he is imprisoned by his own sense of guilt.

Macbeth toasts Lady Macbeth ('Sweet remembrancer'). She drinks. The court applauds. Macbeth empties the cup, speaks ceremoniously, clasps his hands (as did Duncan in the opening scene).

As in the stage version, the Ghost is seen only by Macbeth, who appears ill at ease but restrains himself. Lady Macbeth gets up to pacify the courtiers. She puts one hand consolingly on Macbeth's shoulder. But her husband, now forgetful both of her and of the court, jumps up and rushes around, seeing only the Ghost of Banquo. Zoom in on Macbeth. He stares into the camera, toward us – as though *we* are Banquo. When he toasts Banquo he points to us. After a while he recovers, laughs, orders more wine, drinks. The guests clap their hands in a measured manner. When Banquo appears again, Macbeth has an 'epileptic' fit, sweats, talks in staccato phrases, the saliva dripping from his mouth. He protects himself with his arms, cleaves the air with his dagger in a gesture indicating both murder (of Banquo/the recipient) and suicide.

Thanks to the TV medium – and to superb acting – Nunn is able to focus, in this scene, on Macbeth's *experience* of the Ghost – rather than on the Ghost itself. Macbeth's mental change in the course of this passage from relative equilibrium to hysteria is subtly indicated by having him – and us – experience the guests' applause as normal the first time and as ghostly (measured) the second time. Similarly, by placing the recipient on Banquo's chair, so to speak, Nunn brings us inimically close to Macbeth.

Gold's approach is rather different:

1 *Long dining-table, seen from one of the short ends. All
   chairs are occupied except the two at either short end.* LADY
   MACBETH, *in a purple dress, crown on head, is sitting in FG
   R,* ROSS *behind her,* LENNOX *opposite her.* MACBETH, *in grey
   coat-of-mails, crown on head, walks up to empty chair in
   BG.*

   MACBETH. Here had we now our country's honour roof'd,
   Were the grac'd person of our Banquo present;
   Who may I rather challenge for unkindness,
   Than pity for mischance!

2 ROSS, *carving steak* (LADY MACBETH *behind him*), *looking up
   at* MACBETH.
   His absence, Sir,
   Lays blame upon his promise. *Smiling.* Please't your
   Highness
   To grace us with your royal company.
   Begins to eat.

3 *Table, empty chair in FG.*
   MACBETH. The table's full.

4 LENNOX *in FG L of table.*
   Here is a place reserv'd, Sir.

5 MACBETH. Where?

6 LENNOX *pointing to empty chair in FG.*
   Here, my good Lord.

7 MACBETH *staring before him, sighing. Rumbling of 'thunder'.*

8 ROSS *in FG and* LADY MACBETH *in BG. Thunder'.*

9 TWO THANES *in FG and* LENNOX, *concerned, in BG next to
   empty chair.*
   LENNOX. What is't that moves your Highness?
   'Thunder'.

10 MACBETH. Which of you have done this?

11 *Table in cold, bluish light, empty chair in BG. Guests turn*
    their heads toward chair.

12 ROSS *in FG and* LADY MACBETH *in BG turn their heads toward*
    chair.

13 *Zoom-in on empty chair. Eerie, shrill sound.*
    LORDS. What, my good Lord?

14 MACBETH *and 'drumbeats'.*
    Thou canst not say, I did it: . . .

15 ROSS, *sceptical, in FG and* LADY MACBETH, *her mouth open,*
    in BG. 'Drumbeats'.

16 MACBETH *and 'drumbeats'.*
    . . . never shake
    Thy gory locks at me.

17 *Empty chair. Eerie, shrill sound.*

In this version there are two vacant chairs, not one. The sequence
opens with a long shot of the table. Macbeth, next to his chair in
the background, is seen from the empty chair obviously intended
for Banquo. The intention here, strengthened by the fact that both
chairs are in focus (deep-focus shot), is clearly to bring the chairs –
i.e. Macbeth and Banquo – visually together. Since the Ghost in
Gold's version – as in Nunn's – never materialises, there is a risk
that we identify ourselves not with Macbeth, but with his guests;
neither they nor we see the Ghost. When Macbeth states 'The
table's full', our eyes have already told us that he is wrong and we
are as surprised as his guests are.

The reasoning behind this solution may have been that presenting
the Ghost means paying too much attention to what is, after all,
merely a concretisation of Macbeth's inner experience. What is
important here, Nunn and Gold may have argued, is not the
object seen (Banquo) but the reactions of the viewer/experiencer
(Macbeth) – especially since a teleplay, unlike a stage version,

allows both for close-ups, revealing such reactions, and technical devices, indicating that we are faced with a subjective vision. Or, to put it in negative terms: precisely because the TV medium leans toward realism, is it much riskier to present the Ghost on television than on the stage.

Actually, Gold has divided the quoted passage up into two distinct parts, an initial objective one (shots 1–6), in which we share the vision of the guests, and a subjective one (shots 7–17), in which we share Macbeth's vision. It begins with startling non-diegetic sound-effects, reminiscent of the thunder we have earlier heard, suggesting that there is witchcraft in this vision; continues with a marked change of light and even more disturbing sounds in crescendo, mingling with Macbeth's voice; and ends with a zoom-in to a close-up of the empty chair, as the sound reaches a painful climax. In this manner Gold has, within his medium, attempted to find an equivalent – or even superior – way of making Macbeth's emotions palpable.

But here we may note an interesting difference. While it is clear from the text that only Macbeth sees the Ghost, and that the Ghost thus represents an inner reality, it is not clear in the teleplay whether the ghostly substitutes – the sound-effects and the bluish light – are experienced by him alone or not. Assuming that they are, the latter part of the sequence demonstrates the following pattern:

	guests	spectator	Macbeth
sound-effects	−	+	+
light-effect	−	+	+
close-up of chair	−	+	+
Ghost of Banquo	−	−	+

It should be clear from this that, although Banquo's Ghost is never presented, Gold nevertheless by other devices manages to establish a close rapport between the spectator and the protagonist.

That Ross carves the steak and starts to eat before Macbeth has sat down at table casts an ironic light on his readiness to blame Banquo: if the latter appears to be lacking in manners, so does Ross. But more important is the fact that his carving of the red steak at this moment must be disturbing to Macbeth, who has just been told that Banquo has received 'twenty trenched gashes on his head' from the knives of the murderers. Toward the end of the scene Macbeth tries to defend himself against the Ghost by seeking protection behind his hired tools, the murderers ('Thou canst not say, I did it'). This statement evokes a sceptical reaction from Ross and surprises Lady Macbeth (shot 15). The point is, of course, that neither of them realises that Macbeth is referring to Banquo. Lady Macbeth undoubtedly thinks he is referring to Duncan, whom she knows Macbeth has killed; she has every reason to worry if he is on the point of revealing the crime which she herself has instigated.

Film

Polanski's handling of the banquet scene is cinematically broad-canvased:

1 MACBETH *in white, with a golden goblet in his hand, by the table R, where* ROSS *is sitting.*

ROSS. Please't your Highness
To grace us with your royal company?

2 MACBETH *by table L.*
The table's full.

3 SEYTON *as major-domo, with staff.*
Here's a place reserv'd, Sir.

4 MACBETH. Where?

5 SEYTON. Here, my good Lord.

6 ROSS *indicating with his black-sleeved arm the chair next to him, which is occupied by a turned-away figure. Another black-sleeved arm shoots out from the other side of the table, pointing in the same direction.*

7 SEYTON *and* MACBETH, *the latter smiling.*

8 *Zoom-in on* MACBETH, *now puzzled.*

 9 *Black-sleeved arms. Pan R to turned-away figure, who raises his hand to his face. Bluish light. Zoom-in on figure, now turning his head around. It is* BANQUO.

10 MACBETH, *scared.*

11 *His ringed hand.*

12 *His goblet falling to the floor with a clinking sound, swirling around, wine pouring out of it.*

13 SEYTON'*s hand picking up the goblet, drying up the spilt wine. Tilt up to his face.*

14 MACBETH. Which . . . which of you have done this?

15 BANQUO'*s face, now stabbed, bleeding, in bluish light, his hand shielding his eyes, nodding as* MACBETH *says*
       Thou canst not say, I did it:

16 MACBETH.   never shake
       Thy gory locks at me.

A comparison with the play text reveals, first of all, that Polanski has cut Macbeth's first speech and one sentence in Ross's and Lennox's speeches; the latter, in fact, does not say anything at all in Polanski's version, since his words are given to old Seyton, '*an Officer attending on Macbeth*'.

Unlike Nunn and Gold, Polanski presents the Ghost, thereby strengthening our identification with the protagonist. Thus, when Macbeth declares that the table is full, we already share *his* vision rather than that of the guests. Without resorting to any 'ghostly' effects at this point (shot 6), Polanski is nevertheless attuned to Shakespeare when he has Seyton and Ross indicate an empty chair which is empty neither to us nor to Macbeth. We are forced to question either the vision of the guests or Macbeth's and our own eyesight. Polanski further underscores *our* sense of hallucination by showing how two identical, black-sleeved arms from either side of the table keep pointing in the same direction. Mabeth's change from trust to doubt in his own vision is registered in shots 7–8, followed by his subjective vision (ghostly light, zoom-in) in shot 9. He now sees Banquo as he was when still in good health. Macbeth's terror at this sight is indicated both by his face and by his dropping of the goblet. The spilling of the red wine on the floor, quickly wiped up by his faithful servant, corresponds to the spilling of Banquo's blood in the scene before, a deed covered up by Macbeth's hired murderers. The connection is made clear through the quick transition from the spilt wine to Banquo's bleeding face, a testimony to Macbeth's rapidly increasing pangs of conscience.

It is interesting to compare Polanski's version of the banquet scene with the very different approach in Orson Welles's highly stylised, 'expressionist' black-and-white film of 1948. Here

[Macbeth's] face blenches at the sight of the ghost, and the scene cuts to the astonished, staring faces of the guests. Back in close-shot on the face of Macbeth ('Never say I did it'), he raises his finger, the shadow of which, pointing, takes the camera round until we see the table empty except for Banquo's ghost seated at the far end. Macbeth's drunken face sweats.[19]

Let us imagine a *stage* version in which the Ghost is not presented. 'Thou canst not say, I did it: never shake/Thy gory locks at me' will certainly be understood by the spectator to refer to the murder of Banquo. But the mere fact that the guests, who cannot understand the lines this way and must react accordingly, are kept visibly before us when Macbeth utters these words means that our attention as spectators will be divided.

If, by contrast, in a *screen* version the lines are matched by a close-up of the murdered Banquo in bluish light and the guests at this point are off-screen, we are completely at one with Macbeth's vision, even to the point of noting, with him, that Banquo 'replies' to his statement with a gesture of denial. From this we may conclude that, generally speaking, empathy is more easily stimulated by the screen than by the stage.

Macbeth's death

Text

Muir's text suggests that Macbeth is killed on the stage: Macbeth
and Macduff '*Re-enter fighting, and* MACBETH slain' (v.viii.35). Yet
in some texts (and many stage productions) he is killed off-stage.
An important consideration here is whether there is a scene-
change at this point, as Muir's text suggests, or not. For, if there
is not, keeping the killed Macbeth on stage creates problems for
the following relevant acting-direction: '*Re-enter* MACDUFF, *with*
MACBETH's *head*' (v.ix.19).

Stage

It is certainly not impossible to create the illusion that Macbeth is
decapitated on the stage. The severing of his head from his body
has at times been projected in shadow, or it has been disguised
by fighting soldiers surrounding Macbeth and Macduff.[20] Yet a
decapitation *in full view* would be exceedingly difficult to re-create
on the stage. Not so on the screen.

Television

In Nunn's TV version, the last we see of Macbeth is a medium
shot as he attacks Macduff with the words 'And damn'd be him
who first cries "Hold, enough!"' (v.viii.34). The next shot shows
the royal crown and shroud, before which the victorious Malcolm,
now entering the castle, stops. Only from the final shot, showing
Macduff's bloody hands and daggers next to the golden crown – a
shot pointing back to Macbeth's killing of Duncan – can we infer
that Macbeth has been slain. Nunn thus ends his teleplay with an
emblematic picture suggesting that in the neighbourhood of power
(the crown) we shall always find the temptation to usurp that
power (the daggers). The emblematic nature of this closing shot
is stressed by its being frozen. This is an emphatic device, the
counterpart of which on the stage would be a sustained spotlight
on crown, hands and daggers – a rather artificial solution.

In Gold's teleplay Macbeth and Macduff fight alone in the
throne-room of the castle, and – as with Nunn – we never witness
the actual killing of Macbeth. The last glimpses we get of him

alive are a series of close-ups as he fights with Macduff.

Film

In the film, by contrast, Macbeth and Macduff, when fighting with one another, are not alone but surrounded by soldiers who form a circle to watch them. Polanski's version of the sword fight has been criticised for being so long that it invites 'attention to technique, rather than to drama'.[21] But this is ignoring the true significance of the fight in the film, where what is traditionally depicted in a tragic–heroic vein is turned into an unheroic spectacle. The combatants use any weapons they can find; they clumsily fall on top of each other and are praised or jeered by the surrounding onlookers. We are not far from the Roman gladiatorial contest or the modern boxing-arena. The scene is in fact anticipated by the one in the English camp showing two soldiers fighting – for fun or as training – surrounded by their fellow soldiers.

By turning the sword fight into a rather long affair – with Nunn it is remarkably short – Polanski heightens the suspense, giving us time to empathise with the onlookers on the screen and to view the enacted events with their eyes. The fight ends in a most brutal way. While in the play text Macduff alone is responsible for Macbeth's death, Polanski's Macbeth is first stabbed in his back by the villainous Ross. The sequence is so swift that it is difficult to see that it is Ross who actually gives him the mortal wound – a very functional way of illustrating the sly nature of treachery. The wounded Macbeth symbolically creeps up the steps from which he has come down. Macduff follows him with raised sword. When the King reaches a landing, Macduff lets his sword fall, severing Macbeth's crowned head from his body. The head falls straight to ground level, while the harnassed body tumbles down the steps which it had just tried to ascend – again a symbolically pregnant situation.

The actual decapitation has derogatorily been called 'a grand-guignol effect',[22] but the point of it is that it involves us directly in the action. It is seen from the low-angle viewpoint of the multitude (the screen audience) below the landing; the logical extension of this viewpoint is that of the cinema audience. And the decapitated head falls not only downwards but also forwards, in the direction of the double audience. What Polanski – presumably influenced

by Artaud's ideas of maximum audience participation – has here
tried to depict is a form of public execution, recalling the hanging
of Cawdor at the beginning of the film. It is of course only natural that the screen audience should
welcome the killing of the enemy tyrant. But what about the real
audience? Do we, too, enjoy this cruel public spectacle? If so, is
it because we too feel that the tyrant gets what he deserves? Or is
it because there is a primitive thirst for blood in all of us, linking
us with the (more honest) audiences at former public executions
or at present-day bullfights? Or, on the contrary, are we, who
know Macbeth so much better than the screen audience does,
shocked by the brutality of the scene and the reaction of the
multitude? The answers to these questions depend, in part, on
whether or not we experience this screen multitude as akin to the
archetypal one which once shouted 'Let him be crucified'. In any
case, there can be little doubt that Polanski has designed the final
scenes as a provocation, allowing us to test our own reactions.

The ending

Text

Macbeth's death signifies the end of an era of tyranny; with
Malcolm as ruler a new democratic era begins. Shakespeare's
drama ends on a harmonious note:

> *Re-enter* MACDUFF, *with* MACBETH's *head.*
> MACDUFF. Hail, King! for so thou art. Behold, where stands
>   Th'usurper's cursed head: the time is free.
>   I see thee compass'd with thy kingdom's pearl,
>   That speak my salutation in their minds;
>   Whose voices I desire aloud with mine, –
>   Hail, King of Scotland!
> ALL. Hail, King of Scotland! *Flourish.*
> MALCOLM. We shall not spend a large expense of time,
>   Before we reckon with your several loves,
>   And make us even with you. My Thanes and kinsmen,
>   Henceforth be Earls; the first that ever Scotland
>   In such an honour nam'd. What's more to do,
>   Which would be planted newly with the time, –

As calling home our exil'd friends abroad,
That fled the snares of watchful tyranny;
Producing forth the cruel ministers
Of this dead butcher, and his fiend-like Queen,
Who, as 'tis thought, by self and violent hands
Took off her life; – this, and what needful else
That calls upon us, by the grace of Grace,
We will perform in measure, time, and place.
So thanks to all at once, and to each one,
Whom we invite to see us crown'd at Scone.
Flourish. Exeunt.

(v.ix)

The ending demonstrates how hubris has been punished and how justice is restored. The unrightful king (Macbeth), murderer of the rightful king (Duncan), is defeated by Duncan's son (Malcolm), the king-to-be. The wider implication of this has succinctly been described by Peter Hall: 'The play charts the progress of Scotland – which is a metaphor for the society of the audience who is watching it – from disease, sickness, corruption, terror, lies, hypocrisy, evil, back into health or – at least – the possibility of health.'[23] The historical significance of the change from evil tyranny to benevolent democracy is indicated by the raising of the thanes to the rank of earls, 'the first that ever Scotland/In such an honour nam'd'. Just as Malcolm, the good king, is to replace Macbeth, the evil tyrant, so a new nobility is to replace the old one.

It is noteworthy that an expectation that has been raised earlier in the play is not fulfilled at the end. In I.iii.67 the Third Witch told Banquo, 'Thou shalt get kings, though thou be none.' Yet in the end Banquo's son Fleance is not present, nor does Malcolm make any reference either to him or to Banquo. Part of Shakespeare's audience would undoubtedly have known that the witch would eventually prove right, that the Stuarts, descended from Banquo, many years later would become kings of Scotland. But this can hardly have been a reason for excluding Fleance. His absence in the ending is rather a sign of the playwright's wish not to disturb the impression of health restored. After all, any reference to Banquo's heirs at this point would have suggested a new rivalry, this time between Malcolm, elected by the people, and Fleance, 'elected' by the witches. Shakespeare apparently did not want a resigned *perpetuum mobile* ending of this kind. He settled for a more hopeful variant, feeling perhaps that the cleansing of evil on the stage would give the audience an appropriate sense of catharsis.

Television

By keeping the ending somewhat cryptic, Nunn does not radically depart from Shakespeare. In this version, the final impression seems to be: health is restored – but for how long? We do not doubt the honesty and democratic mind of Nunn's Malcolm, but he seems more a Hamletian thinker than a man of action. If we have doubts about his ability to establish a new and better regime, it is because he does not give the impression of being forceful enough. He may well fall a victim to a new brutal usurper. The emblematic final shot showing the crown next to the bloody hands holding the daggers may legitimate an interpretation along such lines.

A more definite departure from Shakespeare we find in Gold's version:

1 MACBETH *lying dead, sword in hand, on the red carpet covering the steps leading up to his throne.* MACDUFF, *standing L of him, takes the crown from his head, holds it in his hands, looks at it. Sound of harsh 'drumbeats'.*

2 MALCOLM *and attendants approach. Harsh 'drumbeats'.*

3 *Dead* MACBETH.
  MACDUFF, *next to him, turning to* MALCOLM.
  Hail . . . King! . . . for so thou art. The time is free.

4 *Pan with* MACDUFF *descending steps, walking up to* MALCOLM, *surrounded by thanes and kinsmen.*
  MACDUFF. I see thee compass'd with thy kingdom's pearl,
     That speak my salutation in their minds;
     Whose voices I desire aloud with mine, –
     Kneeling. Hail, King of Scotland!
  ALL *kneeling.* Hail, King of Scotland!
  MALCOLM, *receiving the crown from* MACDUFF, *turns around and gives attendants sign to stand up.*

MALCOLM *matter-of-factly.*
We shall not spend a large expense of time,
Before we reckon with your several loves,
And make us even with you. My Thanes and kinsmen,
Henceforth be Earls; the first that ever Scotland
In such an honour nam'd. What's more to do,
As would be newly planted with the time, –
As calling home our exil'd friends abroad,
That fled the snares of watchful tyranny;
Turning to MACDUFF.
Producing forth the cruel ministers
Of this dead butcher, and his fiend-like Queen,
Who, as 'tis thought, by self and violent hands
Took off her life; –
Zoom-in on MALCOLM, *crown in hands*
                    this, and what needful else
That calls upon us, by the grace of Grace,
We will perform in measure, time and place.
So thanks to all at once, and to each one,
Whom we invite to see us crown'd at Scone.

5   *Dead* MACBETH *on steps.* FLEANCE *enters from R, stops, his glance fixed on* MACBETH.

6   FLEANCE *looks at* MALCOLM. *Muffled 'drumbeats' until the end.*

7   MALCOLM *meets* FLEANCE's *glance, lowers crown in his hands.*

8   ANGUS.

9   LENNOX.

10   CAITHNESS(?).

11   MENTEITH(?).

12   ROSS.

13   FLEANCE *looking at* MALCOLM.

, 14   *Zoom-in on* MALCOLM, *looking at* FLEANCE.

15   *Dead* MACBETH *and* FLEANCE *standing R of him, still looking at* MALCOLM. *Picture turns yellowish red. Fade-in to white paper announcing final credits.*

In Gold's teleplay, we have observed, Macbeth is never decapitated, never degraded as he is in the play text. He dies a heroic death. The contrast between him and his 'democratic' successor is indicated by their positions: the dead Macbeth alone on the 'bloody' steps leading to the golden throne; Malcolm on ground level, surrounded by his thanes and kinsmen, all of them in grey chain-mail against a sombre grey background, their bodies throwing ominous black shadows on the ground as they approach us – much as Duncan and his attendants did in I.ii.

The matter-of-fact tone employed by Malcolm reveals that we are not here faced with the speech of a king intent on settling matters for the best. Rather we are confronted with a piece of rhetoric by a shrewd politician. In such a context, the raising of the thanes to earldoms will be felt as a pacifying piece of strategy. This impression is confirmed by the series of close-ups showing the sceptical faces of Malcolm's attendants, a series which calls to mind the earlier series of close-ups, showing the envious reactions of Duncan's attendants to his announcement that his eldest son, Malcolm, will henceforth be named Prince of Cumberland (I.iv.39). History repeats itself.

Unlike Shakespeare, Gold includes Fleance in the final scene. Just as Macbeth earlier questioned Malcolm's princely status, so Fleance now questions his royal one. After all, the witches had prophesied that Banquo, not Duncan, would 'get kings' (I.iii.67). Placed between the dead Macbeth and Malcolm, turning his glance from one to the other, Fleance seems to ask himself if Malcolm is not another usurper.

Malcolm seems to sense this. It is significant that he never puts the crown on his head, a pacifying non-gesture completely in line with his diplomatic way of addressing the attending noblemen. It is also significant that he lowers the crown as he meets Fleance's glance. In the closing shots Fleance's sceptical face (shots 6 and 13) brackets those of the attending noblemen – as though he incarnated a general distrust. At the end he and Malcolm face one another as two rivals. Fleance has taken Macbeth's place and the struggle that has just ceased can begin again. The change of colour in the concluding shot, corresponding to the one in the very first shot of the teleplay, takes us from the dark world in which we have been dwelling back into the supernaturally light one where we started out. There is also a telling contrast between the greyness surrounding Malcolm and his new regime and the red light in which the fallen warrior is bathed.

Film

Again, Polanski's version of the ending differs markedly from both Shakespeare's, Nunn's and Gold's:

1 *LA of* MACDUFF *on landing.*
   MACDUFF. Hail King! for so thou art.
   Pointing downwards with his sword.
   Behold where lies th'usurper's cursed head:

2 *Tilt down to* MACBETH's *severed, crowned head.*
   Two black gloves grip the crown. Tilt up to

3 *their owner:* ROSS. *Pan with* ROSS *as he walks R,*
   raising crown high above him.

4 MALCOLM *taking off his soldier's helmet.*
   ALL *off-screen.* Hail!

5 *HA of* ROSS, *smiling.* Hail, King of Scotland!

6 *LA of* MALCOLM *receiving crown.*
   ALL *off-screen.* Hail, King of Scotland!

7 MALCOLM *putting on crown.*

8 *Out-of-focus flash shots panning with* MACBETH's *severed head as it is carried on a pole along the crowd of soldiers mockingly laughing at it. Loud shrill sound.*

9   SOLDIERS *on wooden erection shouting.* Hail!

10 MACBETH's *head waved on the pole high above the walls of the castle. Zoom-out. Acclamation of multitude below.*

11 *Establishing-shot of the ruin of the* WITCHES *on the heath. Heavy rain. Sombre music of bagpipes.*

12 *A rider in black cloak and hood on a white horse approaches the ruin.*

13 *The face of the rider:* DONALBAIN. *Neighing of horse, crooning of* WITCHES *inside ruin.*

14 DONALBAIN *on horseback. Crooning.*

15 *The face of* DONALBAIN. *Crooning.*

16 DONALBAIN *by crooked branch of a tree.*

17 *The back of* DONALBAIN, *limping down to* WITCHES' *smoking cauldron.*

18 *The ruin. Ominous, sombre music mingling with sound of 'heartbeats'.*

Even more than the teleplays, the film departs from Shakespeare's positive conclusion. In a number of ways Polanski suggests that, if the new regime differs from the old one, it is merely in being petty, mediocre, totally lacking in grandeur. Our scepticism about what is to come is nourished from the moment that Macbeth is 'dethroned': Polanski shows us two black-gloved hands taking the crown off the severed head. It is the treacherous villain in the film, Ross, the tool first of Duncan, then of Macbeth, finally of Macduff, who is now the first to hail Malcolm as king of Scotland. The indications of a new and better regime found in Malcolm's speech are missing in the film for the simple reason that the whole speech has been cut.

Unlike Gold's Malcolm, Polanski's does not hesitate to put the crown on his head. The whole situation comes ironically close to the crowning of Macbeth at Scone which we have witnessed earlier. Polanski has, as it were, designed an inverted *le roi est mort, vive le roi* scene: that is, we move from Malcolm putting the crown on his head to the crownless head of Macbeth carried on a pole along the multitude, from the hailing of one head to the mocking of another. As we have already noted, the whole situation at the end carries overtones of the Crucifixion. We have soldiers mocking the victim and an easily swayed multitude, and, just as the mocked King of the Jews hung on a cross high above his blasphemers, so Macbeth's severed head is waved high above the mocking crowd, a sign of how he, despite his crimes, towered above the petty men who have now conquered the stage.

The film ends with an epilogue (from shot 11), partly harking back to the prologue with which it began. In the opening the witches had asked, 'When shall we three meet again/In thunder, lightning, or in rain?' Now we are back with the witches in a very Scottish setting – heath, bagpipes, rain – indicating the sombre future for the country.

Donalbain's visit to the ruin is suggestive in several ways. It recalls Macbeth's earlier visit to the ruin and thus links him with the ambitious usurper; we sense that he is as eager to replace his brother Malcolm on the throne as was Macbeth with regard to Duncan. Donalbain's ugly limping puts him on a par with Richard III, his black figure on a white horse with Ross – both indications of his treacherous nature. His all-black appearance and his stopping by the branch of a *dwarf* birch (reminiscent of the crooked stick seen in the beginning) turns him, as it were, into the deadly old First Witch of the prologue, while his walking-away into the distance recalls the receding of the Second Witch at the end of the pre-credit sequence. The end of the film shows us another 'walking shadow' (v.v) – Macbeth's image of man – with the difference that this one is limping. The concluding shot is a long shot of the witches' ruin, isolated on the heath, a Dunsinane *in petto*.

Macbeth **and the media**

In my examination of *Macbeth* I have focused on three passages in the play text: the opening, the beginning of the banquet scene, and the ending.

In relation to these passages, I have deliberately abstained from discussing the translation problems involved in, for example, Bergman's version, since it would have been very difficult to clarify to readers unfamiliar with Swedish what is here at stake.

While stage versions have been discussed only in passing (except for Bergman's treatment of the opening scene) and radio versions not at all, the focus has been on two TV versions (Nunn, Gold) and one film production (Polanski).

Are media differences more fundamental than differences in directorial approach or is it the other way around? Do we agree with Marshall McLuhan that 'the medium is the message'?[24] Or do we think that the directorial approach determines the message? The preceding pages should have convinced the reader that this is not a question of either–or but of both–and. A director will on the one hand always try to bend a medium to his vision; on the other hand, he has to adjust his vision to the capabilities of the chosen medium.

When comparing the two TV versions, we must take into account that Nunn's version was an adaptation of his stage production, whereas Gold's was made directly for television. From this one might be tempted to draw the conclusion that Gold's version is better suited to the TV medium and therefore superior to Nunn's. The opposite is true. Both Nunn's stage production and his TV adaptation are generally considered as landmarks in British stagings of Shakespeare. One would perhaps also assume that Nunn's teleplay is very different from his stage version and that this would explain its success. Again, the opposite is true. According to Michael Mullin, 'the television shooting script follows the same staging as that used in the theatre'. Mullin presents five reasons why the Nunn teleplay is a successful adaptation: (i) the production had been tested in repertory; (ii) the small stage created a production style that carried over to television; (iii) the ritual style suited television because the audience was asked to believe only in the reality of the emotions released in the performance; (iv) the rhythm of the camera work followed the emotional rhythm of the script; and (v) special TV effects were avoided – the TV medium was kept subordinate to the drama.[25]

Mullin here tries to steer clear of the Scylla of filmed theatre on the one hand and the Charybdis of screen drama – the naïve exploitation of the technicalities of the TV medium – on the other.

As his point (iv) indicates, Nunn's teleplay is successful not least because the director here proves to be deeply sensitive to the TV medium. By which I mean that he is handling it subtly rather than spectacularly. In the best sense of the word Nunn has adjusted – rather than subordinated – the TV medium to the play text.

Chapter 3

Representing the Source Text: Ibsen's *Et Dukkehjem* / *A Doll's House* (1879)

While *Macbeth* is generally characterised as a tragedy, opinions are more divided with regard to *A Doll's House*. Is Ibsen's play, too, a tragedy, dealing with internal conflicts and universal, inescapable issues? Or is it a problem play, dealing largely with social problems that can be solved? *A Doll's House* has been interpreted both ways. While the generic labelling itself does not concern us, the consequences it has for any transposition of the play do. Obviously, a director who sees *A Doll's House* as a problem play would create a production differing in tone and emphasis from one who sees it as a tragedy. If he is free to choose his medium, his choice may well depend upon the generic approach.

Even if a director of *Macbeth* does not have these problems, he still has to establish the nature of the relationship between Macbeth and Lady Macbeth, since this will directly bear upon the question how flawed Macbeth, the protagonist, is. Similarly, a director of *A Doll's House* must, on the basis of Ibsen's text, specify the relationship between Nora and Torvald Helmer.

Synopsis

Act I. Nora Helmer returns home from a shopping-trip, loaded with Christmas gifts for her three children and for her husband Torvald, who has just been appointed manager of the Credit Bank with a substantial increase in salary. Mrs Linde, an old friend whom Nora has not seen in ten years, makes a surprise call. Nora reveals a secret to her: when she and Helmer were first married, Helmer had a serious illness and was forced to live for a time in Italy. To pay for this, Nora secretly borrowed a sum secured on the signature of her now dead father. Since that time she has been repaying the loan with whatever she has been able to save.

Nora persuades her husband to provide a job at the bank for Mrs Linde shortly after. Nils Krogstad, a bank employee of dubious reputation, calls on Helmer. It is from Krogstad that Nora has borrowed the money. Left alone with her, Krogstad demands to know whether he is to be replaced in the bank by Mrs Linde. (Years ago the two had an affair.) He threatens that, should he be discharged, he will not only reveal Nora's secret to her husband but also disclose that she forged her dead father's signature. When Helmer returns, he declares Krogstad a cunning forger and lectures Nora on the dangerous influence he could exert.

Act II. The following day Nora awaits Krogstad's letter to her husband. She is saddened when Helmer again refuses to spare Krogstad and resolves to ask Dr Rank, a close friend of the Helmers, for money to redeem her note. But, before she has the opportunity to do so, Rank reveals that he is soon to die of an inherited disease. He also reveals that he has been in love with her for many years. These revelations make Nora feel that she cannot ask Rank for any help.

Krogstad returns, secretly to tell her that he has prepared a letter informing her husband of the loan. Nora hints that she is contemplating suicide. As he leaves, Krogstad drops the letter into the letter-box.

Mrs Linde, who is now fully informed, leaves to visit Krogstad in order to plead for Nora. Meanwhile, Nora rehearses the tarantella she is to perform at a fancy-dress ball the following evening.

Act III. While the Helmers are at the fancy-dress ball upstairs, Mrs Linde and Krogstad meet in the living-room. There is a reconciliation between the former lovers, now both widowed and in need of each other. Mrs Linde's faith in Krogstad reawakens the goodness in him. He wants to withdraw the letter, but Mrs Linde feels that Nora must tell her husband the truth.

Back from the party, Helmer claims his 'conjugal rights'. Rank interrupts them. As he leaves, a black-crossed card dropped into the letter-box confirms Nora's suspicion that Rank's 'good night' is in fact a final leave-taking.

When Rank has left, Helmer opens the letter-box. Having read Krogstad's letter, he begins to scold his wife violently for causing such a blow to his pride and position. They must continue with the pretence of married life, he states, but Nora will no longer be allowed to bring up her children. When a second letter from Krogstad arrives, saying that, in remorse, he is destroying the bond, Helmer is relieved. But Nora compels him to sit down for their first serious talk in the eight years they have been married.

She tells him that, having lived first as her father's 'doll child', then as Helmer's 'doll wife', she must now 'try and educate' herself. Moreover, after Helmer's revealing reaction to the two letters, she has discovered that she has been living all these years with 'a stranger'. She leaves the house, telling her husband that reconciliation can come only if their 'life together' could become 'a marriage'. Helmer, left alone, clings to this idea.

Title

Traditionally the English title of Ibsen's play is *A Doll's House.* But Ibsen's title 'does not mean a house of dolls, which in Norwegian is *dukkehus,* or *dukkestue.* Before Ibsen, *et dukkehjem* was a small, cozy, neat home; his play gave it the pejorative meaning.'[1] As a result, one of Ibsen's American translators, Rolf Fjelde, prefers the title *A Doll House* – also because 'one can make a reasonable supposition that Ibsen . . . at least partially includes Torvald with Nora in the original title *Et dukkehjem*, for the two of them at the play's opening are still posing like the little marzipan bride and groom atop the wedding cake'.[2]

However, defenders of the traditional English title could, of course, object that only Nora is depicted as a doll in the play, and that it is she who complains that both her father and, after him, Helmer have been treating her as a doll. Moreover, the singular possessive in 'doll's house' does not automatically imply one possessor (compare 'bird's nest'). Finally, the traditional title is the nearest natural English equivalent to the Norwegian one.

Plot

Reduced to its essence, the plot of *A Doll's House* may be sketched as follows. In Act I, the major question we ask ourselves is: will Nora's forgery be revealed? Already it is apparent that Krogstad (the antagonist) is a threat to her.

Act II deals with Nora's attempts to find an escape from this threatening situation. She first tries to persuade Helmer to let Krogstad stay in the bank. When this fails, she contemplates borrowing money from Rank but (i) his declaration of love and (ii) his revelation of his imminent death make this impossible. She finally tries to prevent Krogstad from revealing anything, this too in vain.

Having failed in all her attempts, Nora in the final act realises that her forgery will be revealed. We now ask ourselves: how will Helmer react to this? The crisis comes as Helmer reads Krogstad's first letter, in which he threatens to reveal the forgery. Helmer, scandalised, attacks Nora. But when he reads Krogstad's second letter, in which the threat is withdrawn, he forgives her (*peripeteia*). Helmer's true nature has now been revealed to Nora. Far from being a noble altruist, he has disclosed himself as an egoist, who only cares about appearances. How will Nora react to this? Resolution: she leaves her husband and children to 'educate' herself.

As is evident from the synopsis, only three of the six characters – notably Krogstad – forward the plot. It is also apparent that Ibsen moves from a fairly superficial type of suspense to more penetrating and worrying questions.

Cue designations

Consistent with Ibsen's own practice, I shall use the surname for the husband, the first name for the wife. In his 'Notes for the Tragedy of Today', which clearly relates to *A Doll's House*, Ibsen had written, 'There are two kinds of spiritual laws, two kinds of conscience, one for men and one, quite different, for women.'[3] No doubt the difference in cue designations serves to indicate the contrast between Nora's (female) individualism – her first name being the only one that is truly hers – and Helmer's socially determined (male) role of *paterfamilias*. The name caption 'Nora' – in contrast to 'Mrs Linde' – may also be seen as an anticipation of her final individualist revolt. To emphasise the doll aspect, Ibsen uses the shortened pet form of the name rather than the full one (Eleonora).

Setting

Text

As usual, Ibsen's description of the setting is fairly detailed:

> *A pleasantly and tastefully, but not expensively, furnished room. A door to the right in the background leads to the hall; another door to the left in the background leads to* HELMER'*s study. Between these two doors a piano. In the middle of the left wall a door, with a window downstage of it. Near the window, a round table with armchairs and a small sofa. In the right wall, slightly upstage, is a door; downstage of this, against the same wall, a stove lined with porcelain tiles, with a couple of armchairs and a rocking-chair in front of it. Between the stove and the side door a small table. Engravings on the walls. A what-not with china and other bric-à-brac; a small bookcase with books in handsome bindings. Carpet on the floor; a fire in the stove. A winter's day.*

When first confronted with this living-room, we find it hard to see much significance in it. It all looks quite attractive and respectable, a 'doll's house' in the pre-Ibsen sense of the term. The piano (music), the engravings (art) and the books (literature) suggest that at least one of the inhabitants has cultural interests. That is about all.

However, when we reread the play, the setting takes on a greater significance. We can now see that the room reveals Helmer's rather than Nora's taste. *He* is the ruler in this household and he is the one who explicitly voices his aesthetic interests.

Therefore, as Helmer is gradually revealed as a man hiding behind a socially impeccable façade, the living-room takes on other qualities. The properties we took to be signs of cultural interests now appear to be merely status objects, social icons. Like the play title, the setting is thus vested by Ibsen with a pejorative meaning.

We may also ascribe the fact that the whole action takes place in one and the same room as a sign that Nora is imprisoned in a doll's house existence – although the room, as Austin Quigley points out, has 'no fewer than four doors, one of which leads to a fifth and a sixth'.[4] This raises the question of whether this is an open or a closed environment.

Even if Ibsen's stage-directions are not followed in productions of the play, directors and scenographers must certainly clarify to themselves what the playwright intends by these directions. As Peter Reynolds observes, you cannot 'understand what the characters *say* . . . unless you can read the visual *context* in which it is said'.[5] This must not be understood as a plea for slavish adherence to Ibsen's stage-directions; it merely means that an awareness of the interplay in the drama text between the characters and the setting is essential for a true understanding of the play and for any production of it.

Stage

In a recent production of *A Doll's House* by the Royal Shakespeare Company, the scenographer, Kit Surrey, departed from Ibsen's realistic interior, yet retained much of its implicit significance:

> Kit Surrey designed a carpet. . . . The carpet emphasized the doors and gave the set a feeling of being surrounded by other rooms – not only in the apartment itself, but also in the rest of the building. Privacy in this environment is at a premium. . . . The couple take great pains not to disturb their neighbours . . . .
> On this brown carpet, Kit Surrey placed furniture and effects carefully chosen to signal the status and image that this couple wish to present to the world and to themselves.[6]

In the 1985 Gothenburg production, the walls of the living-room were merely indicated; behind them a winter landscape could be seen with (the Helmer) children throwing snowballs at one another – in anticipation of conflicts in store. Once the lights were transferred to the interior, the warm orange-red carpet of the living-room vividly contrasted with the bluish cold outside. Very different from these open settings was the one seen in Bergman's highly condensed Munich version of the play. His *Nora* – for his choice of title Bergman adjusted to a practice common in Germany – was one of three thematically related plays produced simultaneously under the title *The Bergman Project*. The others were Strindberg's *(Miss) Julie* and Bergman's stage version of his own film *Scenes from a Marriage*. The setting for *Nora* demonstrated a radical departure from Ibsen's living-room:

> The entire stage space was a limbo cut off from any contact with the world of reality – a void encompassed by an immense, non-representational box that was uniformly lined with a dark-red, velvetlike fabric. Within this vast, closed space, a smaller enclosure was defined by high, dark walls that suggested both the panelled interior of a courtroom and the wainscoting of a polite mid-Victorian parlor. Neither windows nor doors existed to alleviate the impression of solemnity and constrictive solidity conveyed by this maximum-security coffin–prison. . . . At the geometrical center of the stage, a low, quadrilateral platform stood like an island in the midst of this forbidding framework of wallscreens. This was the acting area proper . . .[7]

As often with Bergman, the setting emphasised the idea that marriage is a prison, where one is deprived of one's individual freedom and where the partners constantly sit in judgement on each other – an idea common in modern drama ever since Strindberg's *Dance of Death*, a play Bergman had been rehearsing a few years earlier.

Having reduced the text by nearly a third, Bergman presented the play in fifteen scenes rather than three acts. Central to his production was the idea that 'Nora is conscious from the outset of her frustration and longing to escape from a narrow, constrictive existence that is gradually suffocating her.'[8] Bergman's approach to the play was clearly determined by the fact that it was part of a kind of trilogy:

The important thing to me is to present *A Doll's House* and *Miss Julie* and *Scenes from a Marriage* not as three separate productions, but as one production. What I would have liked to do here [at the Residenztheater] would have been to construct an intimate stage on the big stage, and then play *Scenes from a Marriage* at three in the afternoon. *A Doll's House* at seven and *Julie* at nine o'clock in the evening.[9]

The special question Bergman's version of Ibsen's play poses is the following: how did the production of *Nora* relate to the other two productions of the triad? Presumably it would have turned out differently, had it been an independent *mise-en-scène*.

The opening

Text

Ibsen opens his play on a harmonious note; in Michael Meyer's translation,

> *A bell rings in the hall outside. After a moment we hear the front door being opened.* NORA *enters the room, humming contentedly to herself. She is wearing outdoor clothes and carrying a lot of parcels, which she puts down on the table right. She leaves the door to the hall open; through it, we can see the* PORTER *carrying a Christmas tree and a basket. He gives these to the* MAID, *who has opened the door for them.*

> NORA. Hide that Christmas tree away, Helen. The children mustn't see it before I've decorated it this evening. *To the* PORTER, *taking out her purse.* How much – ?
> PORTER. A shilling.
> NORA. Here's half a crown. No, keep it.

> *The* PORTER *touches his cap and goes.* NORA *closes the door.*

This opening immediately suggests that it is Christmas Eve. It also tells us that Nora is paying the Porter more than one would normally do, but we cannot, as readers, make out why this is so. Is Nora a spendthrift? Is she unusually generous because it is

Christmas? (A third possibility – that Nora is generous, because her husband's financial position has recently improved – is still unknown to us at this point.) In performance, however, it is likely that the exact nature of Nora's 'generosity' will be clarified by the way in which the actress handles the situation. As J. L. Styan observes, 'performance makes the point: does she give the man the larger coin with a careless air, thus declaring her indifference to money, or does she hesitate for just a moment before she says, "keep the change".'[10]

However, Ibsen's opening means more than this. John Northam has drawn attention to the Christmas tree as a 'symbol of family happiness and security'.[11] But, as Quigley convincingly demonstrates, the tree above all relates to what might be termed the mask-versus-face theme of the play as well as to Nora, as an exponent of this theme:

> The Christmas tree . . . is dressed and then stripped – which links it with the later fancy-dress ball and the costume Nora first dons and later discards. . . . The 'real' tree for the children is to be the dressed tree, not its unadorned version. And this links the notion of dress and costume to that of deception and masquerade, which in turn links with Nora's deception of Torvald about borrowing money and Dr Rank's disguising for twenty long years his true feelings for Nora. This, in turn, makes us aware that some kinds of deception, like hiding the unadorned Christmas tree, can be for potentially good purposes. The ambivalent value thus attributed to deception later interacts with Nora's lying in general, with her role-playing for a variety of purposes. . . . the ambivalent values of this home will, we suspect, at some point enable us to link the unadorned Christmas tree . . . with the figure of Nora . . . .[12]

Discerning as it is, Quigley's thematic network may well come close to Ibsen's own experience while writing the play; in both cases we deal with the insight of intense and scrupulous rereaders, a situation very different from that of the ordinary theatregoer.

Translation

The connection between Nora and the Christmas tree is even verbally present in the Norwegian original: in the beginning Nora speaks of the tree being *pyntet* (decorated), while midway in the play Mrs Linde expresses her wish to see Nora *pyntet*. This significant correspondence is – unavoidably? – lost in Meyer's rendering (emphasis added):

NORA. . . . . The children mustn't see it before I've *decorated* it.

MRS LINDE. I did so want to see Nora *in her costume.*

Once we see the significance of the Christmas tree, it makes a difference whether Nora herself is to decorate it – as Meyer has it – or whether, as Ibsen, McFarlane and Watts have it,[13] the question of who is to do it is left open.

Another translation problem in the opening sequence relates to ethnic (national) differences. Whereas Meyer's characters speak of English money, those of McFarlane and Watts retain the Norwegian monetary system. Watts even provides a footnote which informs us that 'fifty øre' is 'the equivalent of a sixpence', while 'a hundred øre equals one krone, then worth just over a shilling' – helpful information for the reader but not for the spectator; the latter runs the risk of missing the whole point of the money transaction. This kind of problem does not exist when we turn to translations from Norwegian into, for example, Swedish, where the monetary system is similar.

Stage

In Bergman's drastically abridged adaptation Ibsen's opening sequence was omitted altogether and, instead of seeing a happy Nora entering her home, the spectator was confronted with a Nora

  already seated, utterly immobile, in the midst of a wilderness of toys, dolls, and other suggestive relics of childhood. Leaning back against the pillows of the plush sofa, she stared out into empty space – virtually the picture of a human doll . . . . The very distant and faintly audible sound of an old-fashioned music-box tune added to the strongly oneiric [dream-like] mood of nostalgia and suppressed melancholy that was created by this silent image of her motionless, oddly dejected figure.[14]

The opening lines were:

NORA. Come here, Torvald, and I'll show you all the things I've bought.
HELMER. Don't disturb me! (*Enters.*) Bought did you say? All this?[15]

Having done away with the 'tipping scene', Bergman nevertheless indicated Nora's spendthrift mentality by surrounding her with Christmas presents. But, with these changes, the situations in play text and stage performance are no longer identical, and to the recipient (as opposed to the re-recipient) Bergman's opening suggested rather that Nora was a loving mother spoiling her children.

Opening his play at a later point than Ibsen, Bergman also lost the symbolic value attached to the Christmas tree; in his version it was already placed and decorated when the curtain rose.

In a realistic performance, one expects the Christmas presents to be hidden in boxes and parcels. This aspect did not interest Bergman, to whom the symbolic connotations of the presents themselves – '*a helmet and sword, two large dolls, a locomotive*' – were of much greater significance. As often with Bergman, his opening presented a visual image – a *tableau vivant*, as it were – setting the thematic keynote for his production. Presented as a doll among dolls, Nora was shown to be treating her children just as she herself was being treated, perpetuating a harmful tradition and at the same time compensating for her own dependent position. (It is interesting to note that Bergman had already utilised the doll symbolism in his film *Cries and Whispers* to indicate the immature, all-too-flexible mentality of Maria.)

Radio

When the opening passage is omitted in abridged radio presentations, it is simply due to fact that plot value – relating to the dramatic build of the play – ranks higher than thematic value, relating to the play texture. And the plot value of the opening sequence is low.

This is how three Swedish radio-script versions open. The first one, from 1944, reads,

NORA. . . . Helene!
HELENE. Yes.
NORA. Pay the porter and hide the Christmas tree. The children mustn't see it until tonight, when it is decorated. You understand?
HELENE. Yes, ma'am! *Out. Door.*

Here the first sign of Nora's spendthrift mentality has been omitted. In another radio version, three years later, the whole opening situation has been cut; the play starts with Nora's 'Come out here, Torvald, and see what I've bought.' A third version, from 1953, begins in a surprisingly conventional manner:

NARRATOR. The action takes place in the home of Torvald Helmer, a lawyer, in the 1880s.

Jingle of sleigh-bells at a distance. An old-fashioned door-bell rings. A door is opened.

NORA *at a distance.* How do you do, Helene! – Hide the Christmas tree well. The children mustn't see it until tonight, when it is decorated.
HELENE. Yes, ma'am.
NORA *approaches humming.*

In this last instance the listener is in very orderly fashioned informed about time and place both by a narrator and by sound-effects (bells).

Television

Turning to the TV medium, we again find a great variety. This is how Brinckman's textually rather faithful Norwegian production opens:

1   NORA *in red coat and* PORTER *with Christmas tree outside door.* NORA *rings the bell.*

2   *CU of* NORA *through glass of door, from inside. Ringing of bell.*

3   HELMER *at desk in his green-walled study, book in L hand, pen in R. When he hears the bell he smiles, gets up, goes to the door of his room, opens it, looks out.*

4   *The hall and behind it a long corridor. A door in BG is opened and the* MAID [HELENE], *approaches.*

5   HELMER *in door opening waves to the* MAID *with his book, indicating that she should open the door.*

6   MAID *opens front door.* NORA *enters with a basket full of parcels in one hand and a big parcel in the other. Behind her the* PORTER *with the Christmas tree and another basket full of parcels.*

    NORA.   Hide the Christmas tree away, Helene.

7   *Pan with* NORA *as she moves into the living-room, where she puts down the parcels; turning to* MAID, *who is still by front door.*

    NORA.   The children mustn't see it before it is decorated this evening.

8   MAID *and* PORTER *with Christmas tree by front door.* MAID *takes tree and basket from* PORTER *and disappears R.*

9   NORA *up to* PORTER, *takes out her purse.* How much – ?

PORTER. Fifty øre.
NORA. Here's a crown. No, keep it.

PORTER *thanks her and leaves.* NORA *closes door.*

In retrospect the first shot is remarkable in that it is the only exterior shot in the whole teleplay. As such it clearly relates to the ending, where Nora leaves her doll's house for the world outside. Within nine shots Ibsen's two-room set (hall and living-room) has been extended with three more areas (exterior, study, corridor).

We may further note that already, in this brief opening sequence, husband and wife are contrasted visually: he is keeping check of the money at his desk; she has just been spending a lot of it. Helmer also immediately establishes his role-play as *paterfamilias*: he knows that Nora is at the front door but it is below his dignity to go to the door himself; he orders the maid to go.

A rather different approach is found in the 1958 Swedish TV script:

During the credits a pair of hands are seen picking up Christmas decorations from a table – Norwegian union flags, balls, flowers, candle-holders, candles. The decorations are neatly arranged in rows. When the credits are finished, there is a momentary switch to ANNE-MARIE's *face, as* NORA *can be heard by the front door.*

NORA. Please put the Christmas tree there in the hall. How much is it?

ANNE-MARIE *alone in picture, busy with the candles.*
The voice of a PORTER. Fifty öre.

NORA. Here's a crown. No, keep it all.

ANNE-MARIE *shakes her head – lovingly – at this generosity. Then* NORA *enters the room.*

NORA. Hide the Christmas tree carefully, Anne-Marie. The children mustn't see it until tonight when it is decorated.

ANNE-MARIE *goes to the hall.* NORA *goes to the door by* HELMER'*s study.*[16]

By means of the little flags the director provides a link between the imbalanced union between Sweden and Norway, on the one hand, and that of the marital partners, on the other: Nora's leaving Helmer anticipating Norway's independence of Sweden, achieved in 1905. The neat arrangement of the Christmas decorations introduces us, as it were, to the aesthetic doll-house world. Nora's generosity is experienced via the nurse Anne-Marie (rather than the maid), who, rather like Helmer, takes a critical–benevolent attitude to her.

Much more removed from the drama text is the opening in the 1970 Swedish TV version. In his script the adapter–director, Per Sjöstrand, has divided the play into no fewer than sixty-five different scenes, each scene shift representing a change of place. In the opening section we move with Nora from the Credit Bank (scenes 1–2), where Helmer has just officially accepted his new post as manager, to a toy shop (3), then to a shop for gloves (4), then back to the bank (5), then to a tea-room (6), then back to the bank again, inside (7–8) and outside (9), and finally to outside the Helmers' apartment house (10). Not until scene 11 do we find ourselves in the hall, where Ibsen's play begins. Once inside the house, we see in turn the various rooms of the apartment; besides the drawing-room and the hall, Helmer's study, the dining-room, the children's room and the kitchen. Toward the end, a couple of scenes take place in the street outside. This arrangement is only slightly simplified in the actual production.

It can be seen from this that Sjöstrand opens his production by cross-cutting between Helmer's masculine world and Nora's feminine one – a contrast that, as Birgitta Steene has observed, the play text already indicates in spatial terms by having Rank and Krogstad but not Nora enter Helmer's study.[17] Nora's doll mentality is demonstrated from the very beginning as she listens *'with childish affection'* to her husband's speech (added by Sjöstrand) about 'trustful collaboration' – a speech which seems utterly hypocritical to Krogstad, who has just learnt that he has been dismissed.

An advantage of Sjöstrand's rearrangement is that the meeting between Nora, Mrs Linde and Rank is made more plausible. The two women simply come across each other in the tea-room, where Rank after a while joins them. Nora's secret eating of macaroons is replaced by her revelling in pastries – against her explicit promise to Helmer. Nora brings Mrs Linde from the tea-room to the bank, in the hope that she can persuade Helmer to find a post for her there. From the bank, Sjöstrand cuts to a shot of Nora with her three children on the sofa in the Helmer drawing-room, the lonely Mrs Linde sitting opposite the happy family.

In Sjöstrand's adaptation not only the initial porter sequence but also the fairly long 'lark-and-squirrel' passage, which establishes the doll-house relationship between Helmer and Nora, has been replaced by a sequence depicting the social environment to which the Helmer household belongs.

Film

The same tendency to incorporate the surrounding environment is found to an even greater extent in Joseph Losey's film (1973), shot on location in Røros, Norway. Here several shots of the church, which towers above the houses of the town but is surrounded by mist, seem to insist on the repressive social role played by religion.

Losey's film opens with a pre-title sequence, taking us back to the pre-scenic events of the play. A few establishing-shots indicate that the time is around or before the turn of the century: men and women (in long dresses!) are skating; there are horse-sleighs with bells. Nora and Mrs Linde take off their skates and enter a coffee-house by the skating-rink. We learn that Nora is getting married to Helmer within a week, while Mrs Linde has been forced to dismiss Krogstad for a husband with a secure income. This prologue outlines the contrasting situations in which the two women find themselves, one joining a man, the other leaving one. The irony is that, despite leaving Krogstad, Mrs Linde is truly in love with him, while Nora, despite marrying Helmer, seems more in love with the status and prospects he offers than with Helmer himself. In this way Losey, unlike Ibsen, interprets the past for us and makes us side with Mrs Linde rather than Nora from the very beginning.

After the credits, we are introduced to the urban environment.

We witness Nora, pregnant, and Rank, the doctor, next to her dying father; the Helmers' departure for Italy and their return from there; the interior of the Credit Bank and of a tea-room; we accompany Nora as she is buying Christmas presents and a Christmas tree. For some of these scenes Losey comes exceedingly close to Sjöstrand's TV script. But, in contrast to the Swedish director, Losey shows Nora entering the hall along with the porter.

Like Sjöstrand, Losey 'breaks up the theatrical time/space continuum by setting the action in a variety of locations and by cross-cutting among them for dramatic emphasis and tension'.[18] In a film Nora can be shown more fully and more convincingly in the outside world than in the most heavily adapted, multi-set stage version; in this sense Losey's presentation seems to have been influenced by his medium. Yet his use of the film medium appears to be in conflict with a major theme of the play. Ibsen's unity of setting strengthens our feeling that Nora is a prisoner in her husband's house; her final exit seems so definite not the least because it is the first time that we see her leave her doll's house. In Losey's film this essential aspect is fatally diluted by the romantic exterior shots of the beautiful wooden houses of Røros, of turn-of-the-century horse-sleighs and of skating ladies.

As Foster Hirsch notes, Losey's version of the Helmers' house

> is a series of rooms that open into one another, so that there is a sense of deep and receding space; behind the living room can be seen the dining room; on the other side of the stairs from Nora's bedroom is the children's room – the physical separation between Nora and her children, the children glimpsed in the rear of the frame with their nurse, makes a telling point about Nora's distance from them. . . . The apartment . . . looks nothing like a doll's house, being clearly the residence of very sober and well-off adults. There is no sign of 'Nora in these stiff and beautifully appointed rooms, no expression of her lightheartedness and charm. The mise-en-scène makes her seem like a stranger in her own house . . . .[19]

A stranger – or a prisoner! In his design for the Helmer residence Losey tries to win back what he has lost by letting Nora out of her doll's house.

In contrast to Losey, Patrick Garland in his film version, also dating from 1973, shows us little of the world outside the Helmers' apartment. And the apartment in a film, Bazin assures us, feels even more cramped than a room on the stage.[20] The most obvious exception to this rule is the opening establishing-shot:

1 NORA *behind* COACHMAN *in a horse-sleigh riding through a snowy landscape. Jingling of sleigh-bells. Music-box music. Children throwing snowballs at the sleigh, which continues into town.*

2 *A front door (from inside). Ringing of doorbell.*
 A MAID *opens the door, which has a Christmas garland on it, and lets in* NORA, *who carries a lot of parcels, including a doll's bed. Music-box music.*

 NORA. Is Mr Helmer in?
 MAID. Yes, ma'am.

The romantic initial shot serves several functions. It introduces us to the protagonist, Nora, as a passive female passenger next to an active male, taking her from the countryside (nature) into the town (society/culture). Somewhere in between they are attacked by the children. The diegetic sound of the sleigh-bell contrasts with the non-diegetic one of the doll-like music-box. In his opening shot the director has obviously tried to present Nora's dilemma in a nutshell.

The tarantella

Text

The tarantella scene is the most spectacular one in the play. In Meyer's translation it reads,

 NORA. . . . Let me start practising now, at once – we've still time before dinner. Oh, do sit down and play for me, Torvald, dear. Correct me, lead me, the way you always do.
 HELMER. Very well, my dear, if you wish it.

 He sits down at the piano. NORA *seizes the tambourine and a long*

*multi-coloured shawl from the cardboard box, wraps the shawl
hastily around her, then takes a quick leap into the centre of the
room and cries.*

NORA. Play for me! I want to dance!

HELMER *plays and* NORA *dances.* DR RANK *stands behind* HELMER
at the piano and watches her.

HELMER *as he plays.* Slower, slower!
NORA. I can't! . . .
RANK. Let me play for her.
HELMER *gets up.* Yes, would you? Then it'll be easier for me to
    show her.

RANK *sits down at the piano and plays.* NORA *dances more and
more wildly.* HELMER *has stationed himself by the stove and tries
repeatedly to correct her, but she seems not to hear him. Her hair
works loose and falls over her shoulders; she ignores it and
continues to dance.* . . .

HELMER. But, Nora darling, you're dancing as if your life
    depended on it.
NORA. It does.
HELMER. Rank, stop it! This is sheer lunacy. Stop it, I say!

RANK *ceases playing.* NORA *suddenly stops dancing.*

HELMER *goes over to her.* I'd never have believed, it. You've
    forgotten everything I taught you.
NORA *throws away the tambourine.* You see!
HELMER. I'll have to show you every step.
NORA. You see how much I need you! You must show me every
    step of the way. Right to the end of the dance. Promise me
    you will, Torvald?
HELMER. Never fear. I will.

On the most obvious level, Nora dances the tarantella to distract
Helmer's attention from the fateful letter-box. Her wild dancing
expresses her fear that he will discover her crime. While Helmer

is unable to guide Nora, Rank, who is himself doomed to die shortly, is more successful. He and Nora understand one another intuitively, both of them being close to death. Helmer understands nothing. The many references to failed attempts at guidance actually help to pinpoint the fact that Nora, although she has herself asked him for guidance, no longer follows his instructions. She is on the verge of breaking away from him. In this scene the tarantella prepares for her discovery at the end that she and her husband have in fact never understood one another.

However, the reason why Nora practises of all dances a tarantella – a dance of death – is that she is contemplating suicide. The tarantella is a sophisticated motif which demands of the audience a certain factual knowledge both of the dance and of the spider that has given the dance its name:

> The tarantula spider is reputedly poisonous, and anyone bitten by it is likely to contract the disease of tarantism. This is 'a hysterical malady, characterized by an extreme impulse to dance'. And the cure for this malady was held to be – dancing the tarantella. Thus, 'the dancing was sometimes held to be a symptom or consequence of the malady, sometimes practised as a sovereign cure for it'. The symptom of the disease and the cure for the disease are one and the same.[21]

Translation

A closer examination of the way in which the theme of guidance is handled in the source text and in two of the English translations, both from 1965, reveals a classic translation problem. (Emphasis is added.)

NORA.   . . . *vejled* mig som du plejer.

NORA.   . . . *show* me *where I'm wrong*, the way you always do. (Watts)

NORA.   . . . *lead* me, the way you always do. (Meyer)

HELMER.   . . . så kan jeg bedre *vejlede* hende.

HELMER.   . . . then I can *show* her better.   (Watts)

HELMER.   . . . Then it'll be easier for me to *show* her.   (Meyer)

HELMER.   Nå, her må rigtig *vejledning* til.
NORA.   . . . Du må *vejlede* mig til det sidste.

HELMER.   Well, you certainly need a lot of *coaching.*
NORA.   . . . You must *coach* me up to the last minute.   (Watts)

HELMER.   I'll have to *show* you every step.
NORA.   . . . You must *show* me every step of the way. Right to
the end of the dance.   (Meyer)

Ibsen uses the word *vejlede* (guide) three times and the corresponding noun *vejledning* (guidance) once. Toward the end of the play
Helmer declares himself prepared to *vejlede* the erring Nora with
the help of another *usvikelig vejleder* (infallible guide): religion.
The meaning of the term has been greatly extended. It is precisely
through these repetitions of the same root in different contexts
that we are made aware of the significant correspondence between
guidance in dance (Act II) and guidance in life (Act III).
    Turning to the translations we discover that neither Watts nor
Meyer retains Ibsen's consistency of vocabulary here. As a result,
the correspondence between the guidance offered in Act II and
the guidance offered in Act III is obscured. Ibsen's *til det sidste* (up
to the end) is rendered as 'up to the last minute' by Watts and as
'every step of the way. Right to the end of the dance' by Meyer.
The delicate, ironical balance in Ibsen's text between a literal level
(Helmer) and a figurative one (Nora), *not understood by him*, is
disturbed in Meyer's wordy, explicatory rendering. The metaphorical significance of the dance guidance has become too explicit.

Stage, radio, television, film

In Bergman's production, Nora's tarantella,

> danced on top of the table to the rebellious pounding of her
> tambourine, was not a coy manoeuvre designed to divert
> Helmer's attention but a hieroglyph of desperation intended to
> attract it. This passionate choreographic outburst, watched
> thoughtfully by Rank and with incomprehension by Helmer,
> was virtually a mute, conscious outcry for help in a situation
> that Nora herself now knew to be beyond help. The dance was
> brief; the clattering tambourine she let fall to the floor signified
> its finality, as the last game in a played-out masquerade.[22]

No piano, no music, no guidance from either Helmer or Rank.
Feeling perhaps that the tarantella can easily attract too much
attention in itself, Bergman stripped the scene of many of Ibsen's
ingredients and condensed it into a Munchian cry of anguish.

Despite the music that goes with it, the tarantella is above all a
visual spectacle. In a radio production it is hard to find acoustic
equivalents for Nora's anguished dancing. In the 1947 Swedish
version the sequence is kept short: Nora's anguish is conveyed by
hysterical laughter; Helmer instructs her more specifically than in
the play text, and it seems as though Rank accompanies her
throughout. In the 1953 version, the music is sombre, the tambourine prominent. In a Dutch version broadcast in 1987, Helmer, at
the piano, slows down markedly as he asks Nora to dance less
wildly. Surprisingly enough, in none of these three versions is
there any clear difference between Helmer's playing and Rank's.

In Sjöstrand's TV version, the tarantella is interrupted near the
beginning by a shot showing how Mrs Linde visits Krogstad in
vain. Helmer rather emphatically instructs Nora, and the scene
ends with Nora throwing the tambourine to Mrs Linde.

In his film version, Garland cross-cuts frequently between Nora's
dancing and Mrs Linde's visit Krogstad. This suggests, in a rather
obvious, medium-oriented way, what is on Nora's mind while she
is dancing. Toward the end of the tarantella, Garland cuts – via
two close-ups of Nora's face – from the rehearsal to the actual
performance of the tarantella at the fancy-dress ball upstairs,
thereby indicating a time lapse. Cross-cutting is again used to

contrast Helmer and Nora, miles apart although dancing together, with Krogstad and Mrs Linde, who are finding their way back to one another. At the same time close-ups of Nora's legs remind us of the erotic 'silk-stocking scene', in which Rank's secret love for Nora was revealed.

The same connection is made in Losey's film. Here Nora, in suicidal black, rehearses a wild tarantella. Helmer objects with words added in the screenplay: 'There's a difference between a dance and a wanton display.' In protest, Nora then starts to dance can-can fashion, very obviously siding with Rank. This provocative Nora is a far cry from Ibsen's heroine, who at this point is torn between her sense of loyalty to her husband and her newly awakened sense of loyalty to herself. No doubt the erotic emphasis in the film has something to do with the casting of an attractive star (Jane Fonda) as Nora, and the ease with which the film medium can offer titillating close-ups.

Since Ibsen has not specified any particular tarantella music, the question arises of whether it should be in the style of the Southern Italian folk tarantella or of its more sophisticated nineteenth-century classical equivalent. Nora's costume and tambourine suggest a folk idiom, which is what all the directors of the productions discussed here have chosen. In Garland's version the tarantella tune has a special appropriateness, since it is an echo, in the minor, of the music-box tune with which the film began.

The ending

Rarely, if ever, has a play-ending aroused so much consternation as that of *A Doll's House*. As Meyer puts it,

> The terrible offstage slamming of that front door which brings down the curtain resounded through more apartments than Torvald Helmer's. No play had ever before contributed so momentously to the social debate, or been so widely and furiously discussed among people who were not normally interested in theatrical or even artistic matters.[23]

Text

Ibsen was himself well aware of the significance of the play's conclusion: 'I may almost say that it was for the sake of the last scene that the whole play was written.'[24] By 'the last scene' Ibsen undoubtedly meant the section that begins with Nora telling her husband to sit down so that they can talk. Her demand at this point signifies a crucial change in the development of the play as well as in her moral and social attitude. But it does not provide an answer to the major question we ask ourselves in the final act: will Nora leave her husband and children? Not until we see her in her outdoor dress and carrying her travelling-bag – in the middle of the night! – is an answer, albeit inconclusive, provided.

Within this larger unit, comprising roughly the last two pages in the standard Norwegian edition of 1933, we may distinguish the *very end*, the actual leave-taking and exit, comprising the last six speeches plus stage- and acting-directions. In the following, I shall focus on this part of the ending; how it was first conceived by Ibsen; how it was later given an alternative shape by him; how it has been translated into English; and how it has been done on stage, radio and screen.

The passage that concerns us is the following:

HELMER. Nora, – can I never be anything but a stranger to you?
NORA *picks up her bag.* Oh, Torvald, then the miracle of miracles would have to happen. –
HELMER. Name it, this miracle of miracles!
NORA. You and I would both have to change so much that – oh, Torvald, I don't believe in miracles any more.
HELMER. But I'll believe. Tell me. We would have to change so much that – ?
NORA. That our life together could become a marriage. Goodbye.
HELMER *sinks down on a chair by the door and covers his face with his hands.* Nora! Nora! *Looks around and gets up.* Empty. She is no longer here. *With a glimmer of hope.* The miracle of miracles – ?!

The sound of a street door being slammed shut is heard from below.

Compare this to the ending in the first complete draft:

> HELMER. Nora, can I never be anything but a stranger to you?
> NORA. Oh, Thorvald, then the miracle of miracles would have
>   to happen. –
> HELMER. Name it, this miracle of miracles!
> NORA. You and I would both have to change so much that; –
>   oh, Thorvald, I don't believe in miracles any more.
> HELMER. But I believe in them! Tell me! We would have to
>   change so much that –
> NORA. That our life together could become a marriage. Good-
>   bye.
> *She quickly picks up her bag, waves and leaves.*
> HELMER *sinks down on a chair by the door.* Nora! Nora! – The
>   miracle of miracles – ?

Although the two texts may seem very similar, there are some notable differences between them. In the draft, Nora's leave-taking is somewhat hesitant: she picks up the bag immediately before leaving, she waves to Helmer and – most important – there is no door slam. In the published version, by contrast, Nora picks up the bag at an earlier point; she no longer waves to Helmer; and her departure not only shows much greater determination on her part, but is also much more definite. Ibsen very specifically informs us that the door not only slams shut but actually locks behind her – as though no return is possible.

While the Nora of the draft may well come back sooner or later, there are thus various indications in the published version that she will not. Her slamming of the door, Quigley rightly observes, 'seems to summarize in a single action Nora's rejection of her husband, her children, her home and her social position, along with the society that taught her to need such things'.[25] Nora's exit through the front door both parallels and contrasts with the opening of the play, when we see her happily returning home with a Christmas tree. 'The unadorned Christmas tree, framed in the doorway at the beginning of the play', Quigley points out, is linked 'with the figure of Nora, no longer in fancy dress, passing through the same doorway at the end of the play'.[26]

As for Helmer, we may note that, whereas in the draft he claims to believe in miracles, in the final version this is weakened to a desire to believe in them; as a result the (added) acting-direction concerning the hope he suddenly clings to seems to be born more out of desperation than out of faith. Taken together the nuances inserted by Ibsen considerably strengthen the ending in the published version, making it harsher, more provocative.

Translation

The problem of translating the play into English is acute in the case of Nora's final speech. In the original this reads, 'At samliv mellem os to kunde bli'e et ægteskab. Farvel.' This is rendered as follows:

> Where we could make a real marriage of our lives together. Goodbye! (McFarlane, 1961)

> That our life together could be a real marriage. Good-bye. (Watts, 1965)

> That life together between us could become a marriage. Good-bye. (Meyer, 1965)

> That our living together could be a true marriage. (Fjelde, 1965)

> That our life together could become a marriage. Good-bye. (Marker, 1983)

It is striking that one of the five translators, Fjelde, omits the final word, perhaps out of a feeling that Nora's exceedingly pungent statement should not be followed by anything at all. In Nora's closing speech *samliv* (literally 'life together') and *ægteskab* (marriage) are seen as two different things which should be integrated, fused. Although legally a marriage, Nora's and Helmer's relationship has in fact, Nora now discovers, never really existed. What Nora means by *ægteskab* is a 'true marriage', a physical and spiritual relationship based on equality and mutual respect. However, by having her refer not to *et sant ægteskab* (a true marriage) but simply to *et ægteskab* (a marriage), Ibsen is showing that to Nora at this point no other form of marriage is valid. Just as with the forgery, she is indifferent to anything other than inner values. It is therefore hardly true to the spirit of her to translate *ægteskab* as 'a real' or 'a true marriage'. As for *samliv*, it is impossible to find an exact equivalent for this concept in English, and the terseness of Nora's speech is lost in translation. Of the variants offered, 'our life together' seems the best.

Stage

In many recent productions emphasis has been placed on Helmer's genuine desire to change, so that 'the miracle of miracles' can happen. Bergman's Munich production, for example, showed a great concern for Helmer's situation, even though the play in this version was entitled *Nora*. At the end of scene 14, after the tarantella, Helmer embraced Nora passionately and started to unbutton her dress. Scene 15 opened with silence and darkness. Then Nora could be seen dressed in a dark coat and carrying a small travelling-bag, while Helmer was lying naked in their double bed. Helmer's final hopeful line was cut. The production ended with Nora's strong curtain speech – 'That our life together could become a marriage. Goodbye' – followed by her exit. Helmer, bathed '*in a searing white light*', was '*left weeping on the bed*'.[27]

In an interview he gave shortly after the staging of his production, Bergman voiced his views of the two characters and described what he had been trying to convey:

> Helmer's tragedy is fully as interesting as the development of Nora. He's a decent man who is trapped in his role of being the man, the husband. He tries to play his role as well as he can – because it is the only one he knows and understands. . . . And then suddenly Nora stands there in front of him with her coat on and her bag in her hand, intending to go away. In my production, Helmer has gone to bed and he's undressed . . . . Then he wakes up . . . – and *everything* pours out from Nora, who is fully clothed, over Helmer, who is sitting there naked in his bed. And when she goes away, with her enormous aggression and her incredible brutality, he collapses completely. . . . He simply lies down on the bed and cries like a very small child.[28]

Despite this Strindbergian defence of Helmer, Bergman declared that he meant the audience to feel sympathy also for Nora, 'for both of them'.

It is noteworthy that the ending of Bergman's *Nora* bore a certain resemblance to the way he ended Strindberg's *Julie* (as he chose to call it), the second play of the 'trilogy'. In that production Jean, after Julie had left to commit suicide, momentarily broke down and started to cry. In both cases the woman turned out to be considerably stronger than the man.

Television

A Nora who does not leave at the end was presented in Rainer Werner Fassbinder's heavily adapted TV version, entitled *Nora Helmer*, in which the play was turned into a power struggle between husband and wife. This was indicated in the opening shot, showing Helmer's hand resting upon Nora's shoulder and her hand resting upon his. Fassbinder's Nora recklessly makes use of radical feminist slogans to create a comfortable position for herself within a society she claims to fight. Her final line was, significantly, cut. At the end of this version it is clear that Nora, having humiliated her husband, is now the stronger of the two. There is therefore no reason for her to leave.[29]

In the script of the Swedish TV version broadcast in 1970 the end reads as follows, in English translation:

NORA. That our life together could become – a marriage. Goodbye.

NORA *leaves the house.* TORVALD *remains standing where he was for a long time, completely still. Then he starts to move, aimlessly, bewildered, and as he now begins to understand what has really happened, he gives way to a genuine desperation. Suddenly he goes to the window, opens it and shouts* Nora!

The street. NORA *moves away.* TORVALD'*s voice echoes between the walls of the houses.* Nora! Nora!

She turns around but does not stop. The picture of her face is frozen.

Here the final shot is of Nora, not Helmer – or Torvald, as he is
called in the script (a cue designation in line with Sjöstrand's
positive view of Helmer). And the final word, '*frozen*', seems to
express Nora's alienation from her husband at this point.

However, in the actual production the script was not followed
to the letter; a transcription of the ending as transmitted might
read:

NORA, *wearing a white shawl, and* TORVALD *by the front door.*

NORA. That our life together could become a marriage.

She opens the door and leaves. TORVALD *remains by the door for
a while, then walks slowly back into the living-room, all the time
fingering the ring he has just got back from her. Quietly desperate
he says to himself* Nora. *He then goes to the window, opens it
and shouts* Nora! Nora! *The name reverberates along the street.
Fade-out.*

Here, as in the play text, the final focus is on Helmer. His walking
through the large living-room accentuates the emptiness of the
room and thereby his (feeling of) loneliness. His desperation is
expressed by his calling for his wife in the middle of the night. We
are here a long way from the Helmer who is afraid of making a
scandal. Something has happened to him.

Much closer to the drama text than this TV version is the
Norwegian one from 1974. Here the whole action, except for the
opening shot, takes place in the Helmers' apartment, albeit in
different rooms. At the end Nora puts on a brown coat with
mournful black-fur trimming – instead of the black shawl called
for in the text or the white one (an ironical bridal veil or a shroud?)
used in the Swedish TV version. As she utters her final, devastating
and yet hopeful exit line, there is a close-up of her, looking down,
disillusioned. Helmer runs after her as she leaves through the
cross-shaped glass-and-wood apartment door. Her steps can be
heard as she walks down the stairs. Helmer turns, closes the door,
looks at the ring she has returned to him, walks back into the
living-room and says, 'Empty.' He sits down in the middle of the
sofa, a position emphasising his loneliness, and says, 'The miracle
of miracles.' Fade-out. There is no door slam.

Radio

Although Ibsen, as always, makes subtle use of visual effects in *A Doll's House*, there is nothing in the play which is wholly dependent on them. More than many other Ibsen plays, therefore, *A Doll's House* lends itself to radio production. Other reasons for this are the unity of time and place, the small number of characters and the strong reliance on the spoken word. The last sequence, the 'discussion', is especially well suited to the theatre of the ear.

This is how the three Swedish radio-script endings are phrased in English translation:

NORA. That our life together could become a marriage. Goodbye, Torvald. *Door.* (1944)

NORA. That our life together could become a marriage. Goodbye, Torvald. (1947)

NORA. That our life together could become a marriage. Goodbye. *Door.*

HELMER. Nora! Nora! Empty. She's gone. The miracle of miracles – ?
The sound of a street door being slammed shut is heard from below. (1953)

After Nora's strong line, which can be rendered in Swedish without any loss, the three versions all reveal slight variations. The second keeps the laconic 'Goodbye' of the original, while the other two add a friendly 'Torvald'. Helmer's final reaction is retained only in the third version. In the first version even the final door slam has been omitted – which is surprising in a medium dependent solely on the aural code. Probably the director wished to keep the door open for a possible return by Nora.

In the Dutch radio version, broadcast in two parts (!), the end is as follows (in English translation):

NORA. Then so much will have to change that our life together will become a true life together. *Door, footsteps, street door, wind.*

HELMER. Nora! *Close to microphone.* Nora! – Gone. She's gone. –
Life together?
Sombre piano music in crescendo.

Here, presumably in an attempt to update the play, the word
ægteskab (marriage) is not, as one would expect, translated with
huwelijk but with *samenleven* (life together), the same word as
used to translate *samliv*. The repetition makes the line seem trite
and vacuous. *Two* doors are closed, and Nora's exit through the
second is followed by the sound of the wind blowing – a sign
perhaps of the hostility of the world outside the doll's house and
thus of the life Nora is now confronting, or, alternatively, of the
fresh air now entering the doll's house as Helmer is left alone.
Yet, far from indicating the dawning of hope, the non-diegetic,
sombre piano music with which this version is concluded stresses
Helmer's desperate sense of isolation.

Film

At the end of Garland's film version Helmer and Nora, both in
black, are seen by the front door. As Nora leaves, we see the door
with a Christmas garland on it closing. A long shot shows Helmer
walking back through the hall – a way of making him seem small
and lonely – into the living-room, where he stops. There is no
need for him to say 'Empty'. A long shot of the big living-room
shows how empty he feels. There is a slow zoom-in to a close-up
of his face as he says, 'The miracle of miracles.' Then comes the
sound of the street door slamming shut, crushing his hope. Fade-
out and, as an ironical footnote, sweet, doll-like music, as from a
music-box – the kind of music that was heard at the beginning of
the film.

In Losey's version the last speech is Nora's comment about 'life
together' becoming 'a marriage'. Having said this, she puts on a
black coat and leaves quickly, without saying goodbye. Helmer
remains standing in the living-room. When he hears her slam the
street door shut, he lowers his head; even when left alone, he
performs a social ritual. There is a shot of the fatal letter-box,
now open, and a final exterior shot of the church in the distance,
swept in mist and snow. The chiming of the church bells mingles
with the sombre brass music that was heard in the pre-title sequence

of the film – two sounds expressing the power of the religious, bourgeois society of which Helmer and Nora have become victims.

A Doll's House and the media

A Doll's House is a good example of a drama text written in a language understood by few people outside the region of origin (in this case, Scandinavia). As a result, the majority of recipients of Ibsen's play experience it not directly, as readers of the source text, but indirectly, via some kind of transposition. It could be a one-stage transposition (translation), a two-stage transposition (translation + stage performance) or a three-stage transposition (translation + radio/screen script + performance). With each stage we are further removed from the source text. Since the last stage is, precisely, that represented by the *mass* media (radio, television, film), it follows that most recipients of *A Doll's House* have experienced the play in a form at several removes from the original.

A Doll's House differs from *Macbeth* in that the play text has undoubtedly been authorised by the playwright himself. This applies especially to the – in comparison with *Macbeth* – ample secondary text. As a result, a new problem arises with regard to the stage- and acting-directions: to what extent does a director need to adhere to these? Even more relevant in our context is the question: to what extent is it possible to adhere to these directions in media for which the play was not written and which were even unknown to the playwright (radio, television, film)? One would here perhaps expect a difference of approach between stage productions, using the medium intended by the playwright, and radio, TV and film productions, using media he did not intend. But, although Ibsen's secondary text, as we have seen, has been handled very differently, the different solutions do not seem closely correlated with the choice of medium. Brinckman's teleplay and Garland's film, for example, follow the secondary text more closely than Bergman's stage version.

Possibly we may expect a more conservative approach from a director who is a countryman of the playwright than from one who is not. Veneration for a national tradition may here play a part – directorial innovations often seem to come from abroad! – but the fact that the native director deals with the source text, the foreign one with a target text, is probably more important. If you are already removed from the source text, you probably feel relatively free to depart from the play text also in other ways – for example, by disregarding much of the secondary text.

As for the primary text, the film medium is particularly likely to make drastic cuts to the dialogue. In this area the drama text is clearly inimical to the film medium and functions more than the other modes merely as a blueprint.

Not only the emphasis on the verbal component but also the unity of time and place and the small number of characters – all aspects which favour adaptations for radio and TV – appear to be far from positive factors when turning the play into a film. Here precisely the opposite characteristics seem to be the rule: frequent changes of environment; a great number of (minor) characters and extras; emphasis on the visual. Yet *A Doll's House* has proved to be very popular with film-makers. By 1978 the play had been filmed no fewer than twelve times, five times in the United States.

Based on a stage production, Garland's film is quite theatrical; because it confines virtually the whole of the action to a few rooms, it seems better suited to TV transmission than to the large screen. The opposite is true of Losey's version, which, however, was first shown on television and only later in the cinema. The two films thus illustrate the range of options open to directors making a film from a play: at the one end of the spectrum are versions with a strong verbal (theatrical) emphasis; at the other, highly visual (cinematic) versions, in which much of the dialogue has to be cut – a considerable problem when one is faced with such a dense text as that of *A Doll's House*.

Because *A Doll's House* is more static than *Macbeth*, film-directors are acutely aware of the difficulty of serving two masters: the play and the film. Garland gives priority to the play text; the result is filmed theatre. Losey gives priority to the film medium; the result is a trivialisation of a richly textured play. In neither case is a successful marriage of text and medium achieved. This raises a question of principle: can plays be successfully transposed into film?

Chapter 4

Between Stage and Screen: Strindberg's *Spöksonaten*/ *The Ghost Sonata* (1907)

Unlike *Macbeth* and *A Doll's House*, August Strindberg's chamber play *Spöksonaten*, usually rendered as *The Ghost Sonata* in English, is hardly intelligible at a literal surface level. When interpreted on a metaphorical level, i.e. when the bewildering *signifiants* are 'translated' into meaningful and coherent *signifiés*, it may be seen as 'the first great absurdist drama'.[1] With his conviction that 'the motif determines the form',[2] Strindberg in *The Ghost Sonata* has created a drama which is more theme- than plot-centred. Like *A Dream Play*, *The Ghost Sonata* is a norm-breaking drama, more epic and more subjective than *Macbeth* and *A Doll's House*. How can a drama of this sophisticated kind be transposed for the screen mass media, accustomed as they are to more immediately intelligible, realistic fare?

Synopsis

Note: Strindberg divides the text into three parts, here called 'acts'.

Act I. On a sunny Sunday morning, a student meets a milkmaid in front of a house by a drinking-fountain. He tells her how on the preceding night he witnessed the collapse of a house and

helped to save many of the victims. The Milkmaid remains silent.
At his request she gives him water to drink, then disappears. The
Student is now addressed by an old man, Jacob Hummel, a cripple
sitting in a wheelchair. Hummel has not seen the Milkmaid. The
Old Man, who appears quite benevolent, claims that he has saved
the Student's father from bankruptcy. He now asks the Student to
do him a favour in return. Will he go to the Opera together with
the Colonel and his daughter, the Young Lady, who live in the
house behind them? In this way he will get acquainted with the
Young Lady, whom he adores. During the conversation between
the two men, the inhabitants of the house appear in the windows
or outside the house, and this causes the Old Man, who knows
them all, to comment on them. The Old Man is wheeled out by
his servant, Johansson, who returns and now paints a very negative
picture of his master. When the Old Man comes back, surrounded
by a crowd of beggars, the Student at his suggestion is hailed by
everyone for his courage during the preceding night. The Milkmaid
again appears, with her arms above her head like a drowning
person. This time not only the Student but also the Old Man sees
her. He shrinks with fear into his chair.

Act II. The evening of the same day, in the Colonel's round
parlour inside the house. Here the ghost supper – so called because
the participants 'all look like ghosts' – is soon to begin. The
Fiancée, the Aristocrat and the Student have been invited. But
the Old Man, too, turns up. He has come 'to pull up the weeds,
to expose the crimes'. The Colonel, he reveals, is neither a colonel
nor a nobleman but a former servant. He seduced the Fiancée
when she was still engaged to the Old Man. And the Old Man
revenged himself by seducing the Colonel's wife, the Mummy.
The Young Lady is the fruit of this adultery. But now the Old
Man in his turn is exposed. He too is a former servant. His name
is false. He is a liar and a usurer. And, worst of all, long ago he
drowned the little Milkmaid, because she had witnessed a crime
he wished to keep secret. The Old Man must now atone for all
this. On the Mummy's orders, he hangs himself up in the closet,
where she has been repenting her adultery for many years.
Meanwhile the Student, unaware of what is happening, is next
door, in the Young Lady's hyacinth room. He recites from *The
Song of the Sun*, an old Icelandic poem: 'Man reaps as he sows.'

Act III. A few days later, in the hyacinth room. In the background the Colonel and the Mummy are sitting silently in the parlour. Inspired by the beauty surrounding him, the Student gives a lyrical description of woman, love and existence. The Young Lady explains that the Cook, who has just appeared, has taken all her strength and that the Student can never have her. In despair the Student declares that all mankind is impure and that life is infernal. The Young Lady collapses and dies. Remorseful, the Student prays that she may be granted a blessed afterlife. He recites again the lines from *The Song of the Sun* quoted at the end of Act II. And the play ends, very spectacularly: '*The room vanishes; Böcklin's* Toten-Insel *becomes the backdrop.*'

Text

Title

The play title has both an exoteric and an esoteric meaning. The exoteric meaning, related to the main theme, is that, since life on earth is a shadow life, a mirage, we are all ghosts – while those who appear as ghosts in the play are the truly living. To the older Strindberg life often seemed synonymous with 'death', death with 'life'.

Esoterically, the title alludes to Beethoven's Piano Sonata no. 17 in D minor (op. 31, no. 2), usually called *Der Sturm* (The Tempest). In a letter to his German translator, Strindberg refers to it as the *Gespenster* (Ghost) Sonata. He had used it in an earlier play, *Crimes and Crimes*, to indicate the pangs of conscience afflicting the protagonist.

Strindberg presumably also wished to indicate in the title that the structure of the play is somehow akin to that of a sonata. The subtitle 'Chamber Play Opus III' suggests this, especially when combined with Strindberg's own definition of the term 'chamber play': 'the concept of chamber music transferred to drama. The intimate action, the significant motif, the sophisticated treatment.'[3]

Theme

In a prologue written for the opening of his own Intimate Theatre in Stockholm, where the play was first performed, Strindberg speaks of the journey that mankind must undertake 'from the Isle of the Living to the Isle of Dead'. He was alluding to Arnold Böcklin's well-known paintings of these subjects; at his request copies of these were placed on either side of the stage in the Intimate Theatre.[4] In *The Ghost Sonata* we witness a similar journey. The house we see on the stage represents the House of Life, which at the end vanishes and is replaced by the Isle of the Dead. Without actually realising it, we have been on our way to another reality. Along with the Student, we gradually discover that the house which on the outside looks so attractive (Act I), is far less attractive inside (Act II). Life may not be what we had expected but *amor vincit omnia* (Act III). Yet even this proves to be an illusion: like everyone else, the beloved Young Lady is tainted by Original Sin ('sick at the core of life'). The stable, attractive house has proved to be a mirage. The true reality – this is what Strindberg wants us to experience – is to be found in the life hereafter.

The fundamental idea of the play, then, is that life on earth is painful and illusory (dream-like) and that when we die we are saved, returning from this pseudo-existence to the original one. Only by hoping for this can we endure life. This ties in with the idea that the living are actually ghosts – as indicated by the cue designation 'The Mummy' and the reference to the 'ghost supper' in Act II.

The Student is 'a Sunday child', who 'can see what others cannot see'; he is a student of languages trying to find the unity behind and beyond the linguistic Tower of Babel that mankind has erected 'to keep the secrets of the tribe'. As Sarah Bryant-Bertail observes, he is the only one in the play who sings, 'matching human language with the "universal language" of music'.[5] At the same time he is Everyman, starting out in life enthusiastically but ending it in disillusion. His hope for a better existence hereafter, justifying the pain of this life, is thus not just an individual hope but – as in *A Dream Play* – a universal one, the hope of mankind.

Time and place

The play loosely adheres to the unities of time and place. Act I opens on a Sunday morning; Act II happens in the afternoon and evening of the same day; Act III is set a few days after Hummel's funeral, about a week later.

The acts are linked together spatially. Along with the Student we move from the street (Act I) through the round parlour (Act II) to the hyacinth room (Act III), from wider to narrower space, a Dantean journey in reverse. By synchronising this inward movement with the Student's increasingly negative view of life, Strindberg indicates a connection between life experience and denial of life.

As Freddie Rokem has observed, Strindberg's use of space in *The Ghost Sonata* is quite cinematic. 'The gradual revelation of the rotten foundations of the house . . . is presented visually by a zoom from act to act towards the center of the house.' The spatial 'turnaround' in Act III has its counterpart in a reversed point of view: that of the young couple in the foreground replaces that of the old people in the background.[6]

Character appearance

In his acting-directions, Strindberg gives rather sparse and somewhat capricious information about his characters' outward appearance. Thus we lack information about how the Old Man is dressed in Act I and what the Young Lady wears in Act III. On her second appearance, we learn that the Young Lady *'has changed her clothes'* but we are not told in what way. In Act I the Colonel appears *'in civilian clothes'*. How he is dressed in the following acts Strindberg does not tell us, but we can assume that he wears his uniform in Act II; here the author could rely on widespread knowledge of Swedish military fashion around the turn of the century.

The opening and the ending

The duplicity characteristic of mankind – the attractive social mask hiding the ugly face – is represented by the *'façade'* of the House of Life. In a fairly literal translation the initial stage-directions

read,

> *The ground floor and the first floor of the façade of a modern*
> *house; only the corner of the house is visible, ending on the*
> *ground floor in a round parlour, on the first floor in a balcony*
> *and a flagstaff.*
>
> *Through the open windows of the round parlour, when the*
> *curtains are drawn, a white marble statue of a young woman is*
> *seen surrounded by palms, brightly lit by rays of sunshine. In the*
> *window to the left, there are pots of hyacinths (blue, white, pink).*
>
> *On the balcony rail at the corner of the first floor there is a*
> *blue silk quilt and two white pillows. The windows to the left are*
> *hung with white sheets. It is a bright Sunday morning.*
>
> *In the foreground in front of the façade is a green bench.*
>
> *To the right in the foreground is a street drinking-fountain, to*
> *the left an advertisement pillar.*
>
> *To the left at the back is the entrance, which reveals the*
> *staircase, the stairs of white marble and the banister of mahogany*
> *and brass; on both sides of the entrance on the pavement are*
> *laurel bushes in tubs.*
>
> *The corner with the round parlour also faces a side street,*
> *which is thought to lead inwards towards the backdrop.*
>
> *To the left of the entrance, on the ground floor, is a window*
> *with a gossip mirror* [enabling people indoors to see what is
> happening outside].

The play opens as follows (figures indicating sequences added):

1   *When the curtain rises the bells of several churches in the*
    distance are ringing.

    The doors of the façade are open; a woman in dark clothes
    is standing motionless on the stairs.

    The CARETAKER'S WIFE *sweeps the entrance hall; she then*
    polishes the brass on the front door; finally she waters the
    laurels.

    The OLD MAN *is sitting in a wheelchair by the advertisement*
    pillar reading a newspaper; he has white hair and beard and
    wears glasses.

2   *The* MILKMAID *comes in from the corner with milk bottles in*

a wire basket; she is in summer clothes, with brown shoes, black stockings, and a white beret; she takes off the beret and hangs it on the fountain; wipes the sweat from her forehead; drinks from the cup; washes her hands; arranges her hair, using the water as a mirror.

A steamship bell can be heard ringing, and the bass notes of an organ in a nearby church now and then break the silence.

3 *After a couple of minutes of silence, when the girl has finished her toilet, the* STUDENT *comes in from the left, unshaven and showing he has not slept. He goes right up to the fountain. Pause.*

STUDENT. May I have the cup? *The* GIRL *pulls the cup towards herself.* Haven't you finished yet?
The GIRL *looks at him with horror.*
OLD MAN *to himself.* Who's he talking to? – I don't see anyone! – Is he crazy? *Continues to watch them in great amazement.*

The theme of food has a prominent place in Strindberg's writings. In *The Ghost Sonata* the antithesis of the blood-sucking vampire is the suckling mother. The Old Man and the Cook are the vampires of the play. The opposite, nourishing archetype we find in the character who is but an apparition: the Milkmaid. It is she who represents the nurturing, loving force in life. When Strindberg provides the Cook with 'a colouring-bottle with scorpion letters on it', he gives her an attribute which blatantly contrasts with the Milkmaid's white milk bottles.

Thematically important are also the biblical allusions in the opening sequence. When, in the opening scene, the Student tells the Milkmaid that he has 'bandaged up injured people and kept watch over the sick all night', we associate him both with Jesus and with the good Samaritan. As John Northam has observed, the scene contains an allusion to John 4:7–14, where Jesus meets a woman of Samaria at Jacob's well,[7] and this provides a key to the meaning of the whole scene. 'Give me to drink', Jesus bids the woman. 'Give me a drink of water', the Student asks the Milkmaid. The contrast in the biblical text between Jacob's earthly water, which only temporarily quenches the thirst, and Jesus's 'living

water', which does so eternally, is latently present in the contrast
between the earthly existence on which Jacob Hummel's power
rests and the heavenly one to which the Milkmaid belongs and for
which the Student finally hopes.

The full significance of the opening is not clear until we reach
the end of the play.

> *The* YOUNG LADY *has drooped, seems to be dying, rings.* BENGTS-
> SON *enters.* Bring the screen! Quickly – I'm dying!

> BENGTSSON *returns with the screen, which he opens up and puts
> in front of the Young Lady.*

STUDENT. The liberator is coming! Welcome, pale and gentle
  one. Sleep, you lovely, innocent, doomed creature, suffering
  for no fault of your own. Sleep without dreaming, and when
  you wake again . . . may you be greeted by a sun that does
  not burn, in a home without dust, by friends without stain,
  by a love without flaw. You wise and gentle Buddha, sitting
  there waiting for a heaven to grow out of the earth, grant us
  patience in our ordeal and purity of will, that the hope may
  not come to nought!

> *The strings of the harp hum softly; the room is filled with a white
> light.*

> > I saw the sun. To me it seemed
> > that I beheld the Hidden.
> > Men must reap what they have sown,
> > blest is he whose deeds are good.
> > Deeds which you have wrought in fury,
> > cannot in evil find redress.
> > Comfort him you have distressed
> > with loving-kindness – this will heal.
> > No fear has he who does no ill.
> > Sweet is innocence.

> *A wailing is heard behind the screen.*

You poor little child, child of this world of illusion, guilt,

suffering and death, this world of endless change, disappointment, and pain. May the Lord of Heaven have mercy on you
as you journey forth . . .

The room vanishes; Böcklin's Toten-Insel *becomes the backdrop;
faint, quiet, pleasantly sad music is heard from outside.*

Böcklin's monumental painting *Toten-Insel* shows an isle with
high, crater-like rocks surrounding a group of tall cypresses. In
the walls of the rocks, there are openings like those of sepulchral
chambers. On the shore below, in the centre, there are stairs of
white marble; here the recently dead are received. '*A black boat
with a black oarsman, carrying a white coffin with a white figure
standing next to it*' – Strindberg's stage-directions for his unfinished
sequel of *The Ghost Sonata*, entitled *Toten-Insel* – approaches the
stairs across the still water.

In *The Ghost Sonata* the final projection of this painting forms
an antithetic counterpart to the solid façade of the play's opening.
The marble stairs of the house – the entrance to Life – correspond
to those of the isle, the entrance to Death. The windows have
their counterparts in the sepulchral openings. The white marble
statue inside the house, '*surrounded by palms*', resembles the erect
white figure in the boat, surrounded by the cypresses of the isle –
evergreen like the laurels outside the house but with a more
'aspiring' shape. The mournful Dark Lady '*standing motionless on
the stairs*' corresponds to the black oarsman in the boat. Even the
fresh water of the street drinking-fountain, which the Milkmaid
'*in summer clothes*' uses as a mirror, has its counterpart in the still
water around the isle, in which the white figure in the boat is
reflected.

It is from this isle of the blessed that the ghostly Milkmaid
emanates. This explains why she wears summer clothes even
though she was drowned in the winter. And it is to this isle that
the Young Lady journeys forth in the final tableau. The house of
earthly existence – the Old Man's realm – has collapsed and in its
place we see its spiritual counterpart, 'a home without dust', the
Isle of the Dead, 'the station of rest or the first summer vacation',
as Strindberg calls it in one of his *Blue Books*.

As Northam has demonstrated, the connection between the
beginning and the end of the play is also underlined by the sound-

effects.[8] When the curtain rises on Act I, we hear the ringing of bells of '*several churches at a distance*'. While the Milkmaid washes her hands – an act of purification – and looks at herself in the 'fresh water' of the street drinking-fountain, '*A steamship bell can be heard ringing, and the bass notes of an organ in a nearby church now and then break the silence.*' By this puzzling combination of sound-effects Strindberg from the very beginning creates a strange and solemn mood. Only in retrospect, when we have witnessed the ending, do we realise their metaphorical significance, do we understand that the ringing of the steamship bell signifies a leave-taking of the shore of life and that the organ music is there to help on the last journey.

Translation

Even theatres have their national conventions. The entrance of the house is placed by Strindberg '*to the left upstage*'. One translator instead places it '*at the rear, right*'. We deal in this case with a consistent principle, accounted for in the 'Translator's Foreword': 'For the purpose of conforming to the American stage custom, I have reversed the author's directions – Right and Left – to their opposites. Thus they are given here from the viewpoint of the actor on the stage.'[9] In not reversing the stage-directions, other translators may have the reader of the play in mind. The remark just quoted calls attention to the fact that playwrights and translators rarely indicate whether their stage-directions are from the viewpoint of the actor or from that of the spectator.

In the initial stage-directions Strindberg three times uses the words *fasad* (façade) and *synes*, which denotes 'is seen' and connotes 'appears', 'seems'. Both words allude to the fact that the House of Life is a mirage. It is therefore regrettable that this idea does not fare well in translation. While *synes* is difficult to render in English, there is no such reason why the translators should either neglect the façade altogether or mention it only once.

Extremely important in Strindberg's plays are the correspondences in the text. As we have seen, the sound-effects at the beginning and at the end of *The Ghost Sonata* correspond with each other: the organ music from a nearby church in the opening has a counterpart in the miraculous sighing of the harp strings toward the end, the chiming of distant church bells in the beginning in the '*soft, quiet, pleasantly sad music*' from the distant Isle of the Dead at the end. It is therefore unfortunate that in one translation the ringing of the bells is said to come not only from distant but also from nearby churches;[10] that another refers to '*the deep notes of the organs in the nearby churches*';[11] and that a third sentimentally renders the final sound-effect as '*the soft strains of ecstatic music, mournfully ending on a note of peace*'.[12]

Another problem concerns ethnic differences. Although Strindberg never explicitly says so, a number of things indicate that the play is set in Sweden. The fact, for example, that the windows are '*hung with white sheets*' is a traditional sign of mourning in Sweden. Three approaches can be distinguished here: (1) the original is faithfully translated; (2) the original is faithfully translated and complemented by a note explaining the significance of the custom; (3) the explanation is included in the main text:

(1) *hung with white sheets*[13]

(2) *hung with white sheets**
    *Sign of mourning.[14]

   *draped with white sheets [in Sweden the
   indication that someone has died]*[15]

(3) *hung with white mourning sheets*[16]

Of these solutions, only (2) is to be recommended. (1) does not help the English-speaking reader understand the significance of something which is obvious to his Swedish counterpart. In a play where 'ghosts' haunt the stage and where the characters speak like parrots, it may be difficult for a foreign reader to know what is realistic and what is not. If no explanation is given concerning the white sheets, there is a risk that they will be taken as nothing more than a bizarre detail. As for (3), it is of course incorrect not to point out what has been added in translation. Our conclusion, then, is that the translator should provide necessary further information but distinguish it from the author's text.

Strindberg's associative way of writing often presents different problems from those presented by Ibsen's work, for example.[17] A revealing example of how Strindberg's habit of expressing himself in metaphorical terms may puzzle translators is the following, from the beginning of the play:

> OLD MAN. Wealthy perhaps?
> STUDENT. Not at all . . . on the contrary! I'm destitute!
> OLD MAN. Wait a moment . . . I think I've heard that voice . . . when I was young I had a friend, who couldn't say 'window' [Swedish *fönster*], he always said 'winder' [Swedish *funster*] – I've only met one person with that pronunciation and that was him; you are the second one – are you possibly related to Mr Arkenholz, the wholesale merchant.

But the Student has never said *funster*! As a result, most translators seem to be of the opinion that Strindberg has been careless. So they emend, either by using a vague paraphrase –

> OLD MAN. Do you know, it seems to me I've heard your voice before. When I was young I had a friend who pronounced certain words just as you do[18]

– or else by making the author's text logical:

> STUDENT. . . . I'm ab-absolutely penniless.
> OLD MAN. Wait a moment! I seem to know that voice. When I was young I had a friend who couldn't say absinthe, he always said ab-absinthe.[19]

But the phrasing of the play text, puzzling though it may seem, is highly meaningful; as Evert Sprinchorn points out,

> If this were a realistic play, there would be no explanation, just as there would be no explanation for the appearance of the Milkmaid as an apparition visible at first only to the Student. On the other hand, if the apparition can be accounted for as a symbol, so can the window. For Hummel is described later as a thief who enters through windows to steal human souls, and here we see him as he first steals into the Student's life by means of a 'window'.[20]

As a matter of fact, the Old Man's statement immediately reveals him as a liar, for, far from being a most unusual way of pronouncing *fönster*, as he claims, *funster* is a very common pronunciation of the word in and around Stockholm. Even when translations come very close to one another, suggestive differences may be discerned. This is how three of the translators render the end of the Student's prayer for the Young Lady, the final words of the play:

You poor little child! Child of this world of illusion and guilt and suffering and death – this world of eternal change and disappointment and never-ending pain! May the Lord of Heaven have mercy on you as you journey forth . . .[21]

Unhappy child, born into this world of delusion, guilt, suffering and death, this world that is for ever changing, for ever erring, for ever in pain! The Lord of Heaven be merciful to you on your journey.[22]

Poor little child, child of this world of illusion, guilt, suffering, and death, the world of everlasting change, disappointments, and pain! May the Lord of Heaven be merciful to you on your journey . . .[23]

Of these versions, the last comes closest to the original, perhaps somewhat at the expense of natural English, as in the plurals 'illusions', 'disappointments'. The maintenance in two of Strinberg's ellipsis (. . .) after the final word is praiseworthy. The sign corresponds to what is being said in the final sentence: that we are dealing with a journey, with something unaccomplished.

In the third version the asyndetic parataxis of the original is retained in the phrase 'illusions, guilt, suffering', while in the first version it is replaced by parataxis through conjunction ('illusion and guilt and suffering'), which gives the line a certain naïveté. The second version in several respects differs from the others. 'Unhappy child' sounds somewhat high-flown next to the more intimate 'you poor little child', but the expression 'born into this world' compensates for this to a certain extent.

Of special interest is the final sentence. Strindberg here has a line consisting of three dactyls and two trochees: 'Hi'mmelens He'rre va're dig nå'dig på fä'rden . . .'. The three dactyls give a harmonious movement to the line suggesting the idea of a voyage to an isle which, although it is called the Isle of the Dead, is in fact, as we have earlier noted, the Isle of the Living. Only in the first version do we find a rhythmic–poetical counterpart of this line, which forms a transition to the final soft music.

Stage

Scenery

In his 1973 *mise-en-scène* of *The Ghost Sonata*[24] – his third production of the play – Ingmar Bergman chose to place the modern house façade not upstage (as Strindberg has it) but in the auditorium. A few years earlier he had done the same with the attic in Ibsen's *The Wild Duck*. A major reason in both cases was that with this arrangement the characters would no longer turn away from the audience. To Bergman, whose interest in the human face is well documented, this was of paramount importance. As he stressed during rehearsals, much more important than what the characters witness is their reaction to it.

In *The Ghost Sonata*, where the house represents Life and its inhabitants stand for humanity, the spatial reversal was meaningful also in the sense that it linked the audience with the characters on the stage. Appearing on either side of the proscenium frame, the inhabitants of the house came to function as mediators between the audience inside the House of Life and the characters out in the street.

At the same time, Strindberg's idea was partly retained. A beautiful *art nouveau* building was projected on the black screens in the rear. As the Old Man and the Student watched the house in the auditorium, the spectators watched the house they were describing on the screens. The result was a dream-like mirror effect, inducing a feeling of being strangely 'face to face', seeing 'through a glass darkly' – to quote two Bergman film titles. The state was further heightened by the similarity between the stage, enclosed by concave screens, and the horseshoe shape of the auditorium, turning the whole locale into a global 'wooden O' or *theatrum mundi*.

At the start of the play the Student relates how he has witnessed the collapse of a house in a neighbouring street the day before; at

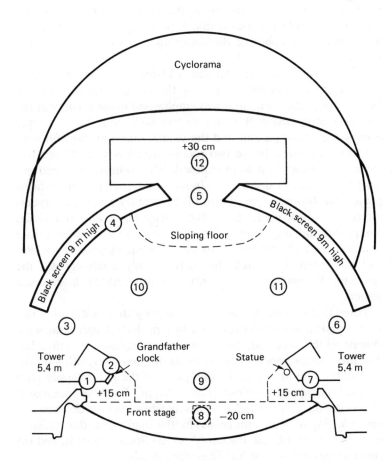

Ground plan for the Bergman production of *The Ghost Sonata* showing the concave screens in the middle of the stage and behind them the rectangular platform used in Acts II and III. Encircled figures indicate entrance/exit areas or central acting-areas. The measurements prefixed + and − apply to raised/lowered areas, and show difference in level from that of the main acting-area. The platforms left and right just behind the proscenium represent part of the house observed by the Old Man and the Student in Act I and entered by them in Act II.

the end, the house on the stage collapses. The implication is that the houses are one and the same: the House of Life. Bergman's scenographic solution meant that Strindberg's partly verbal and partly visual metaphor of the dream-like, illusory nature of life was retained purely visually.

What I have called the Student's Dantean journey in reverse was necessarily obscured by placing the house in the auditorium. Instead the generation motif was emphasised in the scenery of the last two acts, where the old, experienced, guilt-laden people occupy the round parlour and the young, innocent, hopeful ones the hyacinth room. In the two rooms two phases of life and two contrasting views of it were exposed. The contrast appeared not least in the interior decoration. In the round parlour, out-of-focus projection showed a typical turn-of-the-century wealthy bourgeois interior – overloaded, dark; five sturdy black and red chairs completed the impression of sombreness. In the much loftier hyacinth room, by contrast, two slender white chairs and a white-and-gold harp dominated the picture; only gradually did the spectators become aware of a contrasting property: the black death screen.

Three times – once in each act – the projected exterior/interior scenery was momentarily replaced by a projected high stone wall. Whenever this occurred, there was a sound reminiscent of thunder. The projections appeared in moments of intense anguish – on the part of the Old Man (Act I), the guests at the ghost supper (Act II), the Student and the Young Lady (Act III). By these audiovisual effects the director wished to communicate a sense of claustrophobia, a feeling of being imprisoned in 'this madhouse, this reformatory, this charnel house the earth', as the Student puts it, and the concomitant longing for 'the liberator', death.

The contrast between house façade/decorated interiors, on the one hand, and bare wall, on the other, also served to underline the mask–face dichotomy that is so pronounced in the play: the projection of the bare wall signified an unmasking, a laying-bare of hidden ugliness.

The dreamy note struck in the opening sequence was not only maintained but augmented in the course of the performance. Only twice, for a minute or so, did the curtain drop, to allow for necessary changes of scenery and costume. But even during these short intervals the audience was kept in a dream-like mood through a strange 'snowfall' – rising and falling dots of light projected on the curtain – creating a sense of dizziness. The second time the 'snowfall' appeared, the face of the aged Strindberg could be vaguely divined, indicating that the audience was sharing the playwright's 'dream', his experience of life – a surprisingly subjective touch.

Lighting

With regard to the stage lighting we may distinguish between functional, realistic, symbolic and atmospheric lighting. An example of *functional* lighting was provided when the Student started to tell the story about the house that collapsed the preceding day: at this point the lighting on the stage was dimmed, while the Student was strongly lit. As a result attention was focused on him and the story he had to tell. The lighting here helped to emphasise a thematically important passage in the play.

Seemingly more *realistic* was the strong white light directed toward that part of the stage to which the Student was wheeling the Old Man in response to his request to sit 'in the sun'. On closer inspection, however, the (sun)light here had above all a *symbolic* significance: sensing that he is soon to die, hoping for divine Grace, the old sinner is attracted to the warm sunlight.

Especially in Act III *atmospheric* light was important. Here there was a change from warm to cold and back to warm light, corresponding to the three 'notes' the director sensed in this act: tenderness – bitterness – tenderness. The hyacinths mentioned in the play text never materialised in the production. They were merely indicated by the Young Lady's hyacinth-blue dress and in the lighting: mixed blue and white light. As the Young Lady, kneeling on the floor, stretched out her hands, the bluish white light coloured her dress to indicate that 'she surrounded herself with a barrier of colour and warmth and fragrance'.[25] By contrast, an uncharitable cold light accompanied the Student's unmasking of the Young Lady, which directly led to her death.

Costume

The costumes were meticulously designed, sometimes with regard to function but more often with an eye to their symbolic significance. In addition, there was an overall colour pattern. Thus Act I was dominated by greyish tints. In Act II the characters appeared in costumes which were realistic in cut but so glaring that they looked like dresses for a fancy-dress ball; here 'the world of illusions' was at its strongest. In the final act, by contrast, the costumes were pale. The masquerade was over and the characters seemed to incarnate the Mummy's contrite recognition that 'we are poor human beings'.

The Colonel

Strindberg's Colonel incarnates duplicity. Behind an aristocratic mask – moustache, false teeth, wig and corset, a dubious title and a false noble name – he disguises the fact that he is a former servant and a sponger.

In Bergman's production the Colonel first wore a long black-silk dressing-gown, announcing his aristocratic pretensions. In Act II he had dressed up for the ghost supper in uniform. Although he claims to have been 'an acting colonel in the American voluntary service', his gold-braided, scarlet uniform did not seem to fit the claim at all. Instead the glaring 'imperial' colour served to bring out the fact that the Colonel was disguising himself behind a socially impressive persona. In addition, the red colour linked him with his wife, the Mummy, and his servant, Bengtsson.

In Act III, however, his red uniform was replaced by an old, worn, grey velvet dressing-gown, strongly contrasting both with the uniform and with the elegant silk gown he wore in Act I; the boots had been replaced by slippers; the wig and the monocle were gone; so was the iron corset and as a result he had lost his artificial erectness. The stiff gait had been replaced by a tired man's bent shuffling along. At the end he had arrived at a resigned acceptance of suffering and a compassion for all human beings reminiscent of a Buddhist outlook.

The explicit references to Buddha in the play text were all omitted in the production, partly because these ingredients would be alien to a Western audience, partly because the 'message' of

Bergman's version did not allow for any divine superstructure. Instead the Colonel in the final act was turned into a 'Buddhist monk' with shorn head, simple gown, mild voice and radiant face. Sitting next to the death screen in a humble, harmonious position, he incarnated the attitude to life which the Student in the play text prays to Buddha for: 'patience in the trials, purity of will'.

The Mummy and the Young Lady

The change in the Mummy's costume from Act II to Act III was less marked than that in the Colonel's but similar in kind. Her 'ghostly' parrot costume, intensely red below in Act II, became almost colourless in the final act. Sapped of her lifeblood, in her long grey–yellow–white dress she was now proclaimed a living corpse.

Corresponding to the Mummy's dress in Act II was the Young Lady's petticoat in Act III: dirty, blood-stained around the womb, a visual confirmation of the Student's suspicion that the most beautiful flowers – the smeary petticoat was disguised by an ethereal hyacinth-blue dress – are the most poisonous and that the Young Lady is 'sick at the core of life'.

According to Bergman himself, a fundamental idea behind his production was 'the fact that the Young Lady is slowly turning into another Mummy'.[26] To convey this idea to the audience the director had the same actress play the roles of both mother and daughter, assisted by a mute stand-in when necessary. The idea that the Mummy has once been what the Young Lady is now and, conversely, that the Young Lady is an embryonic Mummy was indicated in various ways. By *position*: the Young Lady in Act I and the Mummy in Act II were placed in the same position next to the marble statue representing the Mummy as young; moreover the Young Lady's coiffure was strikingly similar to that of the marble woman. By *gesture*: at times the Young Lady would flutter her hands in a manner reminiscent of the Mummy's 'parrot' gestures. By *costume*: as we have already noted, the Mummy's dirty and tattered grey–yellow dress turning red from the womb downwards resembled the dirty and bloodstained petticoat in which the Young Lady was finally revealed. By *movement*: notably in the following passage in Act III (the acting-directions refer to Bergman's version).

YOUNG LADY. . . . *Turning to the* STUDENT, *thumb in mouth, whispers.* What's the worst thing you know?

STUDENT *whispers.* Counting laundry. Ugh!

YOUNG LADY. That's my job. Ugh!

STUDENT. What else?

YOUNG LADY. To be awakened at night and have to get up to fasten the window-catch . . . because the maid has forgotten to.

STUDENT. What else?

YOUNG LADY. To climb up a ladder and mend the cord of the damper when she has torn it off.

STUDENT. What else?

YOUNG LADY *with a shrill voice, increasingly faster.* To sweep after her, to dust after her, to make a fire in the tile stove after her – she just puts in the wood! *Starts slowly turning around.* To watch the dampers, to dry the glasses, re-lay the table, uncork the bottles, open the windows to air the rooms, re-make my bed, rinse the water decanter (*slowing down, increasingly adopting the* MUMMY'*s tone of voice*) when it gets green with slime, buy matches and soap that we're always out of, dry lamps and trim wicks, so the lamps won't smoke and so that the lamps won't go out, when we have company I have to fill them myself . . .

This passage has long been considered a prime example of how Strindberg could not always keep his own household problems outside his work. We know from his *Occult Diary* that many of the everyday chores mentioned tormented him.

However, in Bergman's production it was made clear that the catalogue of unpleasant chores should be understood not literally but figuratively, as so many examples of the obligatory 'drudgery of keeping the dirt of life at a distance'. In addition to this, the passage became the most telling instance of the thematic connection between the Young Lady and the Mummy, of how the former is destined to turn into the latter. In the Young Lady's speech, as quoted above, the development from childhood (thumb in mouth) to old age (mummification), the gradual 'dying' to which we are all condemned in the course of life, was demonstrated by tone of voice and body language.

The Old Man and the Student

Just as the outward similarity between the Mummy and the Young Lady, between mother and daughter, suggested the frightening destiny of human development, so did the outward resemblance between the Old Man and the Student. Like Strindberg's Old Man, Bergman's was provided with a beard (plus a moustache) and glasses. So was his Student. In this way the idea was conveyed that the Student incarnates an earlier stage in the Old Man's life and that, conversely, the Student is destined eventually to turn into another Old Man – an idea that Strindberg hints at, not least through his age-oriented cue designations. Taken together, the male and the female couples thus presented a picture of the fate of humanity.

In providing the Old Man also with a skullcap and a diamond ring, indicative of his Jewish origin, Bergman certainly took a risk. Turning the most dislikable character into a Jew would inevitably be seen as an anti-Semitic statement by some spectators. Actually the reason was quite the opposite one. The Old Man was meant to appear as a pariah revenging himself on the society which oppresses him. His usurping mentality, his desire to unmask people of higher station could in this way be socially justified or at least motivated.

The opening

Let us now see, more closely, how the opening has been rendered in different productions and media.

Stage

Bergman's stage production began as follows (the position numbers correspond to those on the stage plan on page 109).

1 *Projection on the screens of a beautiful white art nouveau apartment house and on the cyclorama of part of a church. L and R (at 3 and 6 respectively) a banister of silvered brass. R (at 11) a grey street drinking-fountain with pump and cup. L downstage (at 1) a grandfather clock and a black chair, R (at 7) a white marble statue of a beautiful semi-nude young*

woman. Projections of palm twigs on clocks and statue. All projections, in black-and-white, are slightly out of focus. White light, chiming of church bells.

The OLD MAN *sits in a black wheel-chair at 10, reading a paper. His hair, moustache and beard are white. He wears glasses. He is dressed in a black overcoat with a velvet collar, black striped trousers, black boots, black–green neckerchief with a diamond tie-pin, a diamond ring on his pink, a black skullcap on his head, on his knees a grey blanket.*

2   *The* MILKMAID *enters at 5 with milk bottles in wire baskets, which she puts down next to the drinking-fountain. She wears a simple, light-grey cotton dress, a peaked cap of the same material, a white apron, grey stockings, black boots, a black purse hanging at the sash. Her hair is braided into a plait.*
    The OLD MAN *looks worriedly around, tucks the blanket around himself.*

3   *The* COLONEL *enters at 7 with his back to the audience. He wears a black wig and a long black-silk dressing-gown. He pats the statue on the bottom and starts observing it.*
    The MILKMAID *wipes sweat from her forehead, washes her hands, arranges her hair, mirroring her face in the water; then puts the cap back on her head.*

4   *The* DARK LADY *enters at 5, walks back and forth in the opening upstage, looking around. She wears a dark-grey silk coat, a big hat with roses and gauze, dark-grey gloves, and carries a black parasol. Her hair is chestnut red. When she moves, the hem of a bright red petticoat can be seen.*

5   *The* CARETAKER'S WIFE *enters at 3 with a laurel tree. She is poorly dressed in a grey skirt, grey blouse, black-and-grey knitted vest, a black kerchief on her head, slippers. She stops, looks at the* DARK LADY, *exits at 5.*

6   *The* MILKMAID *works the pump and drinks from the cup.*

7   *The* FIANCÉE *enters at 1, sits down on the chair, looks at the (imaginary) gossip mirror, starts to crochet. She wears a*

*black–violet silk dress from the 1880s, a black laced shawl,
and a black laced cap. Her hair is grey.*

8 *The* STUDENT *enters at 5. He has a reddish-blond moustache
and beard. He wears glasses, a light-grey linen jacket, grey
striped waistcoat, unbuttoned white shirt, grey shoes, everything a bit torn and dirty. Around his left hand he has a
bandage. His head is bare. He walks right up to the fountain.*

STUDENT. May I have the cup?
OLD MAN *shudders, looks R.*
MILKMAID *pulls cup toward herself.*
STUDENT Haven't you finished yet?
MILKMAID *looks at him with horror.*
OLD MAN *to himself.* Who's he talking to?
STUDENT. What are you staring at? Do I look so terrible?
OLD MAN *to himself.* Is he crazy?

A comparison with Strindberg's text reveals that the number of
sequences there (three) was increased to eight in Bergman's
production; seven of these occurred before a word had been
uttered. (For the play as a whole, the total is 49 sequences in the
play text as against 94 in the production.) The difference indicates
the cinematic swiftness with which Bergman opened his production.
Unlike Strindberg, he began the play with the Old Man alone on
the stage. When the Milkmaid entered, the Old Man sensed her
presence; he looked around worriedly and tucked the blanket
around himself – as though he suddenly felt cold. The Milkmaid,
Bergman thereby suggested, had been evoked by the Old Man's
guilt-feelings.

While Strindberg opens the play with several sound-effects,
Bergman limited himself to one: the chiming of the church bells –
a very natural sound since it is Sunday morning and, moreover,
time for the dead Consul's funeral. The mournful sound faded
away as the Milkmaid left, returned briefly when the dead Consul
appeared, and was heard for the last time when the Milkmaid was
represented as drowning. (Significantly, she was drowned on a
Sunday.) Since the Old Man has 'murdered' both of them, the
mournful chiming of the bells was actually not so much a realistic
sound as an expression of his pangs of conscience. The handling

of this sound-effect seemed well attuned to Strindberg's drama of half-reality.

Radio

As we have seen, the visual code is exceedingly important in *The Ghost Sonata*, where visions form an integral part of the central thematic pattern: the contrast between what seems to be and what is, between appearance and reality. It is therefore a delicate task to adapt the play for the non-visual radio medium.

This is how Per Verner-Carlsson's Swedish radio version opens (I translate from the script):

1 *Chiming of church bells from three churches at different distances. When the nearest has almost finished, the* OLD MAN *starts to speak. The other bells finish their tolling one after the other during the first part of his speech.*

OLD MAN. Sunday. Quiet Sunday morning on the little square. I'm sitting here in my wheelchair, keeping watch in front of the house, the respectable house with the round parlour at the corner, with marble and brass and laurel trees. Well, well! They are sweeping and polishing. The caretaker's wife. *Laughs.* I'm waiting. Watching and keeping watch. Sunday. You see, I am interested in the destinies of people! I observe. What else? Talk about the weather, which we know, ask how we are, which we know? I prefer silence, then you hear thoughts and see the past. Yes – what has been and what shall –

Organ music from the nearby church during the following speeches.

2 OLD MAN. Someone is coming! It is him! It *is* him! The student. At last! Sleepless, unshaven . . . Of course! He walks straight up to the fountain.
  STUDENT *at some distance.* May I have the cup? – Haven't you finished yet?
  OLD MAN *to himself.* Who's he talking to? I don't see anyone.
  STUDENT. What are you staring at, girl? Do I look so terrible?

> Well, I didn't get any sleep last night. I suppose you think
> I was out making a night of it. Drinking punch, eh? Do I
> smell of punch?
> OLD MAN *to himself.* But who's he talking to? Is he crazy?

The need to inform the listener about where the action takes place
has here resulted in a somewhat artificial soliloquy by the Old
Man, consisting partly of verbalised stage-directions, partly of a
dialogue fragment from his speech at the ghost supper in Act II.
His 'you see' implies that he is addressing the listener directly, in
the manner of the classical *prologus*.

Naturally, the greatest problem, in a non-visual medium is
presented by the exclusively visual, pantomimic elements in a play
text. Since *The Ghost Sonata* is unusually rich in such elements –
besides the two mute 'ghosts', several other characters are silent
for long periods – it follows that the drama text does not lend
itself easily to radio adaptation. Obviously, the presence of the
silent characters has to be indicated, somehow, by the speaking
ones. As a result, the dialogue here and there tends to be
unnaturally informative.

Thus there is an attempt to make the listener sense the presence
of the mute Milkmaid by having the Student add the word 'girl'
and by having the Old Man ask himself twice whom the Student
is talking to.

The presence of the Milkmaid is also indicated by the celestial,
harmonious organ music. When she has left and the Old Man
starts to attract the attention of the Student, the music significantly
changes, receives an *'instrumental effect'*, as it says in the script,
and turns disharmonious.

There is no steamship bell, presumably because it would be
difficult for the listener to identify this sound. (In fact, all the
visual presentations discussed here also omit the steamship bell.)
As a result, the symbolic significance of Strindberg's sound montage
is lost.

Television

Shortly before Bergman's production of *The Ghost Sonata* opened,
a Swedish TV version of the play, directed by Johan Bergenstråhle,
was transmitted. The actor who had played the part of the Old

Man in the 1962 radio version took the same role in Bergenstråhle's
TV version, playing it in a more Mephistophelian manner.
The TV version opens as follows.

1   *Fade-in to credits (THE GHOST SONATA. Chamber Play
    by August Strindberg) on patterned wallpaper. Organ music.
    Dissolve to*

2   *LS of a choir dressed in black (six female, four male singers,
    five on either side of the organ). The organist, his back
    turned to the spectator, conducts with his L arm. Organ
    music and singing in the same manner until shot 7.*

3   *Tilt down to the* OLD MAN *in light, yellowish summer clothes
    and hat (with a black ribbon) and black gloves. His face is
    hidden behind a newspaper. The street drinking-fountain in
    FG. Splashing of water.*

4   *Slow zoom-in on the* OLD MAN, *who lowers his paper and
    looks up, so that his face can be seen. He wears glasses.
    Splashing of water.*

5   *A section of a grey apartment house with high windows, one
    L with flowers in it (the hyacinth room) and a double bay-
    window R, covered with white curtains (the round parlour).
    Pan R to*

6   *Open front door with laurels in tubs on either side. A window
    R of door (*FIANCÉE'S *window). Inside the door the* DARK
    LADY *is standing, in black with mourning crape over her
    face. The* CARETAKER'S WIFE *is scrubbing the floor.*

7   *The* OLD MAN *looks up from his paper, then disappears again
    behind it. High organ notes followed by* a capella *female
    voices and, finally, a single female voice.*

8   *The* MILKMAID *walks down a stately grey staircase from L to
    R. She wears a grey dress and beret and carries milk bottles
    in wire baskets. Turns L when she reaches ground level.
    Organ music until shot 12. Footsteps.*

9 *Zoom-in on* MILKMAID *as she walks up to the drinking-fountain and puts the wire baskets next to it.*

10 *The* MILKMAID *wipes the sweat from her forehead, picks up the cup, fills it with water from the fountain and drinks. Dissolve to*

11 *The* STUDENT *walking down a stately grey staircase (like the one we have just seen) from R to L. He wears a Swedish student's cap, black waistcoat and trousers, white shirt with rolled-up sleeves. Footsteps.*

12 *The* MILKMAID *washes her hands in the fountain. Behind her a poster, advertising the programme at the Royal Theatre, and part of the staircase. She leans on the fountain with her arms, mirroring her face in the water. Splashing of water. Chiming of church bell until shot 15.*

13 *The* STUDENT, *who is unshaven and whose cap is dirty.* May I have the cup?

14 MILKMAID *looks at him frightened.*

15 STUDENT. Haven't you finished yet?

16 OLD MAN, *muttering to himself.* Who's he talking to? *Lowers paper, looks up, turns his head R. To himself.* I don't see anyone. *Turns head back, to himself.* Is he crazy?

In Bergenstråhle's scenographic solution there is no indication, as in the play text, of an inward movement. The whole play is acted out in one huge space, in which the high–low dichotomy is essential. The setting is in itself dream-like in the sense that we do not know whether it is an exterior (a street) or an interior (a church), whether the prop in the foreground is a street drinking-fountain or a baptismal font.

Our first impression, as we see a huge organ with organist and choir, all placed on a raised area in the background, and as we hear the music and the singing, is indeed that we are inside a church. The director seems to have incorporated into the organ music Strindberg's *'steamship bell'*: the monotonous notes played remind one of steam puffing from a chimney, but also of the regular ticking of a clock, relating the sound to the ghost supper in Act II, or the beating of a heart (the Old Man's pangs of conscience). The plaintive, wordless singing from the very beginning intones the mood. We are in a world in which 'det är synd om människorna' (meaning both 'humanity is to be pitied' and 'humanity is sinful'), the central line of *A Dream Play*, a drama which looms large in Bergenstråhle's production. (He later produced it for television.) The sound of murmuring water from the fountain – an unrealistic sound – helps emphasise the biblical connotations of the 'fresh water'. It is significant that Bergenstråhle manipulates this sound, which becomes particularly loud when the Milkmaid, the good Samaritan, in a long take, bathes the Student's eyes.

While in the play text we move from (love of) the world to (love of) heaven, from blindness to seeing – at the end we are, as it were, blessed with the Student's second sight – Bergenstråhle makes the heavenly aspect immediately explicit. Instead of a play beginning in a physical reality and ending in a spiritual one – Strindberg's idea – we are presented with a 'medieval', allegorical construction with heaven above and earth-*cum*-hell below. The Milkmaid and the Student both enter the ground level (the world) from the organ loft above (heaven) in virtue of their child-like innocence – much as, in the words of the Student, 'Jesus Christ descended into hell. That was his pilgrimage on earth' – a speech that apparently has been decisive for Bergenstråhle's scenographic solution.

Once we see this, other things fall into place – the dominance of greyness, for example, which not only indicates the drabness of human existence but also is the colour of stone, the material with which the Old Man, akin to the biblical Tempter, builds his world. When the camera tilts down from the organist – the praiser of God – to the satanic Old Man, it makes a clear statement of the metaphysical polarity.

The Old Man appears in yellowish summer clothes, black mourning ribbon and black gloves: a non-realistic costume bringing out his corpse-like nature; his pretence to mourn the Consul, whom he has 'murdered'; and (as signified by the gloves) his feeling of coldness – i.e. his lack of warmth and love and his sense of approaching death. By showing the Old Man first hiding behind his paper, then lowering it so that his face can be seen, Bergenstråhle not only indicates his deceitful nature but also introduces the central theme of seeming versus being.

If Bergenstråhle's production is characterised by theatricality, symmetry, a subtle use of colours, Philip Saville's, transmitted eight years later, is dynamic, cinematic, variegated. Of the ten published English translations of the play, Saville has settled for the very actable and frequently used one by Michael Meyer.

Saville's version opens with a pre-credit sequence, based on two events that are related in the play text. The first one concerns the collapse of a house; says the Student to the Old Man:

> Well – yesterday, for example, I felt myself drawn to that quite ordinary little street in which, in a few minutes, a house was to collapse. I walked down it and stopped in front of this building – I'd never seen it before. Then I noticed a crack in the wall and heard the floorboards snapping. I ran forward and snatched hold of a child who was walking close by the wall. The next moment, the house collapsed. I was safe. But in my arms, where I thought I was holding the child, there was nothing.

The significance of this situation does not appear until the end, where the Student tries to save the Young Lady from this sinful world but discovers that innocence does not exist. In other words, the death – actually disappearance – of the Young Lady corresponds to the disappearance of the child. This is partly why the Student at the end speaks of the Young Lady as a 'poor little child, child of this world of illusion'.

As long as the illusory child is merely mentioned – as is the case in the play text – it fully retains its symbolic significance of 'child of man'. When presented as by Saville, it can no longer be just a child; it receives a gender, becomes a little girl – dressed in blue. Although this links the child with the Young Lady, via the blue hyacinth associated with her, the universality provided for by the play text – the child as a representative of mankind – is gone.

The collapse of the house is shown in a swift sequence where Saville cross-cuts between the collapsing house and the reactions of the people in and around it. In this way he heightens suspense – much as in an adventure film.

Then follows the title of the play, in 'trembling', ghost-like lettering combined with a picture of a nude young girl who seems to come out of the water only to be pushed back into it. This shot relates to the Old Man's crime against the Milkmaid, revealed at the ghost supper: 'he was accused of having lured a young girl out on the ice to drown her, because she'd been witness to a crime he was afraid might get discovered'. The shot – out of focus, in slow motion – is accompanied by non-diegetic, eerie music. All these unrealistic effects obviously serve to suggest that we are concerned with a nightmarish inner reality: the Old Man's traumatic guilt-feelings.

Summarising, we might say that in the pre-credit sequence Saville shows us (i) the Student saving a little girl from being killed, and (ii) the Old Man killing a young girl. Innocence saved versus innocence killed is thus established as the central opposition in the production.

Having devoted close to fifty shots to the pre-credit sequence, Saville begins the teleplay proper as follows:

1   *Window with shutters.*

2   *The* DARK LADY *inside the shutters. Zoom-in.*

3   *Profile of the* OLD MAN *reading a Swedish newspaper* (Dagens Nyheter). *He wears a black coat and beret. The* MILKMAID *approaches from the bluish background with two buckets on a yoke. She wears a white-and-yellow 'folk costume' and a white bonnet.*

4   *The* OLD MAN *turns round to the front. Zoom-out revealing a barrier behind him. Zoom-in on the* MILKMAID *who, now nude, gains superhuman size behind the barrier before she disappears L.*

5   *HA CU of drinking-fountain. Reflection of the* MILKMAID'S *face in the still water.*

6   *The water splashes as the* MILKMAID *pumps water into the fountain.*

7 *LS HA of the* OLD MAN, *in a wheelchair, reading his paper, a blanket over his legs, a grey shawl round him. R FG white-and-red [Danish] flag of the consulate. The stones of the little square form circular patterns.*

8 *The* STUDENT, *dark-haired, dressed in white, approaches the pump and the* MILKMAID, *who has put her white bonnet on the pump. Blue sky behind them.*

9 STUDENT *to* MILKMAID. May I have the cup?

10 MILKMAID. STUDENT *off-screen.* What are you staring at?

11 STUDENT *to* MILKMAID. Am I so repulsive? Oh, I see. I haven't slept all night, so of course you think . . .

12 *CU of* MILKMAID, *frontal.* STUDENT *off-screen.*
    . . . I have been boozing.

13 *CU of* OLD MAN *with glasses.* STUDENT *off-screen.*
    Give me a drink of water, girl – I've earned it. I've been bandaging wounds all night, and tending the injured; . . .

14 STUDENT *alone by pump in BG,* OLD MAN *in FG.*
    STUDENT. . . . I was there when the house collapsed yesterday evening. Now you know.

Although Saville suggests by certain signs – *Bagarbod* (Bakery), *Dagens Nyheter* (Daily News), *Kungl. Teatern* (Royal Theatre) – that the action is set in Sweden, there is little else to verify this. Unlike Bergenstråhle's Student, Saville's lacks a Swedish student cap – for natural reasons, since this badge of status would probably not be recognised by a British audience and so might merely confuse. The Student's all-white costume, apart from indicating his purity, suggests that he is a 'Samaritan' of sorts. The Milkmaid wears what looks like a South German folk costume and her yoke and water buckets turn her into a Gretchen of the early nineteenth century rather than a Swedish milkmaid of the early twentieth. Of Strindberg's Milkmaid there remains only a maid; an essential aspect of the figure is lost. Possibly Saville wanted to universalise the play and at the same time indicate the connection with the Samarian woman fetching water from Jacob's well.

Rather than in a street we find ourselves in a square, surrounded by a barrier; what is behind it we do not know. Saville presumably intended the barrier to indicate the border between consciousness and subconsciousness. This is suggested by the fact that the drowned Milkmaid grows to gigantic size behind the barrier, thereby reflecting the Old Man's growing guilt-feelings. The stones of the square, indicating this grey world, are effectively linked with the Old Man and contrasted with the blue heaven (compare the little girl in blue), against which the Student and the Milkmaid are silhouetted.

In a stage performance a director can choose between presenting and not presenting the Milkmaid; in the former case we would share the Student's point of view, in the latter the Old Man's. Since Saville's version was made for the screen, he is able to present a third alternative. The spectator alternates between the two viewpoints. But, since the Student, as we have seen, takes a very special place, functioning as our guide, it is essential that we should immediately be able to identify fully with him. Saville's alternating-viewpoint version makes this more difficult.

Some notable deviations from the play's stage-directions may be due to Saville's reliance on a target text. Thus while Strindberg's Caretaker's Wife is '*sweeping the entrance hall*', Saville's – doubtless as a result of Meyer's incorrect rendering – is '*cleaning the front steps*'. And, while Strindberg calls for '*a couple of minutes of silence*' before the Student enters, so that the impression that the Milkmaid is somehow linked to the Old Man can sink in, Saville, possibly misled by the translator's '*a few moments of silence*', makes the interval considerably briefer than Bergenståhle does.

The ghost supper

Stage

For the ghost supper in Act II Bergman's idea was that,

> when Hummel in his long monologue reveals the hidden crimes of the others, the audience must feel how he is growing like a toad inflating itself. Then comes the Mummy's counter-attack.

She gives Hummel three pricks. Now it is his turn to shrink. When he has just received the third prick, he thinks: all right, I can stand this, as long as you don't mention the Milkmaid whom I have murdered. At this moment the Milkmaid appears, called forth by Hummel's anguish.[27]

By choreographing it in this way, the Old Man's long monologue, which easily becomes monotonous on the stage, was made dramatically arresting. Throughout the monologue the struggle between him, acting as judge, and his victims could be sensed.

In the background the Student and the Young Lady were seen as a loving couple, in blatant contrast to the depraved old people in the foreground.

Television

In Bergenstråhle's version the young couple do not appear at this point; instead the white marble statue behind the guests, centre, seems to represent their youthful innocence. As in Act I the arrangement is highly symmetrical. The director alternates between long shots of the five guests and medium close-ups of the speaker, the Old Man.

With regard to the dialogue, the production was criticised for its use of old-fashioned language. As a matter of fact, the language is varied in a considered way. Thus the extreme formality of the Old Man's language in his monologue – the verbal forms he uses, for example – suggests that he has learned his speech by heart in advance. His unmasking of the others is in other words carefully prepared. To give his condemnation of them the appearance of objectivity he speaks like a law book. When his true self later comes to the fore, he reverts to a plain way of speaking. The monologue is delivered as a crescendo, with the right arm raised a couple of times (in contrast to the organist, who raised his left arm?), reminding us of a certain rhetorical dictator, the prime satanic figure of our time. (Bergman resorted to the same 'Heil!' gesture in the celebration scene at the end of Act I.)

The emphasis in this version falls on the Mummy's speech of contrition ('we are miserable human beings', etc.), delivered with the crucified Christ as background and with a strong light turning her hair into a halo.

Again, Saville's version demonstrates a very different approach. Unlike Bergenstråhle, he breaks the monologue up into a great many shots, some of which depict what is on the minds of the characters. This is how the Colonel is revealed:

CU of COLONEL *with monocle* [= mask].

LS of COLONEL *naked on stairs, moving away from camera* [= hiding].

CU of COLONEL *looking down* [= ashamed].

And this is a portrait of the Old Man:

CU of the OLD MAN *breathing heavily* [= guilt-feelings, thinking of . . .].

LS of the MILKMAID, *nude, swimming by a landing-stage, surrounded by green, coming out of water, approaching camera, happily smiling.*

CU of the OLD MAN.

LS of landing-stage, now empty [= Milkmaid drowned].

The two sequences are linked by contrasts: the Colonel is ashamed of his nakedness, whereas the Milkmaid is happy with hers (relating her to the nude marble woman); his environment (stone house, stately staircase) is in marked contrast to hers (simple wooden landing-stage, nature); he moves away from the camera, whereas she approaches it.

More ambiguous is the following sequence:

LA CU of the OLD MAN.

LS of a YOUNG MAN *in grey suit in green meadow.*

CU of the FIANCÉE.

LS of the YOUNG MAN *running towards the camera.*

CU of the FIANCÉE

The first shot of the Young Man is inserted between close-ups of the Old Man and the Fiancée, the second one between two close-ups of the Fiancée. This indicates that he represents their memory of Hummel as an innocent and attractive young man. With this interpretation the shots of the Young Man are flashbacks. Alternatively, they may be seen as flash-forwards, representing the Old Man's dreams of a bright future for the Student and the Young Lady; the shots, be it noted, accompany his statement about how he has tried to find a friend for her.

In the play text the Milkmaid *'appears in the hallway door, unseen by all but the* OLD MAN, *who shrinks back in horror'*. This happens as the Mummy rings for Bengtsson, the only person who knows about the Old Man's crime against the Milkmaid. Bergman had the Milkmaid appear by the grandfather clock. After a while she raised her arms like someone drowning. Bengtsson's revelation was followed by a *'thunderclap'*. The Old Man uttered a stifled cry. The Milkmaid lowered her arms and left.

Bergenstråhle has the Milkmaid appear on the stairs and sink down there as if she were drowning. Saville has her appear at an earlier point, just before the Old Man strikes the table with his crutch:

1 *LA of the* OLD MAN, *a big wall clock behind him with a moving pendulum. Ticking of clock. Shadows. Slow zoom-in on* OLD MAN.

2 *The* MILKMAID *in white dress and bonnet in a green meadow.*

3 *Hand of clock. Loud ticking.*

4 OLD MAN *raising his crutch.*

5 MILKMAID *coming out of water, out of focus, in slow motion. Eerie music.*

6 OLD MAN.

7   *Zoom-in to ECU of* MILKMAID, *coming out of water, hand pulling her down* [= title shot].

8   OLD MAN *striking crutch on table.*

In the play text, the Old Man's hubris culminates with his striking of the table, which he compares to the striking of the clock, thereby equating himself with Fate. With Saville, by contrast, the striking of the table is an expression of the Old Man's attempt to repress the painful memory of the drowning Milkmaid. The clock figures prominently with Saville, and in his production the Mummy's stopping of it is the climax of Act II. The reversal of power is indicated by low-angle shots first of him, then of her. The Mummy is dressed like a nun to illustrate her 'nunnery existence' in the wardrobe, her many years of penance.

The ending

Stage

Bergman rearranged the end even more than the opening:

COLONEL *goes up to the* YOUNG LADY, *puts one arm around her shoulder, tenderly.* The liberator is coming. Welcome, pale and gentle one.

He moves the YOUNG LADY *behind the screen. A little later her hand is seen falling on the floor R of screen. The* COLONEL *sits down on the floor, takes her hand.*

Sleep, you lovely, innocent, doomed creature, suffering for no fault of your own. Sleep without dreaming, and when you wake again . . . may you be greeted by a sun that does not burn, in a home without dust, by friends without stain, by a love without flaw.

STUDENT, *standing by the harp, recites in a toneless voice.*

I saw the sun. To me it seemed
that I beheld the Hidden . . . seemed?

Men must reap what they have sown,
blest is he whose deeds are good . . . Good?
Deeds which you have wrought in fury,
cannot in evil find redress.
Comfort him you have distressed
with . . . with loving-kindness – this will heal.
No fear has he who does no ill. *Looks at the* COLONEL.
No fear has he who does no ill . . .
Sweet is innocence . . . Innocence? *Shakes his head,*
   exits R.

MUMMY *comes in from the rear, pushes the screen gently away,
sits down on the chair next to it, looks at the* YOUNG LADY *(who
is lying on the floor, her back to the audience), puts one hand
on the* COLONEL'*s shoulder.* You poor little child . . .

*Light in rays from above. Occasional harp notes during the
final speech.*

   . . . child of this world of illusion, guilt, suffering and death,
this world of endless change, disappointment, and pain. May
the Lord of Heaven have mercy on you as you journey
forth . . .

   A final harp-note. Slow black-out. Curtain.

The conception of life underlying Bergman's production was
almost the opposite of Strindberg's; in the director's own words,
'the only thing that can give man any salvation – a secular one – is
the grace and compassion that come out of himself'.[28] In line with
this view, the projection of *Toten-Insel* had to be omitted. *The
Song of the Sun*, which the Student had recited in a romantic–
idealistic way, to the accompaniment of occasional harp notes,
at the end of Act II was now recited tonelessly, without any
accompanying music, the harp having turned 'deaf and dumb' to
him. Bergman: 'If the Student reads the poem with a sceptical
tone the second time he recites it and recognises that it turns to
dust, then it seems to me meaningful. . . . Every sentence in that
stanza seems dubious.'[29]
   The final speeches of the play text express compassion for the

dead Young Lady and faith in a (better) life hereafter. Strindberg, who has the Student deliver these speeches, stresses the latter; Bergman, who gives them to the Colonel and the Mummy, the former. In the performance the divine aspect was constantly toned down in favour of human love and compassion. In the text the Colonel and the Mummy seem to share a mummified matrimonial existence. In the production they were turned into two people who despite their crimes – or because of them – were tied to one another in a feeling of mutual loyalty. Thus when the Old Man during the ghost supper revealed that the Young Lady was *his* daughter, not the Colonel's, the Mummy grasped the Colonel's hand. A little later, when she testified to the misery of mankind, she stood behind the Colonel with a protecting gesture, while he in turn grasped her hand.

In the final act of the play text the Colonel and the Mummy are seen in positions illustrating that they have drifted away from each other: they are sitting close to the death screen in the round parlour, '*inactive and silent*' – a pre-Beckettian couple waiting for death, 'the liberator'.

In Bergman's version, by contrast, they were reunited at the end. By giving the Student's concluding prayer for the dead woman to *both of them*, the director was able to stress their unanimity. This was strengthened by the choreographic pattern in the final picture. The Mummy's hand rested tenderly on the Colonel's shoulder. He in turn lovingly held the hand of the Young Lady. Both of them regarded their dead 'daughter' – a secular holy trinity harking back to Jof (i.e. Joseph), Mia and their little son Michael in Bergman's film *The Seventh Seal*, the loving trinity that is saved from the Black Death.

In the closing moments of Bergman's performance the harp that had been 'deaf and dumb' to the Student began to play. In addition there was a combination of soft light, representing the love and compassion experienced at this moment by the Colonel and the Mummy, and strong light from above, indicating the spiritual nature of their state of mind, and perhaps also their hope – Bergman did not cut this religious reference – that 'the Lord of Heaven' would show the Young Lady the same compassion as they now did.

'We have broken up and left each other infinitely many times, but then we're drawn together again', the Mummy states in Act

II, referring to her marriage to the Colonel. Bergman demonstrated how the two were 'drawn together' first when Hummel threatened them, then when the Young Lady was taken from them. Her death had not been in vain.

Radio

At the end of Verner-Carlsson's radio version the Young Lady can be heard wailing – letting us know that she is dying – while the Student is concluding his monologue. After she has rung the bell and asked for the death screen, the Student's 'the liberator is coming' speech is accompanied by what in the script is referred to as '*music: the theme of death*', cool electronic music. This is replaced by '*humming, unrealistic harp chords*' when he recites *The Song of the Sun*. A final wailing informs us that the Young Lady is giving up her ghost. And the performance is concluded with the Student's prayer for the dead woman, followed by harp chords which, '*mingled with the sound of bells, swell into a mighty tone block*'.

As already indicated, the three visions of the play – the Milkmaid, the Dead Man, *Toten-Insel* – are the greatest stumbling-blocks for anyone adapting *The Ghost Sonata* for radio. While Verner-Carlsson manages to draw attention to the first two by having the speaking characters comment on them, this is hardly possible in the case of *Toten-Insel*. Strindberg's spectacular conclusion cannot be transmitted to the listener. Instead he is provided with a musical equivalent of the *changement à vue*, signifying the Young Lady's transference from a painful life to, one hopes, a blissful hereafter. In the final sound-effect, the director has abstained from Strindberg's '*soft music*' coming from the Isle of the Dead, since this is only effective if the recipient is aware of the isle. Instead the chiming of the bells from the beginning of the performance returns in the concluding tone block, but now mingled with the celestial harp chords – an acoustic circle composition with a significant close.

Television

Towards the end of Act III, as the Student speaks his sombre monologue, Bergenstråhle has him walk up the stairs, pass in front of the organ and then walk down the stairs left, stopping on the way by a mirror, by the choir and by the crucifix. He has made his pilgrimage through life and now quickly retraces it as he summarises his negative experience of it. His movement is a spatial counterpart of the coda-like repetition of earlier motifs in his monologue. Bergenstråhle's handling of the death screen is inventive. Bengtsson approaches the camera with the red-and-black screen; since we only see his hands and feet, there is something mystifying about it.

The Student does not recite *The Song of the Sun* from memory (as in Act II) but reads it from a book, as though he were distancing himself from it; Bergenstråhle's solution is here close to Bergman's. The Student's concluding prayer for the Young Lady is omitted; death is no 'liberator' in this version.

The performance ends with a long shot of Bengtsson, in black livery and with clasped hands, in front of the death screen – like a priest officiating in front of the altar. The camera tilts up to the choir and the organist; there is white light from above and plaintive singing. The ending is thus a symmetrical reversal of the opening, Bengtsson (the servant) now taking the place of the Old Man (the master). As it says in the play text, 'the roles of life alternate'.

Unlike Bergenstråhle, Saville omits *The Song of the Sun* but retains the Student's prayer. With Bergenstråhle the Student's outburst '[I saw] a virgin – by the way, where is virginity? Where is beauty? In nature and in my mind when it's in Sunday clothes' is uttered as he is standing next to the crucifix. Thus, by way of contiguity, 'virginity' becomes associated with Christ and, obliquely, with his mother, the Virgin Mary.

Saville, by contrast, places the Student next to the nude marble statue as he utters Meyer's rendering of this passage: 'Where is virginity to be found? Or beauty? Only in flowers and trees . . . and in my head when I am dressed in my Sunday clothes.' Since the marble statue represents Eve before the Fall, what is here suggested is rather that innocence cannot be found after the Fall. In the text the implied opposition is between 'nature' (innocence) and 'human nature' (sinfulness). Meyer obscures this with his free rendering 'flowers and trees', which may well have inspired Saville in his choice of an Edenic context.

The play text does not state that the Young Lady is dying, merely that she '*seems to be dying*' (by Meyer tritely rendered as '*has crumpled in her chair*'). What Strindberg is suggesting here is that we, the living, are deluded. Like the characters on the stage we mistake seeming for being. Actually, the death of the Young Lady is no death at all, only a transformation, a rebirth to the true life. This appears also from the acting-direction referring to the Young Lady's manner of 'dying'. '*A moaning is heard behind the screen*', Meyer translates, but Strindberg's *kvidande* could better be rendered as 'whimpering' or 'wailing', i.e. a sound suggesting both birth and death. (In *A Dream Play* – I quote from Walter Johnson's translation – 'the newborn whimper [Swedish *kvida*],/wailing, screaming/over the pain of existence.') If in Saville's rendering the Young Lady's dying seems commonplace, it may have something to do with the difficulty of preserving Strindberg's meaning in translation.

Saville ends the play by placing the Student, in white, in front of a red death screen, his back to the camera. There is then a dissolve to a painting with a white figure in the centre – as though the Student had entered the picture. A zoom-out verifies that the painting is indeed Böcklin's *Toten-Insel*, hanging on a wall – as it did in the pre-credit sequence. Suddenly the wall cracks and the painting falls down. The final shot shows it next to a candelabrum on the floor. There is a pan and zoom-in on the little girl in blue whom the Student tried to save from the collapsing house in the pre-credit sequence. The End.

In retaining *Toten-Insel*, Saville may seem to follow the play text more closely than the other directors. Yet even his version is rather different from Strindberg's. In the text it is the white-shrouded corpse in the boat – reminiscent of the milkmaid and of the white mourning-sheets at the beginning – which represents the recently 'dead' Young Lady; it is she who is taken to a blissful hereafter – at least in the Student's imagination. In Saville's version, on the other hand, it is the Student himself who is taken there – while the little girl in blue (representing the Young Lady) remains among the ruins of the collapsed house. Whereas Strindberg holds open the possibility that the idea of a blessed afterlife is not merely another illusion, Saville dismisses it as just that.

Schematically the differences between the two TV productions may be summarised as follows:

	Bergenstråhle	*Saville*
Text	Original	Translation
Changes	Slight (end)	Moderate (beginning and
		end)
Scenery	Uniform	Varied
Colour scheme	Sparse	Varied
Sound-effects	Sparse	Varied
No. of shots	Low	High
Camera angles	Neutral	Spectacular
Flashbacks	None	Many

The difference may be summed up as one between homogeneity (Bergenstråhle) and heterogeneity (Saville). Bergenstråhle's production is in the Swedish Molander tradition of heightened or magic realism, with strong religious overtones and sparse effects. Saville's version, on the other hand, may perhaps be located in the Reinhardt tradition, in the sense that it is nightmarish, expressionistic, out of touch with recognisable reality.

Saville's version may seem preferable in that it makes fuller use of the capabilities of the TV medium, but one might as plausibly argue that the best radio plays have the most sound-effects or that the best films have the least dialogue. Much more relevant is the question: are the visual and verbal elements properly balanced? The lack of visual fireworks in Bergenstråhle's production means that the exceedingly compact and polysemic dialogue receives due attention; we are given time to ponder and feel the effect of the words. In Saville's version the visual elements obtrude, attract too much attention, while the subtleties of dialogue are harmed by a sometimes defective translation. Both productions lack the inventive power and choreographic subtlety that characterised Bergman's stage version, one of his most successful *mise-en-scènes*.

What the three productions have in common is that they do not adhere to Strindberg's ending. From this we may possibly conclude that the ending of the play text is not ideologically in tune with our time – a sweeping generalisation which may well be proved untrue in future productions.

The Ghost Sonata and the media

With its playing time of merely about an hour and a half and its cinematic touches, *The Ghost Sonata* may seem better suited to media transposition than both *Macbeth* and *A Doll's House*. Yet, unlike Shakespeare's and Ibsen's plays, Strindberg's chamber play has never been filmed for the big screen and has rarely been televised.

One reason for this is undoubtedly that the play still seems too sophisticated to be appreciated by a mass audience. Much the same applies even in the theatre. At least outside Scandinavia, *The Ghost Sonata* has more often been performed by small *avant-garde* groups, such as O'Neill's Provincetown Players, than by well-established theatre companies of the West End or Broadway type. It is decidedly a *rive gauche* play. With few exceptions – Max Reinhardt being the most notable – major stage directors outside Scandinavia have avoided *The Ghost Sonata*. It is evident that a play as difficult to perform as this one, with a cast largely consisting of aged people, cannot gain a firm stage reputation from, say, drama-school productions, in which the actors are much too young and inexperienced to do the play justice.

Other aspects, though of less significance, may add to the problems of transposing the play to a mass medium. Thus for the TV producer the relatively large cast – fourteen *dramatis personae* – may be a stumbling-block. For the film-director the unity of setting may seem uninspiring. And, as we have seen, the purely visual elements create special difficulties for someone who wants to make a radio adaptation.

Yet the question can be put more broadly: why have Strindberg's so-called naturalistic dramas – *The Father, Miss Julie, The Dance of Death* – frequently been transposed to the screen, while his 'dream plays', seemingly much more obviously cinematic, have been largely disregarded by film-makers? The reason, I believe, must be sought in the fact that theatre tends towards the universal and stylised, whereas film tends towards the individual and realistic. Re-creating *The Ghost Sonata* as a film would mean that the characters, instead of appearing as representatives of mankind, would be seen as individuals; and that the dream-like atmosphere, instead of conveying the feeling that life is a dream, would merely convey the impression that the central character and narrator, the Student, experiences life as such.

As we have seen, Bergenstråhle tries to circumvent this difficulty by explicating the play's implicit religious themes, while Saville does it by opting for an expressionist technique. Since Bergman's production was a stage version – in the medium intended by the playwright – he could stay closer to the border area between the real and the surreal evoked in the original text.

Strindberg's use of the Unknown in *To Damascus*, of Indra's Daughter in *A Dream Play* and of the Student in *The Ghost Sonata* as character–narrators and mediators between stage and auditorium is decidedly an epic device suggesting that whatever surrounds these central figures is filtered through their minds. What we partake of is not reality itself – how could it be? – but an experience of reality. In this sense Strindberg's subjective drama is highly realistic. Nevertheless, and from another point of view, a kind of objectivity – or representativity – is achieved simply by having many characters experience more or less the same; this is why Strindberg needs a fairly long list of *dramatis personae* in his later plays – and why it seems detrimental to the play when even minor figures are left out.

This means that while drama traditionally, unlike the novel, is objective – showing reality from as many points of view as there are characters – Strindberg's late drama tends toward an amalgamation of the objective and the subjective, showing both a representative outer world and a subjective, inner world. And the point is precisely that we can never be certain of where the one ends and the other begins. In his stage production, Bergman maintained this 'double focus', while leaning rather strongly in the direction of subjectivism. This he could do by resorting to the cinematic technique of projections visualising the shameful or claustrophobic feelings of the characters as well as of their author (the projected face of Strindberg). Bergman's successful fusion of theatrical and cinematic devices is a logical development along lines suggested by the playwright himself. Like Bergenstråhle's very theatrical TV production, it points in the direction of intermediality.

Chapter 5

Choosing the Medium: Pinter's *The Homecoming* (1965)

Like *The Ghost Sonata*, *The Homecoming*, considered by many to be Pinter's best play, combines realistic and metaphorical elements. These define its basic character and at the same time are what makes its interpretation so problematic. It is a general feature of Pinter's dramas that they demand from their recipients (be they readers, audience, translators, critics, actors or directors) a great deal of sensitivity to what is between and behind the speeches, and *The Homecoming* is no exception.[1]

Unlike the dramatists hitherto discussed, who wrote their plays solely for the stage, Pinter, belonging to our own era, has had a choice of media. Indeed, he has written not only stage dramas, but also radio plays, teleplays and film scenarios. He has also transposed his own play texts from one medium to another. Thus he has turned *The Collection*, a teleplay, and *A Night Out*, a radio play, into stage dramas. Besides being a playwright, Pinter has occasionally directed or appeared as actor in his own plays.

In view of this versatile, first-hand experience of the theatrical arts, one can expect him to have a great awareness of what is specific to each medium and what is not. The mere fact that he both co-operated closely with the stage director of the first production of *The Homecoming*, Peter Hall, *and* wrote the screenplay for the film version of this drama means that the transposition from one medium to another is likely to have preserved (as it has) the play's basic character. Unlike in the situations we have dealt with earlier, it is in this case one and the same person who is (chiefly) responsible for the transposition. Since director and cast are also virtually the same in the stage and the screen versions, we may conclude that differences between the two versions are largely due to media differences.

Synopsis

I.1. The set represents the living room of an old house in North London. It is evening. Four men are living in the house: Max, aged seventy, an ex-butcher; his brother Sam, sixty-seven, a hire-car driver, and two of Max's three sons: Lenny, whose profession seems uncertain, and Joey, who works for a demolition firm. Max, who cooks for the others, talks about his former love for horses, about his late wife, Jessie, about his late friend and companion MacGregor and about his late father and mother – a world of the past.

I.2. A few hours later. It is night. Teddy, Max's third and eldest son, returns home with his wife, Ruth. They have spent a week in Venice and have now stopped on their way home to the United States to pay a visit to Teddy's birthplace and to introduce Ruth to his family. While Ruth goes for a walk, Teddy meets Lenny, who has heard them entering. Their meeting is surprisingly cool and casual and Teddy soon goes to bed. Ruth returns and informs Lenny that she is Teddy's wife. Without reacting to this, Lenny asks if he may hold her hand. He proceeds to tell her a story about a prostitute he once beat up and another about an old lady who suffered the same treatment from him. Ruth shows no signs of being shocked. On the contrary, she makes Lenny an erotic proposal. She then goes upstairs, to bed. As Lenny keeps shouting after her, he wakes his father up. He does not reveal to Max that Teddy and Ruth have appeared but claims that he has been sleepwalking and been shouting in his sleep.

I.3. Next morning. Max and Joey talk about what they are going to do in the afternoon. Sam enters. We learn that he too was taken into his father's butcher's shop but that he was replaced by

MacGregor. Teddy and Ruth now appear. Teddy explains to Max that Ruth is his wife but Max insists on regarding her as a prostitute. When Lenny appears, all the characters are for the first time together in the living-room. A violent scene follows. Max hits both Joey, who has teased him about his old age, and Sam, who has tried to help Joey. He then turns to Ruth again. When he learns that she is a mother of three children, he softens. He now greets Teddy like a loving father. Teddy responds. And the act ends with Max's triumphant exclamation, 'He still loves his father!'

II.1. The afternoon of the same day. Lunch, prepared by Max, has just been finished. Again everybody is in the living-room. Max reminisces about his late wife, a woman 'with a will of iron, a heart of gold and a mind'. He describes how, as a butcher, he had to support not only his own family but also that of his mother, since she was bedridden and his brothers were all invalids. Then, in a fairly long passage, two contrasting views about life in the United States are presented, a positive one by Teddy and a negative one by Ruth. When Teddy and Ruth are left alone, he tries to persuade her to return with him immediately to the United States, but Ruth does not respond. As Teddy goes upstairs to pack the suitcases, she reveals to Lenny that she was once 'a photographic model for the body'. When Teddy returns with the suitcases, Lenny asks Ruth for a dance before she leaves. They kiss. Joey and Max enter only to discover that 'Lenny's got a tart in here'. While Lenny caresses Ruth's hair, Joey embraces her. Neither Max nor Teddy reacts. Ruth takes on a bossy tone and orders food and drink.

II.2. Evening. We learn that Joey has spent the last two hours upstairs in bed with Ruth without going 'the whole hog'. Lenny concludes that Ruth is 'a tease'. Max suggests that she stay in the house. Lenny, whose profession is now revealed – he is a pimp – has a proposition: Ruth can get a flat from him in Soho, where for 'four hours a night' she can earn her living 'on her back'; the rest of the time she can spend in their home as a housekeeper and collective 'wife'. Far from being shocked at the family's proposition, Ruth accepts it wholeheartedly – but on her own terms. Once the contract is settled, Sam bursts out, 'MacGregor had Jessie in the back of my cab as I drove them along.' He then collapses. Teddy leaves for the plane that will take him back to America. And the play ends with Max, Lenny, Joey and Sam (still collapsed) surrounding Ruth.

Theme

Having discovered that being married to Teddy is in fact equivalent to leading a doll's-house existence, Ruth, like Ibsen's Nora, leaves her husband and her three children. Nora leaves her family for the outside world. Ruth leaves her bourgeois family of five for a '*ménage a cinq*',[2] making it quite clear to her new male family that she is not going to let the men dominate her. Her bossy tone at the end demonstrates how she is fighting for independence, for a right to a room of her own. In Pinter's words, 'At the end of the play she's in possession of a certain kind of freedom. She can do what she wants, and it is not at all certain she will go off to Greek Street. But even if she did, she would not be a harlot in her own mind.'[3]

The ease with which Ruth accepts the idea of becoming a prostitute is not simply a result of her youthful experiences. It is rather a consequence of her experience of married life as a dry desert haunted by insects, the imagery she uses to describe America. Teddy's claim on her as mother, sex partner ('wonderful wife'), social company ('popular woman') and intellectual supporter ('you can help me with my lectures') is so imprisoning to her that the claim of his family appears to be preferable. *They* want her body, Teddy wants her soul – that is the essential difference. By having Ruth choose an alternative which to many recipients would seem not only strange but unjustifiable, Pinter has made her homecoming as provocative to modern audiences as Nora's homeleaving was to those of Ibsen's time. Ruth is certainly a Nora of the 1960s, just as Teddy, who cares only about what is within his province, has much in common with the egocentric and status-minded Helmer.

As has often been pointed out, the homecoming of the play title refers not so much to Teddy – in a deeper sense, he does not come home at all – as to Ruth. There are several senses in which the title applies to her: (i) she returns to her native environment ('I was born quite near here') to take up a profession (prostitution) she has practised before there; (ii) since the male family experiences her as a kind of reincarnation of Jessie, the dead wife/mother, Ruth's decision to stay is tantamount to a homecoming by Jessie; (iii) from the arid existence Ruth has led with her academic husband, she has 'come home to herself, to all of her possibilities as a woman'.[4]

Granted that Ruth can fulfil the role of maternal substitute in a way that Max has never been able to, why does she have to become a prostitute? To answer this question we may consider Sam's revelation that MacGregor 'had Jessie' in the back of his car. This seems a possible indication that Jessie was in fact a prostitute. The same conclusion may follow from Max's statement that he has never had a whore under his roof since Jessie died. It is significant that Max first rejects Ruth as a 'tart', then welcomes her as a 'mother', and finally tries to get her to combine the two roles. By setting Ruth up as housekeeper and whore, the family recognises that Jessie has, as it were, returned to them.

In addition to this 'realistic' explanation, there is Martin Esslin's interpretation of the play in archetypal psychoanalytical terms. According to him Max, the father, and Teddy, the eldest son, represent two aspects of the father figure, Max senility and aggressiveness, Teddy the wisdom of old age. Similarly, Lenny and Joey represent two aspects of the son figure: Lenny is cunning and clever, Joey strong and sexually potent. Jessie and Ruth are, of course, mother/wife figures. In accordance with the Oedipal pattern, we witness in the play how father and son struggle for mother and wife. At the end the father figures are defeated by the son figures. Sam, who finally tells the naked truth about Jessie, represents the family consciousness, the superego; quite logically he collapses when the contract with Ruth is settled. From the son's point of view the action of the play amounts to a wish fulfilment; from the father's point of view it is a nightmare.

But how does prostitution fit into this pattern? Esslin gives the following explanation:

A whore is the most passive of women, the one who can be treated as a sexual object without any consideration of her own feelings or desires. The more helpless a male, the more he will tend to dream of women as obedient slaves – prostitutes. Hence the stern, unapproachable mother image must, in the sexual dreams of the child, tend to turn into the image of the whore.

And that is why both Jessie and Ruth are both mother and whore.[5]

Another possible explanation starts from the definition of a prostitute as a woman who is shared by many men – that is, who is unfaithful to each one of her sex partners. This is what distinguishes her from a monogamous woman, married or not. Yet, in the light of the Freudian Oedipus complex, it might also be claimed that a mother in the eyes of the son is unfaithful to him, 'prostituting' herself, whenever she sleeps with his father. And so the son's attitude to the mother must inevitably be ambivalent: she is both mother and 'whore'. A mother who is a real prostitute, who openly has sex with every male seeking her, it may be argued, alleviates the burden for the son, whose father, in such a situation, is deprived of his sexual prerogative. If the son is one of the mother's sexual partners, the father is even more disgraced.

In short, psychoanalytically speaking the prostitute motif is directly related to the rivalry between father and son(s) that is so central in *The Homecoming*. At the end of the play the traditional roles are reversed. It is now the father who clings to the hope that he will be allowed to share Ruth with his sons. (Max's brother Sam, being a homosexual, is no danger to him.) But the final tableau shows that he has little reason for optimism.

Stage and screen

In the following, I shall refer not so much to the original Aldwych stage production as to the film version based on this production (also with Hall as director and with three of the original Aldwych actors in the cast). In addition I shall consider a Dutch stage version, directed by Erik Vos, and a Swedish TV production, directed by Håkan Ersgård.

As we have already noted, Pinter was not only involved in the original stage production of the play, but also responsible for the script of the film version. It is thus not surprising that he has himself drawn attention to a fundamental difference between the stage and the screen media:

On the stage one of the challenges that faces a director, a writer and the actors is how to focus the attention of the audience, how to bend the focus, how to insist that the focus of the audience goes in one specific direction when there are so many other things to look at on the stage. With a film the audience must attend only to the particular image you're showing them. They have no chance to do anything else.[6]

Naturally, in a stage production our attention would tend to turn to the character who is speaking. In a screen version this is not necessarily so. The camera would decide for us whether the speaker, the listener, both or neither would be in picture at any given moment. And the focusing would vary a great deal, a long shot allowing us more freedom of selection than a close-up.

Not surprisingly – in view of its theatrical genesis – the film version of *The Homecoming* favours medium shots. As a result it retains some of the freedom of choice that the spectator has with a stage production. By contrast the TV version, which excels in close-ups, is more severely edited.

When comparing different versions, it is natural to pose the question: how comparable are they? Have they kept the play text intact or have they cut it? If the latter, what cuts have been made? In the case of *The Homecoming* we may assume that there are usually no significant cuts in the stage versions. The dialogue is so dense that it does not call for cutting, and omissions of so-called daring passages seem out of the question, since the whole situation in the play is more daring than anything that is being said or done. It is more surprising that there are no significant cuts in the film version – probably because the playwright himself acted as script-writer – while there is a substantial omission in the TV version: the passage where Lenny boasts about his violent treatment of two women, which his later meekness towards Ruth ironically contradicts.

While scenery and acting in the TV version are realistic, they are rather stylised in the film: here a very limited number of properties and colours – black, white, grey – are used; the costumes of the characters do not markedly differ; and the three sons, whose names are so similar, are linked with one another also through their dark sideburns.

The erotic element is stressed more in the TV version than in the film. The Ruth of this version has a strong sex appeal, which is frequently emphasised, notably in the erotic sequence with Joey: at one point the camera – like a stand-in for all the men – peeps inside Ruth's dress at her underwear.

Like Eliza Doolittle, the Ruth of the film reveals her social adaptability by speaking with a cultivated British accent. The Ruth of the TV version, by contrast, speaks Swedish with a Danish accent. Did Ersgård look for an equivalent of the difference between American and British English, as a way of suggesting that Ruth, unlike Teddy, has been linguistically very 'adaptable' in the United States? Is he pinpointing Ruth's central statement that the fact that the lips move 'is more significant . . . than the words which come through them'? Or is the difference of accent just another way of setting Ruth off from the male characters, of making her more mysterious in their eyes?

The different interpretations of Max are very striking. In the end he is a garrulous old man, aggressively defending his territory. In the TV version he is softer, more introvert, dreaming about the past, a sulky child who has no faith in his ability to assert himself.

Most remarkable, perhaps, are the different interpretations of Teddy. Witnesses of Peter Hall's stage production in London and New York often saw him as the villain of the play, whereas recipients of various Dutch stage productions have seen him as a victim.[7] In the film he is the cool scholar, who is afraid to become emotionally involved, 'the biggest bastard of the lot'.[8] In the TV version, by contrast, he is quite emotional and soft; as a result he appears here – much as in the Dutch stage productions – as a victim of his family's brutality. Presenting him in this way is not only sentimentalising the play, but actually providing it with a one-dimensional 'message' completely opposed to the complex, open one of the Hall productions.

Translation

The most obvious difference between the film version, on the one hand, and the Dutch and the Swedish versions for stage and television, on the other, is of course the linguistic one: the original English versus a Dutch/Swedish translation. A few examples will indicate the kind of discrepancies between source text and target texts to which this difference gives rise.

Unlike the English, the Dutch and the Swedes can choose between two pronouns of address, the formal *U*/*ni* (comparable to French *vous*) and the informal *je*/*du* (comparable to French *tu*). This forces a translator from English into Dutch/Swedish to choose between the two forms. When the Swedish Lenny first meets Ruth, he addresses her with the formal *ni* rather than the informal *du*, which he later resorts to. In view of Lenny's exceedingly casual manner and desire to dominate, this is surprising: it would seem more likely that he would use the *du* form from the outset.

Ruth's 'an awful lot' is strengthened into the mild oath *en jäkla massa* (a damned lot), making her language more like that of a prostitute, while her desire for whisky in 'a tumbler', by contrast, is understated with the vague *ett riktigt whisky-glas* (a real whisky glass). The slang expression 'go the whole hog' relates to the animal imagery that is central to the play; this imagery is necessarily lost in the Swedish vulgarism *sätta dit 'en* (put it in).

In both the Dutch and the Swedish translations of the play, Ruth's last words to Teddy – 'Don't become a stranger' – have been rendered literally, 'as if Ruth were encouraging Teddy not to become alienated from her and the family'.[9] But such a rendering overlooks the fact that the phrase is used by London prostitutes to encourage a customer to come back.[10]

A more obvious ethnic problem is formed by the connotations pertaining to some urban areas: North London, Blackfriars Bridge, Greek Street, and so on. The connotations these names have for a British recipient, notably a Londoner, would be lost to most Dutch or Swedish ones, had the playwright not indicated it in his context.

Although even British people may not think of it, the names of the characters connote a Jewish environment. When *The Homecoming* was first performed in the Netherlands, in 1966, some of the names were changed. Ruth, Sam and Jessie became Ann, Sid and Rosey – 'alterations that suggest an effort on behalf of the translator and director . . . to steer clear of any Jewish associations the original names might evoke'.[11] Admittedly, such a (dubious) change might have been undertaken also by a director dealing with the source text – in the interests of increased universality.

However, the real problem for the translator of Pinter is to grasp the subtext: the many *double-entendres*, plus what is in the silences between the speeches. One example may stand for many. Sam tells Max and Lenny that he has just driven an American to 'London Airport' – the name, incidentally, situates the play in a pre-Heathrow/Gatwick period – and proudly shows a box of cigars which he has received from him.

> MAX *takes one from the box, pinches it and sniffs it.* It's a fair cigar.
> SAM. Want to try one? MAX *and* SAM *light cigars.* You know what he said to me? He told me I was the best chauffeur he'd ever had. The best one.
> MAX. From what point of view?

Max's final question may seem surprising. Its function is to draw attention to the *double-entendre* of the passage. The American has 'had' Sam, Max suggests, not only as his chauffeur but also sexually. In this second context, the cigars seem an altogether appropriate gift.

This passage is actually fairly easy to translate into Dutch or Swedish. Whether it is understood or not by the recipient is not an interlingual problem. It depends rather on careful attention to the play text and sensitive and suggestive presentation. The phallic quality of the cigars is conveyed in Hall's film by the way the homosexual Sam and the 'impotent' old Max handle them, clearly bringing out the sexual subtext of the passage. In the TV version, by contrast, there are no such kinesic indications. As a result the spectator is not made aware of Pinter's *double-entendre*.

Setting

Text

Like *A Doll's House*, *The Homecoming* is set in only one room; again we find ourselves in the living-room of a family. But, unlike Ibsen, Pinter is not interested in re-creating a realistic environment, which only gradually reveals its deeper significance. Rather, he confronts us with a room, which is hardly recognisable as a living-room. The initial stage-directions read,

SUMMER

An old house in North London.
A large room, extending the width of the stage.
The back wall, which contained the door, has been removed.
A square arch shape remains. Beyond it, the hall. In the hall a
staircase, ascending U.L., well in view. The front door U.R. A
coatstand, hooks, etc.
    In the room a window, R. Odd tables, chairs. Two large
armchairs. A large sofa, L. Against R. wall a large sideboard,
the upper half of which contains a mirror. U.L. a radiogram.

The specification 'North London', which is communicated to the
reader as well as to the film and TV spectator but not to the
spectator in the theatre (unless he reads it in the programme), is
vague. Standing by itself, it may suggest to a Londoner the less-
well-to-do, industrial part of the city Pinter obviously has in mind.
    Why a large room? Hall gives two explanations:

'This is partly because we'd worked together on two of his other
plays at the Aldwych and he'd been rather preoccupied, and
rightly, by the fact that the Aldwych is a very large stage. And
he said to me, 'I think properly speaking that this is a large play
that needs a large room, and it'll go on a large stage.'[12]

Whether Pinter adjusted to the format of the Aldwych stage or
selected this stage because it fitted his idea that the play 'needs a
large room', may be hard to ascertain and is not really important.
What *is* important is the suggestion that the play is large in scope.
This could be suggested by having it staged in a room not unlike
'a spacious hall or a throne room'.[13] Also, a large stage would
enable a director to indicate, spatially, the separateness, the
isolation, of the various members of the family.
    The *'square arch'* within the proscenium arch may suggest a
play-within-the-play idea, helping us to see the family dwelling in
the large living-area outside the square arch as comparable to the
audience dwelling outside the proscenium arch. The arch also
provides a connection with the 'arch' below which Lenny met the
prostitute who offered herself to him – a woman who serves to
link Jessie with Ruth and thus obliquely to reveal Lenny's attitude
to them. This appears once we realise how closely connected the

arch is with the dead mother; as Teddy explains to Ruth, 'there
was a back wall, across there . . . with a door. We knocked it
down . . . years ago . . . to make an open living area. The structure
wasn't affected, you see. My mother was dead.'

Teddy is mistaken. On the contrary, when Jessie, 'the backbone
to this family', died, the family structure was fundamentally
affected. The new 'living area', Quigley points out, 'has neither
the same point of focus nor the same sharply defined boundaries
as the room with the previous structure'.[14]

Of the properties, the *'two large armchairs'* may be seen as
belonging to the parents, the king and the queen of the family,
the *'odd'* chairs and the *'large sofa'* to the children. Since the
mother, Jessie, is long dead, one of the armchairs seems a pathetic
reminder of her absence; when Ruth toward the end comes down
the stairs and *'sits'*, we may assume that she sits down in Jessie's
hitherto vacant chair, showing that she is now replacing the dead
woman. Also the sofa is given a special meaning when 'JOEY *lies
heavily on* RUTH' on it, repeating the sexual act which MacGregor
once performed with Jessie 'in the back of [Sam's] cab'.

Stage and screen

Concerning the realisation of the arch for the original production
Hall reports,

> I remember [Harold] being very concerned about the pillar that
> ran across the top of the set, which is where the wall had been
> knocked down. In our first model it was very roughly hewn; it
> was very obvious that a wall had been knocked down, and a
> large beam had been put in to keep the house up. Harold quite
> rightly said, 'Yes, that's right, but it's too explicit.' When they
> talk about the wall being knocked down and the audience looks,
> *then* they should understand why the wall is like it is; but when
> the curtain goes up they shouldn't look and say, 'Ah, a wall has
> been knocked down and a beam has been put in.'[15]

To John Bury, designer of the Aldwych production, Pinter
explained that he needed a room with an area not in full view.
Neither the window nor the door at the bottom of the staircase
was to be shown.[16] (This arrangement is not specified in the stage-

directions.) In this way, Enoch Brater points out, 'the mistiness of the past is amplified, visually, by the mistiness of a stage environment half-dream, half-real. The suspension of explication and validation on a thematic level is matched by the absence of verification on a visual plane.'[17]

The *'large room'* was realised in an extreme way in the 1984 Dutch production, where the audience sat in two galleries on either side of the huge play area. Six old armchairs and a sofa were placed around two carpets in the centre. The adjacent walls were poorly wallpapered. 'The great distance between the pieces of furniture', one critic wrote, 'represents the silence between the lines. In that silence and below the text the true drama takes place.'[18]

According to another critic, what the director had in mind was the stage as circus arena. Like wild beasts each of the characters would fight for his or her place in the human hierarchy. The men would steal their way to their tamer (Ruth) and then return to their own chair, their own territory.[19]

The seating-arrangements meant that most of the spectators were forced to look down on the actors, while facing the spectators on the opposite side – as in a circus. As a result the audience was alienated from the characters.

The great distance between the characters also worked against a realistic style of acting. Thus the play text's 'RUTH *hands coffee to all the men*' was turned into 'an extended, almost ballet-like ritual, in which the men one after the other slowly have to bridge the distance between their chairs and the table in the middle in order to fetch their coffee from Ruth'.[20]

As the Vos production demonstrates, the *'large room'* need not be a problem on the stage. But how is one to squeeze it into a small TV screen? Clearly, great distances between the characters would be very difficult to retain in the intimate TV medium, which does not favour long shots.

As for the atmosphere of the living-area, the idea behind the Aldwych production was to create a set where the absence of a woman was sensed. In the words of the stage-designer, 'The environment is essentially masculine. That was the whole point about the house. There wasn't anything feminine about it. The set couldn't be dirty. It wasn't squalid because of the reference to cleanliness.'[21] Hall makes the same point: 'It's a sterile world from which women have been excluded; the set has to mirror that.'[22]

The stage, film and TV versions do not differ significantly in what they show of the world of the play. The film is not cinematic in the sense that it takes every opportunity to show the environment around the prescribed large room. Except for two brief views of the exterior of the house, the camera stays inside its walls and only momentarily dwells on areas outside the living-room. The TV version is even more confining: we never move outside the room.

The opening

Text

Let us now look more closely at the beginning of the drama text. This is how Pinter opens his play:

> LENNY *is sitting on the sofa with a newspaper, a pencil in his hand. He wears a dark suit. He makes occasional marks on the back page.*
> MAX *comes in, from the direction of the kitchen. He goes to the sideboard, opens top drawer, rummages in it, closes it.*
> *He wears an old cardigan and a cap, and carries a stick.*
> *He walks downstage, stands, looks about the room.*
> MAX. What have you done with the scissors. *Pause.* I said I'm looking for the scissors. What have you done with them? *Pause.* Did you hear me? I want to cut something out of the paper.
> LENNY. I'm reading the paper.
> MAX. Not that paper. I haven't even read that paper. I'm talking about last Sunday's paper. I was just having a look at it in the kitchen. *Pause.* Do you hear what I'm saying? I'm talking to you! Where's the scissors?
> LENNY *looks up quietly.* Why don't you shut up, you daft prat?
> MAX *lifts his stick and points at him.*
> MAX. Don't you talk to me like that. I'm warning you. *He sits in large armchair.* There's an advertisement in the paper about

flannel vests. Cut price. Navy surplus. I could do with a few of them. *Pause.* I think I'll have a fag. Give me a fag. *Pause.* I asked you to give me a cigarette. *Pause.* Look what I'm lumbered with. *He takes a crumpled cigarette from his pocket.* I'm getting old, my word of honour. *He lights it.*

The contrast between the two men – father and son – is here indicated in a number of ways.

1 *By age/stature:* Max is a man of *'seventy'* with a stick – the icon of old age; Lenny is one in the prime of his life, the *'early thirties'*.
2 *By costume*: old and homely clothes (Max) as against *'a dark suit'* (Lenny). 'Lenny is dressed to leave the house, Max to stay', Quigley concludes. This agrees with the critic's division of the characters into a domestic and an extra-domestic group. Yet before we know that 'the cap is standard indoor wear for Max'[23] – a social icon? – we would tend to associate it with the out-of-doors. His habit of wearing it indoors may be seen either as representing his dream of a life outside the household or as a pathetic demonstration of his male sex despite his female occupations.
3 *By domain:* Max's domain is the kitchen; Lenny is comfortably settled in the socially higher-ranking living-room.
4 *By occupation:* Max roams around looking for an ad that will help him to obtain cheap clothes, while Lenny sits on the sofa looking for a way of making easy money by betting on horses.

In addition to all these visual hints at an unbalanced relationship, there are the many silences, indicating the contempt with which Lenny ignores his father; his *'quiet'* scolding of him, which strongly contrasts with Max's impotent rage; and Lenny's immediate assumption – underscoring the power struggle between the two – that the paper Max wants to cut up is the one he is reading.

In the opening sequence Max and Lenny talk about horses and horse-racing. They argue about whether a male horse called Second Wind is going to win a race at 3.30 the next day. Lenny believes he will win; Max says he will not. This controversy prepares for further events within the family. In the afternoon of the next day we witness how Lenny and Joey win the race, so to speak, against Max and Teddy for Ruth's favour. Max tells Teddy that he used to stroke the manes of the horses to calm them down, that he could 'smell' a good horse and that he could tell whether a filly was 'a stayer' or not by standing in front of her, looking her straight in the eye. The significance of all this emerges at the end of the play.

Film and television

The film opens with a close-up of Max's hand rummaging in a drawer in search of the scissors. In the next long shot we see him standing in the kitchen. Unlike in the play text, Max is here introduced in his proper domain, as the 'cook' of the family. He moves quickly toward the door, and in the next shot, from behind the shoulder of Lenny, sitting in the sofa, we see Max moving into the living-room, to the sideboard, rummaging in a drawer, then moving over to Lenny, finally sitting down in the single armchair. All the time Max is kept small in the background, while the immobile Lenny towers in the foreground. In this way the son becomes even stronger in the film than in the stage version.

Instead of the two armchairs prescribed in the play text, there is only one in the film, grey and worn like Max, high like a throne, making him look small in it. By omitting the second chair it is suggested that the remaining one was once Jessie's chair and that Max is trying to replace her – without success.

The TV version opens with a high-angle long shot of the living room in which the action is to take place. High above it we see the lighting- and sound-equipment and the cameras which are to be used, down below a yellow sofa. Lenny enters and sits down on the sofa. The microphone is lowered to a position above his head. Lenny is zoomed in. Instead of wearing a '*dark suit*', as prescribed by the play text – indicating his concern with presenting a proper appearance – Ersgård's Lenny wears the flashy clothes of a pimp: blue, patterned jacket, red shirt and tie, black trousers, and an arm ring. Max enters, with cap, stick and clothes in beige and brownish tints. He rummages in the sideboard and sits down in a rather slender, velvet-green armchair.

While the Max of the film aggressively *orders* Lenny to give him first a 'fag', then a 'cigarette' (as though the 'proper' word would be more effective), the Max of the TV version plaintively *asks* him.

The two versions, in other words, go in opposite directions. While the film begins realistically in the kitchen and then turns into a stylised presentation – in terms both of setting and of acting – the TV version opens with a reminder that what we are going to see is (TV) theatre, and only later resorts to a realistic presentation.

In contrast to the film, there is no unity of colour in the TV version, and the armchair is not prominent. Finally, the choice of a plaintive rather than an aggressive Max lessens the power struggle between the two men. This is a Max who succumbs to the idea that he is an old man rather than one who fights against it.

Teddy's departure

Text

Teddy's departure toward the end of the play is described as follows (the layout is as in the play text):

> TEDDY *goes to the front door.*
>
> RUTH. Eddie.
>
> TEDDY *turns.*
>
> *Pause.*
>
> Don't become a stranger.
>
> TEDDY *goes, shuts the front door.*
> *Silence.*

This is a good example of Pinter's power to create a pregnant situation with very few words. Even the 'poetical' arrangement of the lines seems to indicate a dense subtext. Throughout the play Ruth, like everyone else, has addressed her husband as 'Teddy'. When she now uses a different, more intimate form of the name, this is startling not only to the family but also to us. In Esslin's words,

> 'Don't become a stranger' is a cliché, an idiom without any emotional force. . . . if one were to explain the phrase in a dictionary of idioms one would translate it with no more than: we might meet again; or: see you some time. This, clearly, is also how Teddy understands it. For he goes and shuts the front door. . . . But . . . surely there will also echo something of the *literal* meaning of that phrase 'don't become a stranger', rather like a last despairing lament of a wife for the husband she has now lost, who has, in fact, at that very moment become a stranger to her.[24]

However, as we have earlier observed, Ruth's leave-taking phrase can also be seen as an expression belonging to prostitute lingo. The actress playing the part of Ruth would here have to choose between contrasting ways of phrasing Ruth's final words to her husband.

Film

In the film Teddy's departure is re-created as follows:

1 TEDDY *leaves in BG with suitcase.* MAX, *in BG, stands looking after him.* RUTH *sits in armchair in FG. She calls.* Eddie. MAX *looks at her.*

2 TEDDY *returns, looks at the armchair (he cannot see* RUTH*).* RUTH *firmly, without looking at him.* Don't become a stranger. TEDDY *leaves again. Sound of footsteps and front door.*

3 *LS of* LENNY, MAX *and* JOEY *standing, triangle fashion, at great distance from one another around the armchair. All three look at* RUTH *(but only* LENNY *and* JOEY*, who stand in front of the armchair can see her).*

The departure is here clearly a very significant event. Teddy not only '*turns*', as in the play text; he actually disappears, only to come back again when Ruth calls him. When he leaves the second time, both his footsteps – not heard the first time! – and the sound of the front door inform us that this time his departure is as definite as Nora's slamming of the front door. The earnest way in which Hall's Ruth phrases her farewell sentence, coupled with the fact that she does not look at him, strongly suggests that this is an altogether serious leave-taking, with the literal meaning that Esslin sees in it. However, there is no note of lamentation. Taking into account the kind of person Teddy is, Ruth's words rather seem to imply: do not become alienated, do not operate on things but in things; do not observe but participate.

Television

In the TV version the departure is re-created very differently:

1   TEDDY *approaches the camera.*

    RUTH, *off-screen, calls.* Eddie.

2   RUTH *sits down on armchair in BG. Zoom-in on her face.*

    RUTH *with a casual smile, looking at* TEDDY. Come and see us some time.

3   *CU of* TEDDY'*s sombre face.*

4   *MCU of* JOEY *(FG) and a triumphant* LENNY *(BG).*

In this version, the leave-taking is sentimental, realistic, lacking in depth. Admittedly there are obvious transpositional problems. The phrase 'Don't become a stranger' is well-nigh impossible to render in Swedish, where, as in Dutch, a literal rendering would forfeit both the psychological connotations of the phrase and its echo of prostitute jargon. 'Come and see us some time' is a faithful translation of the phrase used in the TV version. Rendered thus the phrase, although lacking the complexity of the original, could still be effective if pronounced in such a way as to bring out the irony of the cliché expression used, as here, in an extremely non-cliché situation. But this is not how it is pronounced. The Ruth of the TV version says the line with well-meaning, polite casualness.

The picture of Ruth trying to come home to herself is blurred.

The ending

Text

The Homecoming ends with a striking grouping of all the characters except one:

> *The three men stand.* RUTH *sits relaxed on her chair.* SAM *lies still.* JOEY *walks slowly across the room. He kneels at her chair. She touches his head, lightly. He puts his head in her lap.* MAX *begins to move above them, backwards and forwards.* LENNY *stands still.* MAX *turns to* LENNY.

MAX. I'm too old, I suppose. She thinks I'm an old man. *Pause.* I'm not such an old man. *Pause. To* RUTH. You think I'm too old for you? *Pause.* Listen. You think you're just going to get that big slag all the time? You think you're just going to have him . . . you're going to just have him all the time? You're going to have to work! You'll have to take them on, you understand? *Pause.* Does she realize that? *Pause.* Lenny, do you think she understands . . . *He begins to stammer.* What . . . what . . . what . . . we're getting at? What . . . we've got in mind? Do you think she's got it clear? *Pause.* I don't think she's got it clear. *Pause.* You understand what I mean? Listen, I've got a funny idea she'll do the dirty on us, you want to bet? She'll use us, she'll make use of us, I can tell you! I can smell it! You want to bet? *Pause.* She won't . . . be adaptable?

He begins to groan, clutches his stick, falls on his knees by the side of the chair. His body sags. The groaning stops. His body straightens. He looks at her, still kneeling.

I'm not an old man. *Pause.* Do you hear me? *He raises his face to her.* Kiss me. *She continues to touch* JOEY's *head, lightly.* LENNY *stands watching.*

Curtain

The final tableau, in which everybody except the departed Teddy is brought together to form a family of sorts, is a picture at once of unity and of separateness. Each figure takes a different position: Sam is prostrate on the floor; Max kneels; Joey has his head in Ruth's lap; Ruth sits; Lenny stands. The concluding visual image suggests a hierarchy. The old Sam, who will certainly no more partake of Ruth's (possible) graces than he did of Jessie's, is the most peripheral figure in the new family. Max is reduced to a weak, begging position. Joey is tenderly caressed, like a pet child. As the only comfortably placed person, Ruth in *'her'* armchair – the possessive pronoun is indicative – demonstrates a position of strength. So does Lenny by virtue of standing; but, whereas Ruth is *'relaxed'*, he seems tense. His *'watching'* is that of one who is prepared to defend his territory against his weaker male rivals and against the powerful woman who has entered the family.

In a sense this is an open ending. In the words of Willem van Toorn,

> You never know . . . who wins, who loses. Is Teddy the winner by keeping his distance and returning to America . . .? Or does the filthy, cynical but authentic lifestyle vanquish counterfeit, reason, seeming order? Is the play insulting to the woman, who in the end is put in her place as a whore? Or is the final scene . . . a homage to the woman as queen, unreachable mystery?[25]

In the course of the play text we have partaken of three family situations: the Max–Jessie family, Max's all-male family, the Teddy–Ruth American family. Now we are possibly faced with a fourth type, the Lenny–Ruth family:

> The final tableau emphasises the bond between Ruth and Lenny as she sits surrounded by her children, while Lenny stands watching, arms folded. Max, having outgrown his usefulness as dominant father, sexually potent male, or adequate mother-substitute, is reduced to a child.[26]

This interpretation seems valid – except for one detail: Lenny's folded arms. Is this how the critic herself visualised the final tableau or was she remembering an actual performance of the play? In any case it is an amplification of the play text, where, as we have seen, it merely says, 'LENNY *stands, watching.*'

Pinter's final tableau, like the play as a whole, is open to several interpretations. As Hall comments, 'Harold always refuses to say what his plays *mean*, and I think quite rightly. I don't think one can literally define metaphor. A metaphor reverberates and has many meanings to many people, and that's why it's a metaphor.'[27]

To Quigley the end means that a new system of interaction is established. The bond between Lenny and Ruth, he claims, signifies that 'the prostitute–pimp system of mutual exploitation' is placed 'at the center of the domestic scene'.[28] Richard Hornby gives the following interpretation:

> At the end of the play, Joey kneels at Ruth's feet with his head in her lap, in a kind of Pietà; Sam and Max are on the floor, dead and dying; only Lenny remains standing. . . . The drive for dominance has led to a new family structure, with a new 'father' (Lenny), a new 'mother' (Ruth), and a new 'son' (Joey). All are ersatz figures, compared with their predecessors, who were genuine father, mother, and sons . . .; one can thus interpret the action as being some kind of statement about the breakdown of the nuclear family in modern times . . . .[29]

To this one may object that it is an open question whether the three sons were (all) fathered by Max. The likelihood that Jessie was unfaithful to Max, Max's objection to being called 'Dad' by Lenny, and the disturbing questions Lenny puts to him concerning the moment when he (Lenny) was conceived – all these circumstances seem to suggest that Lenny, at least, may not be Max's son.

But what is especially disturbing in Hornby's interpretation is that here, as elsewhere in his analysis, it is stated that Sam dies at the end – as though this were a fact. Yet the point of the whole passage dealing with Sam's collapse is that he does *not* die; even Max, who wants him dead, has to admit that:

MAX *pointing at* SAM. You know what that man had?
LENNY. Has.
MAX. Has! A diseased imagination.

The last words ironically apply to Max himself, to his readiness to imagine Sam as dead.

Nor does the text indicate that Max, as Hornby claims, is dying at the end. In short, the critic does not distinguish properly between the play text and his own, very special interpretation of it in connection with a production of *The Homecoming*.

Quigley draws attention to the significance of the scenery at the end: 'The arch that had framed the opening family situation now frames the closing family situation, too. It predicts for the latter, as it did for the former, a struggle between continuity and change.'[30] Valid as it is, this observation refers to the play text and, by extension, to stage performances of the play. In the film and TV versions here under consideration, the arch figures much less prominently and is, in fact, not visible at the end. As a result, a recipient of these presentations would necessarily miss the point made by Quigley.

An aspect of the ending that seems hitherto to have been disregarded is its relationship to the horse passage in the opening sequence. In light of the earlier passage, it is natural that Max should, at the end, use words such as 'smell', 'bet' and 'adaptable' in expressing his forebodings that Ruth will not prove a 'stayer' in the family. Even such seemingly neutral acting-directions as

He [MAX] *looks at her, still kneeling.*

LENNY *stands, watching*

become highly significant when related to the horse passage. As with the fillies of his youth, Max tries to look Ruth 'straight in the eye' to see if she is a stayer or not. But his position is the weak one of someone kneeling; the strong position of his youth has been taken over by Lenny, who '*stands, watching*'. The contrast between Lenny as he stands immobile, and Max as he falls helplessly to his knees and loses his support (the stick) – a climactic repetition of their kinesics in the opening of the play – informs us that Max has lost his 'gift' along with his youth, and that Lenny has taken over his hypnotic power.

Film

The contrast just referred to can easily be brought out in a stage production, where both men are visible throughout the final sequence. This would seem unnatural on the screen, with its preference for varying camera shots which would at times exclude one (or both) of the characters. Yet much of the contrast is retained in the film, where, significantly, most of the final sequence is shot from a distance – a rather stagy solution. In the TV version, on the other hand, where medium close-ups or close-ups prevail, the contrast is lost.

In the film, the grouping after Teddy, the rival, has left, suggests that, as soon as the common enemy has disappeared, the rivalry between the men who stay behind is sharpened (compare the situation at the end of the productions of *Macbeth* analysed in Chapter 2). The significance of the *high* armchair is now obvious: it separates the 'father figures' (Max and Teddy), not seen by Ruth, from the son figures (Lenny and Joey), whom she can see and who can see her.

The ending is re-created as follows:

1 *LS. Front of armchair C.* RUTH *sits in it.* JOEY *sits on the floor, his head in her lap. She strokes his hair.* MAX *stands in BG L.* LENNY *stands in FG extreme R.*

2 *MS of* MAX. I'm too old, I suppose!

3 *Back of armchair C.* MAX *stands in FG R.* LENNY *stands in BG L.* SAM's *head is seen on the floor R of chair.*

   MAX *with a senile giggle.* I'm not such an old man. You think I'm too old for you? *Approaches the chair. Shouting.* Listen! You think you're just going to get that big slag all the time? You think you're just going to have him . . . you're going to just have him all the time? You're going to have to work! You'll have to take them on, you understand?

4 *Front of armchair.* RUTH *still tenderly strokes* JOEY's *hair.* MAX, *stick in hand, leaning on L part of chair, shouting*

to LENNY. Does she realize that? . . . Lenny, do you think she understands . . . what . . . what . . . what we're getting at? What . . . we've got in mind? Do you think she's got it clear? . . . I don't think she's got it clear. . . . You understand what I mean? *Gradually moves over to R part of chair.* Listen, I've got a funny idea she'll do the dirty on us, you want to bet? She'll use us, she'll make use of us, I can tell you! I can smell it! You want to bet? . . . *Groaning.* She won't . . . be adaptable?

5   *MS of* LENNY *watching.*

6   *Front of armchair.* MAX *falls to the floor, drops his stick.* RUTH, *still stroking* JOEY's *hair, watches him.*

     MAX *grabs hold of chair and raises himself to a kneeling position, looks at* RUTH, *shouts.* I'm not an old man! . . . Do you hear me? . . . *Spits out.* Kiss me!
     RUTH *continues to stroke* JOEY's *hair.*

7   *MS of* LENNY *watching.*

8   *Back of armchair, a vacant wooden chair next to it.* MAX *kneels L of it.* JOEY *sits on the floor R of it.* SAM's *head can be seen on the floor R of chair. In BG* LENNY *stands watching.*

     Shot is sustained. Fade-out.

Just as in the opening sequence where Max's moving around contrasts with Lenny's immobility on the sofa, so here the old man's moving around contrasts with the immobility of the four other characters. The only one who is not completely immobile is Ruth, who keeps caressing Joey's hair. As at the beginning, Max from a weak position aggressively makes demands – to no avail. Max's weakness, already indicated in the play text by his stammering and his falling and dropping his stick, is further underscored in the film by the senile giggle, which so ironically contradicts his claim of not being old, and by his exhausted leaning on the armchair. His *'shouting'* out his distrust of Ruth to Lenny – rather than whispering it to him in confidence – testifies to Hall's distinterest in a realistic presentation. What counts here is not Max's suspicion but his anguish, the equivalent of an expressionist *Schrei*.

Lenny does not stand with folded arms but with his arms straight down – like a guard. His watchfulness is registered in no fewer than five of the eight shots.

The grouping of Ruth and Joey, we have already noted, carries overtones of the *Pietà*; the tenderness with which she caresses his hair expresses a compassion very much at odds with Max's aggressive egotism. One is reminded of her earlier statement – a central line in the play text – that the fact that the lips move is more important than the words which come through them.

The vacant chair next to the armchair may be viewed in different ways: (i) as a rather uncomfortable chair which Ruth has left for the armchair; (ii) as the chair for which the men now have to compete; or (iii) as the chair where Lenny is welcome to sit, next to Ruth.

Extremely suggestive is the fact that the armchair in the final shot is seen from the back rather than from the front. In this way two related ideas are expressed. One is that the chair is the symbol of power in the household, and that it is around this, rather than simply around Ruth herself, that the family gather. Whoever is in power will be served. More significant, however, is the idea that the chair was once Jessie's and has now, after Max's failure to sit *'relaxed'* in it, become Ruth's. By showing the armchair from the back, the director avoids showing who is sitting in it – so that we can imagine it to be either Ruth or Jessie. By this simple and yet effective device, the final shot marks the 'homecoming' of both women – Ruth, and the dead wife/mother with whom she is identified.

Television

In the TV version the presentation of the ending is very different:

1   *CU of* MAX *looking down, muttering to himself.* I'm too old, I suppose. You think I'm old. But I'm not that old. You think I'm too old for you? Eh? You think you're just going to get that big slag all the time? You think you're just going to have him . . . you're going to just have him all the time?

You're going to have to work! You'll have to take them on, you understand? *Looking up.* Does she realize that?

2   *MCU of* LENNY.

MAX. Lenny (MAX *enters frame from R. Close to* LENNY, *softly*), do you think she understands . . . what . . . what . . . what we're getting at? What . . . we've got in mind? Do you think she's got it clear? . . . You understand what I mean? Listen, I've got a funny idea she'll do the dirty on us, you want to bet? She'll use us, she'll make use of us, I can tell you!

Pan R to

3   *MCU of* MAX *as he walks R.* I can smell it! You want to bet? . . . She won't . . . be adaptable!

RUTH's *face enters frame.* MAX *kneels down beside her, his face and L hand (with a wedding-ring on it) by her bosom. Begins to sob. Camera pans as he creeps behind and around the chair.*

4   *CU of* MAX, *still sobbing, kneeling L of* RUTH, *looking up at her.* I'm not an old man. . . . Do you hear me? *Appealingly.* Kiss me.

5   *CU of* LENNY, *zoom-out to*

6   *LS of* RUTH *in armchair.* JOEY *half-sits on the floor in front of her with his head in her lap.* MAX *kneels L.* SAM's *prostrate legs on the floor can be seen R.* LENNY *stands in BG. Fade-out.*

In this version, the director has to a great extent stripped the play text – and a corresponding stage version – of its silent characters. Being the only speaker, Max is also given visual prominence. In shots 3 and 4 he is reduced to a dog, begging for crumbs from his mistress. His lengthy sobbing does not make his situation tragic or even moving; it is merely pathetic.

By his way of shaping the ending, Ersgård seems to insist that *The Homecoming* is very much Max's play, that the drama is essentially about the problem of ageing, of losing possession, a *King Lear* in drawing-room format.

Starting out as a near-soliloquy in the soft, plaintive tone that he used already in the opening, Max here indeed confides his supicions to Lenny. We must assume that Ruth does not hear what he says. Unlike Hall, Ersgård, in other words, presents this passage in a realistic, conventional manner.

It is a powerful stroke to show Max's wedding-ring – his bond with the departed Jessie – close to Ruth's heart. It is less easy to understand why we are shown Sam's legs rather than his head (as in the film). Lenny's watching is not prominent in this version. Scantily prepared for, this ending seems to signify very little.

However, the ending does mark a striking shift in the style of presentation. Harking back to the theatrical opening, the stylised final tableau indicates the director's intention of providing the realistic mode he has otherwise favoured with a non-illusionistic frame, reminding us that we have witnessed not reality but an imitation of reality.

The Homecoming and the media

The playing time, the unity of time and place and the limited number of *dramatis personae* make *The Homecoming* a play easily transposable to other media – although many directors would consider it unsuitable for film adaptation precisely for these reasons.

It is therefore interesting to note that Pinter himself, who helped to turn *The Homecoming* into a film, rather than into a teleplay, apparently thinks otherwise. However, it is difficult to know whether non-aesthetic (commercial) considerations have played a part here. In view of the high costs involved, it is fairly common nowadays for a screen version to be released first as a film, later as a teleplay. In such cases any director who is at all sensitive to the difference between the small and the large screen would need to have both media in mind in making the film. As a result, the borderline between the two becomes even vaguer than it was. Thus it could be argued that the Hall–Pinter screen version of *The Homecoming*, although technically a film, is dramaturgically a teleplay.

In the course of this chapter we have looked at some of the problems of staging the play, and of rendering it into another language.
However, the main focus has been on two productions – the
Pinter–Hall film version of 1973 and Ersgård's Swedish TV version
of 1972 – and the ways in which they differ.

Apart from the obvious linguistic difference – the film making
use of the original text, the teleplay of a Swedish translation – a
number of other differences between the two versions have been
registered: (i) the TV version omits a significant passage and so is
less faithful to the play text; (ii) it is less sensitive to the subtext
(for instance, in the cigar scene); (iii) it favours medium close-ups
and close-ups, while the film favours medium shots; (iv) it lacks
the unity of colour of the film; (v) the acting in the teleplay is
realistic, while in the film it is stylised. Since Hall's approach has
in every respect appeared to be more rewarding then Ersgård's, it
is difficult not to relate this circumstance to the fact that we are
here comparing one of the leading directors of today, working
closely with the playwright himself, to a Swedish TV director who,
in his essentially realistic treatment of the play has been led by
the natural bias of his medium. The alienating frame of the teleplay
is probably to be accounted for the fact that this version (produced
a year before Hall's) was born in a Brechtian theatrical climate.

In addition to considering the transpositional problems proper,
we have noted the tendency among drama critics to disregard the
distinction between drama text and performance. Not surprisingly,
the danger seems to be greatest when the critic of a play text
happens to have directed the same play.

Chapter 6

Medium and Vision

The emphasis in this book has been on the relationship between four different presentational modes – stage, radio, TV and film production – and source and target texts of dramas written for the stage.

A model for transpositions

In Chapter 1 we distinguished four kinds of transposition: rewriting, editing, translating and transforming. While the first two are not always applicable and have here received only passing attention – the first with regard to *A Doll's House*, the second with regard to *Macbeth* – the last two apply in principle to any drama text. A simple model for these two kinds of transposition is provided by the diagram at the top of the next page. Whereas the source text is unique, fixed in time and place, there is in theory no limit to the number of target texts, which may be in any language but that of the source text and may be created at any time after the writing of the source text.

Since the four dramas we have examined were all written for the stage, stage versions of them will in principle be more in tune with the drama text than radio, TV and film versions will. Between the drama text and the radio, TV or film production there is an intermediate stage: the radio, TV or film *script* – that is, a version of the drama text adjusted to the medium in question. In line with these observations we may speak of *one-stage, two-stage* and *three-stage transpositions*.

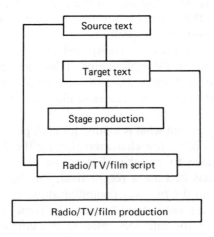

One-stage transpositions
(1) source text – stage production
(2) source text – target text

Two-stage transpositions
(3) source text – radio script – radio production
(4) source text – TV script – TV production
(5) source text – film script – film production
(6) source text – target text – stage production

Three-stage transpositions
(7) source text – target text – radio script – radio production
(8) source text – target text – TV script – TV production
(9) source text – target text – film script – film production

It is obvious that, the more intermediate stages there are, the more removed we are from the source text. Thus a *Macbeth* in the theatre is in principle closer to Shakespeare's *Macbeth* (the original drama text) than a *Macbeth* on radio, TV or film. Yet, unlike the other dramas discussed in this book, *Macbeth* will nowadays rarely be performed on the kind of stage for which it was written. In this sense, even a stage production may, at times, be seen as a two-stage transposition.

While dramas are usually transposed directly from source or target text into radio, TV or film script, at times a stage production – as in the case of Nunn's *Macbeth* and Hall's *Homecoming* – intervenes, and this naturally leaves its imprint on the screen/radio performance.

If we try to pinpoint what is unique for each particular medium, we end up with just a few characteristics: for the drama text, the freedom we have to partake of it as we like – but here the videocassette has become a recent rival; for the stage, the live performance and the two-way communication; for the radio, the exclusively aural presentation; for film, the great mobility in time and space, from the infinitely small to the infinitely large. Yet what is more mobile than the reader's imagination? The medium with the least clearly defined identity is television, serving by far the largest audience. As this list indicates, the media overlap to some degree, but the extent and nature of the overlap varies considerably, depending on the media in question.

Differences between stage, radio, TV and film versions may be categorised under the following headings:

(1) the drama text;
(2) the audiovisual/aural medium;
(3) the production facilities;
(4) the director's vision;
(5) the recipient.

In the following we shall pay attention to all these categories.

Source text and target text: the problems of translation

Whether we are concerned with the drama text, a stage performance, or a radio, TV or film version, we may be confronted by either the source text (the play as written by the playwright) or a target text (a translation of the original play text). Unlike directors, who should be free to deviate from the play text in various ways, translators must try to be reasonably faithful to the source text – and yet create an actable target text. The tendency among some translators to take over the director's job and make omissions, additions and rearrangements *which are not accounted for* can only lead to confusion concerning the nature of the source text.

The problem is most obvious in the case of ethnic circumstances which cannot be readily understood in an alien environment. The reader of a novel can here be helped with an illuminating note by the translator. The spectator of a play, however, must be informed in some other way. A translator of drama can choose between three possibilities. He can (i) translate literally – in which case the ethnic significance of the original is not explained and consequently not understood by the recipient. He can (ii) add an informative note. Or he can (iii) incorporate this information directly into the text. Of these possibilities only (ii) can be recommended. It is true that eventually one will have to resort to (iii) to make the passage intelligible to the spectator, but this is the task of the director, not of the translator.

To be sure, translating is interpreting and many translators do not interpret enough – that is, their renderings are based on a shallow reading of the source text. This explains why significant correspondences in the source text are often obscured in the target texts. The playwright's insistent use of certain key words is, for example, often neglected by translators, on the basis of a misguided argument that stylistic variation is preferable to monotony.

The problem may be schematised as follows. Let us assume that we have a complete formal correspondence between two expressions in the primary text, each consisting of article + adjective + noun: a + b + c. Such a correspondence could in principle be rendered in three different ways:

	expression 1	*expression 2*
(1)	d + e + f ---------	d + e + f
(2)	d + e + f	g + h + i
(3)	d + e + f - - - -	g + h + f

In (1) the correspondence of the source text is retained, whether or not at the cost of idiomatic, actable language. In (2) it has been sacrificed: the translator, who has either been unaware of the correspondence or has found it insignificant, prefers 'variation' to 'monotony'. In (3) the correspondence has been partly retained (the nouns are the same): the translator has settled for a both–and solution – which, however, can easily come over as a neither–nor. Although they may be easier to deal with, one-word correspondences, such as the repetitions of the verbs *pynte* and *vejlede* and their cognates in *A Doll's House*, are not as obvious; as a result they are often neglected by translators.

A special problem, applicable only to the dramatic genre, concerns correspondences between the primary text, spoken in performance, and the secondary text, the playwright's instructions about setting, properties, sound effects and the like. But are such 'intertextual' correspondences not inevitably lost in production and thus irrelevant for the spectator? Certainly not. It is important that the director and scene-designer should be made aware of these correspondences, so that they can find the proper visual and/or aural equivalents for them in their *mise-en-scène* and thereby obliquely suggest them to the spectator. An example of this fairly rare type of correspondence we find in the repetitive use of the Swedish verb *synas* (be seen; seem) in both the primary and secondary text of *The Ghost Sonata*. Relating to the verb *se* (see), which also appears frequently in the drama text, *synas* illustrates the discrepancy between seeming and being. As we have noted, translators have paid little attention to this important correspondence.

A special problem relating to the production of drama is the question of how to present performances in foreign languages. When we watch a TV or film version, we are often confronted by both the source text and the target text, the former aurally, the latter visually, in the form of subtitles. Spectators will react in different ways to this bilingual presentation. While those who do not understand the spoken source language will read the subtitles, those who do will not. Those who have to read the subtitles are doubly discriminated against. On the one hand, they have less time than those who understand what is being said to watch what is happening on the screen. On the other, they are not given the complete dialogue, since only part of what is being said is transcribed as subtitles. Both categories will suffer from the fact that the subtitles prevent us from seeing the bottom of the picture.

For all these reasons, some countries prefer the system of

dubbing to that of using subtitles; that is, the voices of the actors we see on the screen are replaced by voices in the target language. But this system has other, even greater disadvantages. Notably in close-ups there is a disturbing discrepancy between what we see – the movements of the mouth – and what we hear. Clearly, dubbing does not do justice to the paralinguistic aspects of the performance. Moreover, the fundamental idea that everything an actor does, including what he says and how he says it, is part of a created totality is violated by the system of dubbing.

The same drawbacks apply to the system of simultaneous interpretation via earphones, sometimes used when foreign theatre companies are performing on stage. Here again the 'dubbing' separates the visual aspects of the performance from the aural ones. Another possibility – rarely resorted to – is to have part of the target speeches projected on a screen above or next to the stage. But usually – especially where the play or opera is one familiar to most of the audience – one has to rest content with a fairly detailed plot synopsis in the theatre programme.

As a result of technical developments in recent years, the TV spectator in certain countries can choose between source and target language when watching a film. Thus in West Germany, where foreign films are usually shown with dubbed dialogue, it is now also possible to receive some foreign films in the original language. This facility can of course easily be extended to TV and radio plays, by enabling the viewer/listener to suppress the dubbed dialogue in favour of the original one. The problem with this possibility of opting for different languages – generous as it may seem – is that it promotes linguistic polarity among the recipients. What the socio-political consequences of this may be remains to be seen.

Media aspects

The way in which something is presented in a particular medium is obviously determined by the technical/dramaturgical rules governing that medium; in these cases we may speak of *media* differences. But frequently the way in which something is presented is not determined by the medium at all but by the director's own vision; in these cases we may speak of *directorial* differences. The dividing-line between directorial and media aspects is by no means sharply defined.

Is there any relationship between genre (tragedy, comedy, and so on) and media? The problem with this question is that genre labels are far from unequivocal and invite specification. Do we refer to classical, Aristotelian tragedy? To Elizabethan tragedy? To Ibsenite tragedy? Though structurally similar to *Oedipus Rex*, *Ghosts* obviously demands a very different style of presentation from Sophocles' tragedy. There is little doubt that the naturalistic prose drama *Ghosts* is better suited to the small screen than is the stylised verse drama *Oedipus Rex*. Our conclusion must be that the question of genre is subordinate to that of the actual dramaturgical circumstances – such as the number of *dramatis personae* and settings – the chosen style of presentation: illusionistic or non-illusionistic.

Whether we speak of realism, naturalism, symbolism, expressionism, surrealism or absurdism, the fundamental distinction between different styles of presentation is the one between *illusionism*, which attempts to create the illusion that the events and characters we witness are real, and *non-illusionism*, which reminds us that they are not. While drama texts may exemplify either of these basic 'isms', stage and radio productions nowadays tend to favour non-illusionism, while the screen media tend to favour illusionism. Obviously, the performance is more likely to be illusionistic if the play text is – as is certainly the case with *A Doll's House*. But since many plays – *Macbeth*, *The Ghost Sonata* and *The Homecoming*, for example – combine illusionistic and non-illusionistic elements, they leave a director with considerable freedom of choice.

A very noticeable difference between stage and screen versions is that the former tend to show fewer locales than the latter. Here we must be aware, however, that 'genuine' films usually have a much greater variety of settings than films based on drama texts.

The four play texts we have looked at are themselves far from uniform in the number of locales they specify. Thus *Macbeth* contains no fewer than twenty-nine scenes, and, although some locales are visited more than once, there are still a great many different environments, a fact which, combined with the great amount of action, makes this play very cinematic. *The Ghost Sonata*, by contrast, calls for only three sets (or four, if we choose to count the final *Toten-Insel* as a separate one). And in *A Doll's*

House and *The Homecoming* there is only one set. TV or film versions of these latter plays will therefore tend to be rather theatrical (I use the term in a neutral sense) if they adhere closely to the play texts – as do Brinckman's and Garland's *Doll's House*, Bergenstråhle's *Ghost Sonata*, and Hall's and Ersgård's *Homecoming*. Making them more cinematic involves a great deal of rearrangement – as we have seen in our discussions of Sjöstrand's and Losey's *Doll's House*, and Saville's *Ghost Sonata*. A similar contrast emerges when we compare Gold's *Macbeth* (more theatrical) with Polanski's (more cinematic).

Since the limitation to one setting is often thematically determined, usually connoting a feeling of being imprisoned,[1] turning a one-set play into a film with a variety of sets signifies a considerable thematic transposition. Or, looked at from the opposite direction: a marked difference between a 'genuine' film and a film based on a drama text is that the former will tend to make a much greater use of discontinuous editing – sudden spatio-temporal changes – than the latter.

The difference between a stage and a screen version often appears quite emphatically in the first few seconds, since in recent years it has become common to show the first sequence of a film or teleplay before the opening credits – incorporating the name of the author and the title. Such a pre-credit sequence may fulfil several functions. It enables people to be late for the performance without missing the film/play proper. It may stimulate our curiosity and prevent us from switching off the TV. It may inform us of events before the beginning of the play text (as in Losey's *Doll's House*). It may function as a kind of establishing-shot with regard to the style of presentation (Ersgård's *Homecoming*), or as a didactic pointer to the main theme (Fassbinder's *Doll's House* adaptation, Saville's *Ghost Sonata*) of the story to be presented. Possibly influenced by this practice, stage directors nowadays often open their productions with a 'playlet' before the play proper – as when Bergman began his 1988 production of *Long Day's Journey into Night* with a pantomime demonstrating the family unity of the Tyrones that is to be destroyed in the course of the performance.

The absence/presence of the editing-camera undoubtedly signifies the principal difference between stage and screen versions. In all the plays we have considered, there are some elements which are thematically important: the hands and the crown in *Macbeth*, the Christmas tree in *A Doll's House*, the Isle of the Dead in *The Ghost Sonata*, the armchair in *The Homecoming*. It is obvious that these *visual* elements are difficult to communicate to a radio listener; here a subtle adjustment of the dialogue is called for. The audiovisual media, by contrast, can show us these elements, but there are fundamental differences in the way they do so.

While the Christmas tree is on the stage for most of *A Doll's House* – both in the text and in stage versions – it would appear only momentarily in a screen version. As a result the spectator would tend to forget about it and fail to relate the tree to the dialogue. This can of course be counteracted by showing the tree at strategic moments – that is, when the dialogue calls for it. And a screen director might indeed argue that on stage the omnipresent Christmas tree becomes redundant, inexpressive. Nevertheless, as spectators of the stage tree we have the freedom to pay attention to it as much as we like and whenever we like; this freedom, for what it is worth, is denied us on the screen.

On the other hand, while *small objects* tend to be lost to view on the stage, they are easy to highlight on the screen. Not only can they be enlarged (in extreme close-ups) but they can also be framed and ordered in such a way that their symbolic significance is strongly suggested. It is, for example, difficult to make 'hands' a significant *Leitmotiv* in a stage presentation of *Macbeth*. On the screen, by contrast, it is easy to select just those hands (Macbeth's, Lady Macbeth's, those of the witches) which are symbolically relevant, and show them in illustrative close-up positions.

Similarly, in Polanski's *Macbeth* the connection between Macbeth and the (hanged) Thane of Cawdor is indicated in a striking two-shot; on the stage it is difficult to suggest this connection visually without being disturbingly emphatic.

Visual contrasts are easy to create in the screen media simply by placing one figure close to the camera in the foreground (big) and another far away in the background (small) – as in the opening of Hall's *Homecoming*. Or by using a high or low camera angle – as when Saville reverses the angle to illustrate the reversal of power between the Old Man and the Mummy in Act II of *The Ghost Sonata*. On the stage such contrasts would necessarily be much less emphatic. Antitheses are here brought out in other ways: by means of scenery (stairs, for example, to bring out a proxemic high–low contrast), costume (rich versus poor), kinesics (condescending versus humble gestures), and so on. In radio versions none of these means are available. Visual contrasts can here be indicated only indirectly – by having the characters describe what they see. One has to rely mainly on aural contrasts, in the way the characters express themselves and their tone of voice; in addition contrasts can be brought about by means of sound-montage and non-diegetic music.

Montage is often considered a prime characteristic of the film medium, be it solely visual (silent film) or audiovisual. Thus in Polanski's *Macbeth* we have the sequence of (i) Banquo's face, (ii) Macbeth dropping his golden goblet, spilling his wine, and (iii) Banquo's bleeding face – a montage which relates the murderer to his victim by means of the blood–wine connection. This is, clearly, unstageable.

We may also note that the device of discrepancy – words contradicting action – is hardly applicable to radio drama, where one of the elements to be contrasted (the visual one) is lacking. It is, however, very common on the stage, where it is nourished by the current vogue for non-illusionism.

Of great importance is the question of point of view or focalisation. In narrative texts we are used to distinguishing between an authorial and a figural point of view, with the character who acts as narrator taking an intermediate position. It is a common misconception that the authorial point of view is altogether lacking in drama texts. For what else is the secondary text but the text of the author–narrator – less obtrusive, to be sure, than that of the epic narrator, who can look into his characters' souls, but nevertheless reflecting a view different from that of any of the characters. By this criterion, *Macbeth* is the most character-oriented of our plays, since the sparse secondary text here has largely been added by other hands.

With Ibsen the situation has changed. The very first sentence of the stage-directions in *A Doll's House* reveals the author–narrator's point of view: '*A pleasantly and tastefully, but not expensively furnished room.*' The playwright here makes the *reader* visualise a pleasant and tasteful room. At the same time he suggests to the director and the scene-designer that they re-create a pleasant and tasteful room on the stage for the *spectator*. While the reader can easily accept the idea, since the narrator's description allows him to imagine whatever *he* finds pleasant and tasteful, the spectator who is confronted with a visual concretisation of the room may experience it as unpleasant and tasteless. Judging by the way people furnish their living-rooms, taste varies considerably.

Whereas the living-room in the Helmer apartment is undoubtedly there – to all the characters – the rooms in *The Ghost Sonata* may be seen, in part, as a product of the Student–narrator's imagination. With Strindberg we arrive at a more subjective type of drama. In *The Ghost Sonata* the Student's point of view overrules those of the other characters. He is the pilgrim we accompany from beginning (birth) to end (death); he is Everyman, the mediator between stage and auditorium. With him Strindberg has inserted an epic element into his drama.

It is not easy to make the Student's overruling point of view clear to an audience – especially since he is not visible throughout the play. As we have seen, Bergman indicated the subjective point of view by projecting Strindberg's face on the curtain, thereby identifying the author with his character–narrator.

In a radio version it is even more difficult to bring out the Student's dominant point of view, since he is *verbally* even more absent from the drama text than he is visually.

In this respect television and film offer better opportunities. As Seymour Chatman points out, a film-director who wishes to underline a character's point of view has two options:

> The actor can be so placed in the frame as to heighten our association with him. For example, his back or side profile may appear on an extreme margin of the screen. As he looks into the background we look with him. The other (or 'montage') convention uses a simple match-cut: if in the first shot the character looks off-screen, to right or left or front or back, and there follows a cut to another setup within his eyeshot, we assume that he has in fact seen that thing, from that perceptual point of view. And we have seen it with him.[2]

What we have here – 'a character who is both object and mediator of our vision'[3] – is a phenomenon that regularly occurs in the screen media and occasionally in drama texts, as in the case of Strindberg's Student.

A more specific point concerns the handling of apparitions. Ghosts such as Banquo in *Macbeth* and the Milkmaid in *The Ghost*

Sonata can, in principle, be either presented or not presented on the stage. On the screen there is a third possibility, utilised by Saville in his TV version of the Strindberg play; they can be alternately visible and invisible. Technically an asset, the alternating point of view is, however, in this particular case disturbing, in that it alienates the audience from the protagonist, the Student. As for the aural aspect, we may note that stage presentations, generally speaking, use music quite sparsely compared to the screen media – not to speak of radio performances. Especially when it is non-diegetic – as is usually the case in the screen media – mood-creating background music will inevitably help to 'colour' the 'bare' speeches/situations of the play text and stage representations.

Production facilities

The range of possible production facilities is very wide, and all of them have their limitations. Some factors apply to all the media; others are more specific. To the former category belong such things as the range and quality of the technical equipment and the nature and competence of the team responsible for the production. Irrespective of the medium, it obviously makes a difference whether we deal with first-rate actors or ham actors, talented and experienced directors or amateurs. (This is not saying, of course, that some actors and directors do not function better within one medium than within another.)

Next to these general aspects we find more specific, media-oriented ones. Thus the way in which a play is staged partly depends on the size of the theatre, the kind of stage used (end stage, thrust stage, in-the-round), the capacity of the lighting equipment, and so on. A monophonic transmission of a radio play differs from a stereophonic one. With the introduction of the tape recorder new possibilities for radio drama have been created; voices can now, for example, be modulated and edited in such a way that different time levels are paralinguistically suggested. The facilities to hand in a 'live' TV-studio production are very different from the ones utilised in a taped and edited, 'filmed' production. A silent black-and-white film is obviously very different from a colour talkie.

Directorial aspects

When we turn to the directorial aspects, there is a wealth of examples to choose between. At almost every point in a performance – especially in screen versions – the director's vision will be discernible. However, if we wish to isolate those aspects which are *purely* directorial, the number of convincing examples shrinks considerably. But they are there.

In their productions of *Macbeth*, Gold identifies the Third Murderer with Seyton, while Polanski identifies him with Ross. The reason in both cases is the director's desire better to integrate the Third Murderer (otherwise an extraneous figure, appearing in just one scene) into the play. The fact that they identify the Third Murderer with different characters has to do with their differing interpretations of the roles those characters play in the overall development. In both cases the medium is irrelevant; the same identifications could have been made in a stage version.

Similarly, in Bergman's production of *The Ghost Sonata*, the device of having the same actress play both the Mummy and the Young Lady had nothing to do with the requirements of the stage. In fact, it could have been more easily effected in a screen version. Nor does Bergenstråhle's setting for the same play seem to be designed specifically for television. On the contrary, his reduction of the text's three sets to one – an unconventional choice – makes his version very stageable in the theatre.

Most proxemic and kinesic choices are of a directorial kind. Whether Malcolm at the end of *Macbeth* puts the crown on his head (Polanski) or refrains from doing so (Nunn, Gold) obviously has nothing to do with the fact that in the former case the medium is film and in the latter television. Similarly, the fact that Nora makes a final exit in most performances of *A Doll's House* but refrains from doing so in some has nothing to do with the chosen medium; as we have noted, Ibsen himself devised both types of ending. Whether Ruth in *The Homecoming* does (Ersgård) or does not (Hall) speak with an accent distinct from that of the other characters is clearly a directorial, not a media, question. When Polanski gives Lennox's lines to Seyton, and Bergman those of the Student to the Mummy and the Colonel, these rearrangements are purely directorial.

However, as already stated, in many cases there is an overlap between directorial choice and the character of the medium. Thus obvious deviations from the play text – such as cuts – are found in all presentational modes, but stage performances will tend to retain more of the drama text – both the primary and the secondary text – than screen productions, and TV versions will tend to retain more than film versions. It is important to remember that different productions will rarely retain the same amount of dialogue; and, even when they do, it is probable that they differ somewhere in what they have retained. When we deal with productions within different media, the dialogue may, in fact, differ so much that one begins to doubt whether they are productions of the same play. As we have seen, the three productions of *The Ghost Sonata* that we have examined differ considerably, both from the play text and from each other, in their versions of the concluding dialogue.

Often a certain directorial approach will lend itself better to one medium than to another and will therefore be chosen. Take the 'tomorrow' speech in *Macbeth*. When delivering this speech, Gold's Macbeth remains sitting on his throne, while Polanski's moves about. The difference seems to be determined both by directorial and by media preferences, film being a more dynamic medium than television.

To make matters even more complicated, there are very different approaches within each medium. Thus, although Garland's and Losey's productions of *A Doll's House* are both film versions, the former is theatrical, the latter cinematic. There is a like contrast between the two TV versions of *The Ghost Sonata*. Technically, these alternative versions using the same medium differ more from one another than do Hall's and Ersgård's versions of *The Homecoming*, using different media; here the differences are largely directorial.

The recipient

Closely connected with both the medium and the director's vision is the question of for whom the transposition is made: the intended recipient. In addition to the fundamental media question – *how* is the play produced? – we need to take into account the spatio–temporal distance from sender (playwright) to recipient (reader/spectator/listener). This distance can be quite short, as when Pinter directs a play of his own for a London audience. But it can also be exceedingly long. An interesting comparison may be made here between Bergman's and Polanski's versions of *Macbeth*:

	Bergman	*Polanski*
Language	target text	source text
Medium	stage	film
Time of reception	1948	1972 onwards
Audience	Swedish	international

Without arguing for or against the desirability of staying close to the Shakespearian source text – the harpsichord–piano controversy mentioned in the first chapter – we may still inquire which of the two versions has the greater affinity to Shakespeare's *Macbeth*. Polanski is naturally closer to Shakespeare in that he uses the source, and not a target, text, but his choice of medium means that he is forced to cut much of Shakespeare's dialogue – as Bergman was not. The diction of *Macbeth*, most people would say, is better suited to the stylised form of acting we find on the stage than to the realistic acting characteristic of the film medium. While Bergman *had* a select, largely upper-class audience for his time-and-place-bound production, Polanski *has* an international mass audience for his production, which transcends spatial, temporal and even media borders (as when his film is shown on television).

This difference is important in two respects. First, whereas the stage director, like the playwright, usually has a fair idea of what his audience will be like, and so can to some extent tailor his production to his audience, the film-director, working in a mass medium, does not usually cater for a specific audience. Secondly, this means that the film, unlike the stage performance, can be seen at virtually any time and in virtually any place; as a result it can have an impact on spectators far removed in time and space from the original recipients. In that sense a film is like a book. With regard to *durability*, screen and radio versions are much closer to the textual medium than stage versions are.

Recipients can be divided into different categories according to different criteria: age, gender, nationality, and so on. These are clear-cut categories, easy to document statistically. Another basic factor is cost: it is more expensive to go to the theatre or cinema than to read a play, watch the television or listen to the radio. Inevitably the economic factor has a differentiating effect. We may also think of social stratification. For some people, going to the theatre is above all a symbol of status. Opera ranks even higher in this respect.

The term 'mass medium' implies that there are also minority media. What, then, is a mass medium? When defining this term, we have to consider both production and consumption. Drama texts, we could claim, are published and sold in thousands of copies; *ergo* the printed drama text is a mass medium. Radio plays are transmitted to millions of people; *ergo* radio drama is a mass medium. And, indeed they are, if we focus on the *production* aspect.

Yet how many of the drama texts bought are also read? And how many of the potential listeners listen to a radio play? Clearly, from the *consumption* point of view both drama texts and radio plays are rather sophisticated modes – minority media – compared to TV plays and films.

If we include in the notion of a mass medium the idea that the performance is *experienced collectively*, we have to distinguish between performances in a theatre or cinema, where the audience is gathered into one place, and those in television or radio, where the audience is composed of individuals watching or listening alone or in groups. Clearly, it is only in the former case – the public situation – that the audience always shares a truly *collective* experience.

Besides distinguishing between mass and minority media, we can distinguish between productions which are embedded in a continuous flow of programmes (radio, TV) and 'independent' productions (stage, film) – although Bergman's stage adaptation of *A Doll's House* was, as we have seen, 'embedded' in a trilogy. We can also distinguish productions according to the degree of conscious choice exercised by recipients in selecting them: with radio and television this is at a minimum – one has only to turn a knob or push a button – while with theatre or cinema one usually makes a conscience plan to attend. However, with the growing number of channels on TV, we may speak of an increasing *possibility* within this medium of making a definite choice. The more TV breaks up into different channels, the less it becomes a *mass* medium.

Variations within one and the same medium may be considerable. Consider in this respect the difference, earlier referred to, between dubbed and subtitled film versions, or between uninterrupted teleplays and teleplays fragmented by inserted commercials.

From statistics we know that visitors to the theatre tend to be (i) members of the educated upper middle classes, (ii) mostly middle-aged, (iii) mostly women. Does that mean that playwrights and directors cater especially for this group? Sometimes. But, as we all know, there is a Broadway, an off-Broadway and an off-off-Broadway – and the visitors to these three archetypal kinds of theatre differ a great deal from one another.

Irrespective of medium, the kind of play that is being presented will have a differentiating effect on the audience: *A Doll's House* will attract other, and more, recipients than *The Ghost Sonata* – except, possibly, in Sweden. Here the nationality of the playwright may play a part. On radio and television the time of transmission would be of importance – but peak listening-time is not the same as peak viewing-time.

Starting out from such obvious, measurable data, one may, by means of questionnaires or in other ways, gather information about how recipients experience drama as presented in the various media. Although this has frequently been done for individual media, I know of no empirical study that focuses on the reception of the same dramas as realised by *different* media. Such an investigation – the logical continuation of the approach followed in this book – might tell us a lot about what the various media can and cannot communicate.

The spatio-temporal dimension

Two different but connected issues are suggested by this topic: one relating to the concepts of space and time employed in the drama text and the production based on this text; the other relating to the time and place of conception, publication, translation, production, and reception.

A recurring problem with regard to the first issue is indicated by the contrast between a universal and a local environment.

This raises the questions of intelligibility and of recognition/ identification by the audience.

It goes without saying that plays with a geographically vague setting are more easily transferable from one country/culture to another than those which are firmly rooted in a particular ethnic environment. In these latter cases, the question arises: should one retain such an environment or should one adjust it in space, in time, or both, to the situation of the intended recipient? While adjustment should be banned in translation proper – when this occurs we speak of *adaptations* – it may well be accepted in production.

Should *Macbeth* be set (i) in an exotic, alien environment, (ii) in a more recognisable one, close to our time, or (iii) in a timeless environment? In an attempt to secure both universality and identifiability, Trevor Nunn combines (ii) and (iii) – that is, he avoids a specific historical *environment* but has his characters appear in early-nineteenth-century *costumes*.

Should a performance of *A Doll's House* make it clear that the action takes place in Norway or not? In Garland's version, the Norwegian setting is conveyed mainly by the opening shot; in the rest of the film, which takes place inside the Helmer's house (rather than an apartment, as in the original), the place seems of little significance – there are in fact ingredients which seem more English than Norwegian. Losey's version, by contrast, shows quite a bit of the wider environment, reflecting his decision to shoot the film in a genuine Norwegian town with a nineteenth-century look. However, setting the play in such an exotic, picturesque environment may detract our attention from the central issues in the play. A different, somewhat bewildering approach is found in Saville's version of *The Ghost Sonata*. Here bits of Swedish (a shop sign, a poster, a newspaper) have been included in an otherwise rather un-Swedish milieu.

The second issue involves the many problems related to ethnic differences between the world of the drama text and the world of the recipients of a production based on this text. In this context we may recall Ibsen's claim that most ideas have a lifetime of about thirty years. With even greater justification one should claim the same for drama translations and especially for play productions. Since languages are continually changing, every generation needs its own translation. This is especially true of drama translations, for the simple reason that spoken language changes more rapidly than written one. As a result of this we get a marked contrast between linguistically 'dated' source texts and updated target texts. Shakespeare in a recent translation is by definition more our contemporary than he is in the First Folio.

Even so, it is hard to see that translations are significantly influenced by changes in the ideological climate. Play productions, by contrast, certainly are, as the history of the theatre proves. Because many theatregoers around 1880 were shocked by the conclusion of *A Doll's House*, Ibsen offered an alternative, conciliatory ending. When Fassbinder and Bergman a hundred years later created their own alternative endings, it was certainly not because they found Ibsen's original ending too provocative; it was rather because their ideology, attuned to the 1970s, led to a different interpretation. In Bergman's 1948 production of *Macbeth*, the protagonist was – not surprisingly, considering the date – seen as a kind of Nazi dictator. Artaud's 'theatre of cruelty' can be sensed behind Polanski's *Macbeth*. It is interesting to note that, in contrast to the endings of the play *texts* of *Macbeth* and *The Ghost Sonata*, the endings of the *productions* of them that we have examined (Nunn's Gold's and Polanski's *Macbeth*; Bergman's, Bergenstråhle's and Saville's *Ghost Sonata*) are all pessimistic. It may well be that we here deal with a fundamental contrast in *Zeitgeist* between former believers (Shakespeare, Strindberg) and present-day sceptics, between a faith in harmony restored and the lack of such a faith, resulting in disharmonious endings. Even in the relatively short period since *The Homecoming* was first published and produced, there have been marked ideological changes in Western Europe, and these have had repercussions on productions of that play.

How does the transposition of a seventeenth-century drama text compare with that of a play from the twentieth century? Obviously, the Elizabethan theatre, for which Shakespeare wrote, is further removed from the TV screen than the Intimate Theatre, for which Strindberg wrote, not only in time but also in style of presentation. In the Intimate Theatre, the audience was considerably closer to the actors than was the audience in the Globe. Strindberg's medium shots, so to speak, are halfway between Shakespeare's long shots and the close-ups of the TV screen. Similarly, the theatricality of classical drama is obviously further removed from the realism currently favoured by the screen media than is the illusionism catered for by the naturalists of the nineteenth century.

Generally speaking, we would also expect the ideology of plays which were composed long ago to be more foreign to a present-day audience than the ideology of fairly recent plays. Transposing classical drama might therefore involve changing its message. However, as we have seen, this can happen even with a relatively modern play such as *The Ghost Sonata*. On the other hand, when the ideology (ethics) of a recent play such as *The Homecoming* is being questioned, the reason is obviously not that it seems dated, but that it seems too bold, undermining social *mores*.

Since classical plays tend to be fairly long – the serious one-act play was created by Strindberg at the end of the nineteenth century – they are more likely to be drastically shortened than many modern ones. A special problem is created by the fact that many classical plays are written in verse. As verse dramas they have held their place on the stage, but they do not readily appeal to a TV mass audience. Here the great number of *dramatis personae* may also be a hindrance. A film of such a play is likely both to condense the verse dialogue and to try to make it fit a realistic style of presentation. The director opting for such an approach is faced with considerable problems in making it work.

Since the development of film, radio and television, playwrights have had the opportunity of adapting their stage plays for these media, which were not available to their predecessors. Of the playwrights whose work is discussed in this book, only Pinter has had this opportunity. He has also, like other modern dramatists, been able to choose which medium to write for; earlier playwrights had no such choice. What we now see emerging is a new, media-oriented generation of playwrights, writing sometimes for the stage, sometimes for TV, sometimes for the radio – even, as in the case of Pinter, for film. As a consequence, plays written today will not lend themselves to transposition to the same extent as plays written in the past. One could also put it like this: the form and content of plays written for live performance would necessarily be less specific to the medium where there was no other medium of representation than where the playwright could choose among several media. Just as the new medium of photography replaced a realistic manner of painting and thus indirectly contributed to the development of new artistic styles (impressionism, symbolism), so the new medium of film, with its superior ability to create illusion, has led the theatre to become more self-consciously theatrical. In a sense, the arrival of the narrative film meant the death of illusionistic play production, and illusionistic *mise-en-scène* has survived largely by being transplanted from stage to screen. Similarly, the arrival of television has had a definite effect on film production, resulting in lavish, spectacular films, sometimes with thousands of extras – that is, the kind of productions to which the intimate TV medium does not readily lend itself. It is interesting to note that this preoccupation with the masses in a mass medium was anticipated long ago both in the Hollywood films of Cecil B. de Mille and in the Soviet films of Sergei Eisenstein. While Eisenstein's collectivism was ideologically determined, that of the modern film-makers seems determined more by a de Millean desire to show that there are things that film can do better than any other medium.

Today live theatre struggles with increasing economic problems. With a TV set in almost every home, the role of radio drama is diminishing. Film and television are highly competitive. On the one hand, cinemas are struggling to survive; on the other, television would not be as popular as it is if it did not have ample access to cinema films. There is also strong competition between purveyors of the same medium. Thus the contrast between the big, comfortable, well-equipped cinemas catering for a mass audience and the small cinemas catering for a more sophisticated minority duplicates the contrast in the theatrical sector between Broadway and off-off-Broadway. In either case, spectators may feel torn between the professionalism and technical facilities of the big houses and the commitment and pioneering spirit of the small ones.

In such a period, it is to be expected that drama texts when transposed for the various media will result in highly different products. But this tendency is counteracted by joint undertakings. Thus a successful stage run of a play will frequently result in a film version with more or less the same cast (the Pinter–Hall production of *The Homecoming* provides an example). And, owing to the high costs of film-making and the popularity of television, film-directors will tend to aim at star-studded productions which can pay for themselves first on the big and then on the small screen. Naturally such joint undertakings do not contribute to a differentiation of the individual media.

Drama criticism

The inclination among some translators to confuse their own job
with that of the director applies also to many drama critics. As we
have seen, notably in connection with *The Homecoming*, critics
do not always distinguish between text and performance. They
argue as though they were dealing with the same object, whereas
in fact they have different texts and/or productions in mind. Also,
it is frequently uncertain whether their comments and hypotheses
are based on a reading of the text or on impressions from one or
more productions. If these impressions are based on screen or
radio versions – as may nowadays well be the case – the failure to
acknowledge this is all the more disturbing.

Connected with this problem is the tendency not to mention
which play text one is referring to. Here the difference between
source text and target text is of importance. If a Swedish critic,
commenting on the text of *Macbeth*, does not tell us whether he
is referring to the source text or a target text, we are at a loss,
since the title, being a name, is the same in both English and
Swedish. If he is basing his statements on the source text, we
should certainly like to know which edition he has used. If, more
doubtfully, his comments rely on a Swedish translation, we should
like to know which one.

If an English critic comments on the text of *Spöksonaten* we are
a little better off, since Strindberg's play text does not give rise to
the same sort of editorial problems as Shakespeare's; and the use
of the original play title should mean that the critic knows the play
in Swedish and is not merely pretending that he does. If his
comments concern a play entitled *The Ghost Sonata*, we are also
a little better off, since the play title in this case indicates that we
are dealing with an English or American translation, not with a
German translation (*Gespenstersonate*) or a French one (*La Sonate
des spectres*). We may also conclude that the critic is not referring
to the first translation of the play into English, since this was
entitled *The Spook Sonata*. But, unless he informs us which target
text he is referring to, we are still left with nine different translations
of the play into English, all of them entitled *The Ghost Sonata*.

We must also be aware of the difference between explicit and
implicit evaluations. In the former category we find statements
such as 'Nora/Ruth did the right thing', or 'Nora/Ruth should not

have left her family (as quickly as she did).' In the latter category we find statements such as 'Nora/Ruth will stay single and make the best of it', or 'Nora/Ruth will be back within three days.' Unless they can be supported by the play text, the implicit statements, unlike the explicit ones, are not valid; they merely pretend to be objective.

Transposing drama – desirable?

In studies devoted to one particular medium – be it drama text, theatre performance, radio drama, teleplay or film – it is common to find the medium praised at the expense of its rivals. As should be clear from the preceding pages, each medium has its own pros and cons, its own capabilities and limitations. But this circumstance does not mean that we can reach a general conclusion about the relative efficacy of the different media as vehicles for transposing drama. Left with the apparently insoluble question of whether Bach should be played on a harpsichord or on a piano, it seems wise to join Rudolf Arnheim in his solomonic judgement, 'There is no point in comparing the relative value of the various media. Personal preferences exist, but each medium reaches the heights in its own way.'[4]

As for the desirability of transposing a play intended for one mode of presentation into other modes, let me end with two contradictory statements. In a letter to his American publisher Samuel Beckett once wrote,

> *All That Fall* is a specifically [*sic*] radio play, or rather, radio text, for voices, not bodies. I have already refused to have it 'staged' and I cannot think of it in such terms. . . . I am absolutely opposed to any form of adaptation with a view to its conversion into 'theatre'. It is no more theatre than *End-Game* is radio and to 'act' it is to kill it. . . .
> . . . I can't agree with the idea of *Act Without Words* as a film. It is not a film, not conceived in terms of cinema. If we can't keep our genres more or less distinct, or extricate them from the confusion that has them where they are, we might as well go home and lie down.[5]

Severe words from a distinguished playwright and from an author who has tried his hand at all the modes we have here examined.

At the other pole we find the film theoretician André Bazin, who in 1951 claimed that 'there are no plays that cannot be brought to the screen, whatever their style, provided one can visualize a reconversion of stage space in accordance with the data', and who even went so far as to state that 'it may also be that the only possible modern theatrical production of certain classics would be on the screen'.[6]

Neither of these standpoints does justice to the situation we experience today. Bazin's sweeping statement disregards the many problems involved in a transformation from stage to screen, problems which are only rarely successfully overcome. Beckett's comment, on the other hand, is of limited range. It applies to his own plays and, obliquely, to those written in the media era; it does not indicate how one should deal with plays written before this era.

Beckett's insistence on keeping the media distinct and recognising their differences draws attention to an exceedingly important matter: the difficulty of transforming a drama written for one medium into a drama in another medium. The problem is not that plays are transformed but that often they are transformed in a superficial, unimaginative way. Only rarely do we witness a true *re-creation*.

However, the fact that most plays are transformed in a mediocre way – just as most play translations are clearly deficient – should not make us lose sight of the fact that plays are occasionally transformed with great success, just as they are sometimes admirably translated. Disclaiming the value of transformation is like repudiating that of translation. There is indeed a danger that the recipient will take the transformation/translation for the real thing and feel that, if he has seen *A Doll's House* in the cinema, he need not see it on the stage, or read the play, or learn Norwegian to be able to explore the source text. But there is also the hope that, having familiarised himself with the transposed version, he will turn to the 'original', be it the play text or the play performed in the medium for which it was intended. It is possible that a transformed and even adapted version will work better than the original. It needs to be said, too, that it is not through 'originals' but through transpositions – translations and/or radio, TV and film versions – that we usually partake of plays. And, when it comes to the study of drama, there is the challenging fact that it is by examining drama in transposition, rather than by studying the text on its own, that we come to perceive what this hybrid art form is really all about.

Notes

Chapter 1 Textual, Aural, Audiovisual

1. August Strindberg, *Letters to the Intimate Theatre*, tr. Walter Johnson (London, 1967) p. 37.
2. Cf. Keir Elam's distinction between *dramatic text* ('that composed *for* the theatre') and *performance text* ('that produced *in* the theatre'): *The Semiotics of Theatre and Drama* (London, 1980) p. 3. Similarly, Erika Fischer-Lichte contrasts the *literary text* (*literarische Text*) with the *theatrical text* (*theatralische Text*): *Semiotik des Theaters* (Tübingen, 1983) III, 10–22. We may, in addition, distinguish between the *performance text* (the species) and the individual, factual *performance*.
3. Anne Ubersfeld, *Lire le théâtre* (Paris, 1977) p. 8.
4. Ibid., p. 16.
5. Ibid.
6. Eric Bentley, *The Life of the Drama* (London, 1965) p. 148.
7. Julian Hilton, *Performance* (London, 1987) p. 6.
8. Cf. Wiebe Hogendoorn, *Lezen en zien spelen: een studie over simultaneïteit in het drama* (Leiden, 1976); with a summary in French.
9. Peter Pütz, *Die Zeit im Drama: zur Technik dramatischer Spannung* (Göttingen, 1970) pp. 15–16.
10. Cf. Seymour Chatman, *Story and Discourse: Narrative Structure in Fiction and Film* (Ithaca, NY, 1978) pp. 62–84.
11. Manfred Pfister, *Das Drama* (Munich, 1977) pp. 73–9.
12. A recent contribution is Egil Törnqvist and Barry Jacobs, *Strindberg's 'Miss Julie': A Play and its Transpositions* (Norwich, 1988).
13. Most studies of adaptations concern the transposition from prose work (usually novel) to teleplay (TV series) or film. Thus, of the twenty-three film adaptations analysed in Andrew S. Horton and Joan Magretta (eds), *Modern European Filmmakers and the Art of Adaptation* (New York, 1981), only two are based on plays.
14. Fischer-Lichte, *Semiotik des Theaters*, I, 82.
15. Elam, *The Semiotics of Theatre and Drama*, p. 15.
16. Roman Ingarden, *Das Literarische Kunstwerk*, 2nd edn (Tübingen, 1960) p. 120.
17. Fischer-Lichte, *Semiotik des Theaters*, I, 28.

18. Patrice Pavis, *Languages of the Stage: Essays in the Semiology of Theatre*, tr. Susan Melrose *et al.* (New York, 1982) p. 141.
19. Cf. Törnqvist and Jacobs, *Strindberg's 'Miss Julie'*, pp. 138–41.
20. For useful surveys of theatrical proxemics (shape of theatre and spatial organisation), see Elam, *The Semiotics of Theatre and Drama*, pp. 56–69; and Hilton, *Performance*, pp. 19–26.
21. Stanley Wells, *Literature as Drama* (London, 1970) p. 7.
22. Martin Esslin, *Mediations: Essays on Brecht, Beckett and the Media* (London, 1980) p. 177.
23. Ibid., p. 183.
24. William Ash, *The Way to Write Radio Drama* (London, 1985) p. 43.
25. John Fiske and John Hartley, *Reading Television* (London, 1978) p. 109.
26. George W. Brandt (ed.), *British Television Drama* (Cambridge, 1981) p. 27.
27. Werner and Rose Waldmann, *Einführung in die Analyse von Fernsehspielen* (Tübingen, 1980) p. 110.
28. Brandt, *British Television Drama*, p. 8.
29. Jan Bussell, *The Art of Television* (London, 1952) p. 103.
30. Ibid., p. 105.
31. David Bordwell and Kristin Thompson, *Film Art: An Introduction*, 2nd edn (New York, 1986) pp. 147, 387.
32. Sergei Eisenstein's *Film Form* (1949) and *The Film Sense* (1942), ed. and tr. Jay Leyda in the same volume (New York, 1957), penetratingly discuss problems related to these aspects of film-making.
33. S. A. Elghazali, *Literatur als Fernsehspiel* (Hamburg, 1966) p. 79.
34. André Bazin, *What is Cinema?*, tr. Hugh Gray (Berkeley, Calif., 1967) I, 102.
35. Peter Szondi, *Theorie des modernen Dramas (1880–1950)*, 7th edn (Frankfurt, 1970).
36. Bazin, *What is Cinema?*, I, 99.
37. Th. Borup Jensen, *Roman og drama bli'r til film* (Copenhagen, 1975) p. 30.
38. Elam, *The Semiotics of Theatre and Drama*, p. 47.
39. Ibid., p. 46.
40. Paris, *Language of the Stage*, p. 126.
41. Ibid., p. 111.
42. Elam, *The Semiotics of Theatre and Drama*, pp. 184–207. For a less formal and detailed attempt at close-reading notation of a play-opening (in this case of *The Dance of Death*), see Egil Törnqvist, *Strindbergian Drama: Themes and Structure* (Stockholm, 1982) pp. 119–47.
43. Bordwell and Thompson, *Film Art*, p. 388.

Chapter 2 Variations on the Audiovisual: Shakespeare's *Macbeth* (c. 1606)

1. William Shakespeare, *Macbeth*, Arden edn, ed. Kenneth Muir (London, 1986) p. xxxii.
2. John Russell Brown (ed.), *Focus on 'Macbeth'* (London, 1982) p. 243.
3. A. M. Nagler, *Shakespeare's Stage* (New Haven, Conn., 1958) p. 29.
4. Jack J. Jorgens, *Shakespeare on Film* (Bloomington, Ind., 1977) p. 171.
5. Quoted ibid.
6. Quoted from Muir's edition of *Macbeth*, p. 3.
7. Marvin Rosenberg, *The Masks of Macbeth* (Berkeley, Calif., 1978) p. 21.
8. Ann Fridén, *'Macbeth' in the Swedish Theatre 1838–1986* (Malmö, 1986) p. 190.
9. Ibid., p. 205.
10. Ibid., p. 204.
11. Gordon Williams, *'Macbeth': Text and Performance* (London, 1985) pp. 61–2.
12. Gareth Lloyd Evans, *'Macbeth: 1946–80 at Stratford-upon-Avon'*, in Brown, *Focus on 'Macbeth'*, p. 107.
13. Jorgens, *Shakespeare on Film*, pp. 161–3.
14. Wolfgang Clemen, *The Development of Shakespeare's Imagery* (Cambridge, Mass., 1951) p. 101.
15. Rosenberg, *The Masks of Macbeth*, p. 315.
16. Muir (ed.), *Macbeth*, p. 91.
17. A. C. Bradley, *Shakespearean Tragedy*, 2nd edn (London, 1963) pp. 425–6.
18. Michael Mullin, 'Stage and Screen: The Trevor Nunn *Macbeth*', in Robert L. Erenstein (ed.), *Theatre and Television* (Amsterdam, 1988) p. 108.
19. Roger Manvell, *Shakespeare and the Film* (London, 1971) p. 58.
20. Rosenberg, *The Masks of Macbeth*, p. 648.
21. Ibid., p. 647.
22. Ibid., p. 649.
23. Quoted from Brown, *Focus on 'Macbeth'*, p. 232.
24. Marshall McLuhan, *The Medium is the Message* (London, 1967).
25. Mullin, in Erenstein, *Theatre and Television*, pp. 107, 110.

Chapter 3 Representing the Source Text: Ibsen's *Et Dukkehjem/A Doll's House* (1879)

1. Einar Haugen, *Ibsen's Drama: Author to Audience* (Minneapolis, 1979) p. 103.
2. Introduction to Henrik Ibsen, *The Complete Major Prose Plays*, tr. Rolf Fjelde (New York, 1965) p. xxxvi.
3. Henrik Ibsen, *Samlede Verker*, ed. Francis Bull *et al.* (Oslo, 1933) VIII, 368.

4. Austin E. Quigley, *The Modern Stage and Other Worlds* (New York, 1985) p. 93.
5. Peter Reynolds, *Drama: Text into Performance* (Harmondsworth, 1986) p. 78.
6. Ibid., p. 79.
7. Frederick J. and Lise-Lone Marker, *Ingmar Bergman: A Project for the Theatre* (New York, 1983) p. 20.
8. Ibid., p. 19.
9. Bergman as quoted ibid., p. 3.
10. J. L. Styan, 'The Opening Moments of *A Doll's House*: For Performance and Analysis in Class', in Yvonne Shafer (ed.), *Approaches to Teaching Ibsen's 'A Doll's House'* (New York, 1985) p. 94.
11. John Northam, *Ibsen's Dramatic Method* (London, 1953) p. 19.
12. Quigley, *The Modern Stage*, pp. 99–100.
13. Henrik Ibsen, *A Doll's House*, tr. James W. McFarlane, in *The Oxford Ibsen*, v (London, 1961); Henrik Ibsen, *A Doll's House and Other Plays*, tr. Peter Watts (Harmondsworth, 1965).
14. Marker and Marker, *Ingmar Bergman*, p. 23.
15. Ibid., p. 49.
16. Quoted from Gunnar Hallingberg, *Radio och TV-dramatik* (Lund, 1973) p. 172.
17. Birgitta Steene, 'Film as Theater: Geissendörfer's *The Wild Duck* (1976) from the Play by Henrik Ibsen', in Horton and Magretta, *Modern European Filmmakers*, p. 297.
18. Foster Hirsch, *Joseph Losey* (Boston, Mass., 1980) p. 200.
19. Ibid., pp. 202–3.
20. Bazin, *What is Cinema?*, p. 90.
21. Quigley, *The Modern Stage*, p. 107.
22. Marker and Marker, *Ingmar Bergman*, p. 27.
23. Michael Meyer, *Ibsen: A Biography* (London, 1971) p. 454.
24. Quoted from Northam, *Ibsen's Dramatic Method*, p. 25.
25. Quigley, *The Modern Stage*, p. 91.
26. Ibid., p. 100.
27. Marker and Marker, *Ingmar Bergman*, p. 99.
28. Bergman as quoted ibid., pp. 12–13.
29. C. Braad Thomsen, '*Et Dukkehjem*. R. W. Fassbinder: Nora Helmer', in Ulla Strømberg and Jytte Wiingaard (eds), *Den levende Ibsen: analyser af udvalgte Ibsen-forestillinger 1973–78* (Copenhagen, 1978) p. 82.

Chapter 4   Between Stage and Screen: Strindberg's *Spöksonaten/The Ghost Sonata* (1907)

1. Ingmar Bergman as quoted in Egil Törnqvist, 'Ingmar Bergman Directs Strindberg's *Ghost Sonata*', *Theatre Quarterly*, III, no. 2 (1973) 3.
2. Strindberg, *Letters to the Intimate Theatre*, p. 19.

3. Ibid.
4. August Falck, *Fem år med Strindberg* (Stockholm, 1935) p. 53.
5. Sarah Bryant-Bertail, 'The Tower of Babel: Space and Movement in *The Ghost Sonata*', in Göran Stockenström (ed.), *Strindberg's Dramaturgy* (Minneapolis, 1988) p. 307.
6. Freddie Rokem, *Theatrical Space in Ibsen, Chekhov and Strindberg: Public Forms of Privacy* (Ann Arbor, Mich., 1986) pp. 66–8.
7. John Northam, 'Strindberg's *Spook Sonata*', in Carl Reinhold Smedmark (ed.), *Essays on Strindberg* (Stockholm, 1966) p. 41.
8. Ibid., pp. 41, 48.
9. Arvid Paulson (tr.), in August Strindberg, *Eight Expressionist Plays* (New York, 1965) pp. viii, 463.
10. Elizabeth Sprigge's translation in *Six Plays of Strindberg* (Garden City, NY, 1955).
11. Evert Sprinchorn's translation in August Strindberg, *The Chamber Plays* (New York, 1962).
12. Paulson's translation in Strindberg, *Eight Expressionist Plays*.
13. Translation by Erik Palmstierna and James Bernard Fagan in August Strindberg, *Easter and Other Plays* (London, 1929).
14. Sprigge's translation and note in *Six Plays of Strindberg*.
15. Harry Carlson's version in August Strindberg, *Five Plays* (Berkeley, Calif., 1981).
16. Carl Richard Mueller's version in August Strindberg, *The Ghost Sonata* (San Francisco, 1966).
17. For an extensive discussion of problems related to the translation of *The Ghost Sonata* into English, see Törnqvist, *Strindbergian Drama*, pp. 220–42.
18. Sprigge's translation in *Six Plays of Strindberg*.
19. Michael Meyer's translation in August Strindberg, *Plays: One* (London, 1964).
20. Sprinchorn, Introduction to Strindberg, *The Chamber Plays*, p. xv.
21. Sprinchorn's translation in Strindberg, *The Chamber Plays*.
22. Meyer's translation in Strindberg, *Plays: One*.
23. Walter Johnson's translation in August Strindberg, *A Dream Play and Four Chamber Plays* (Seattle, 1973).
24. For a full discussion of this production, see Egil Törnqvist, *Bergman och Strindberg: 'Spöksonaten' – drama och iscensättning. Dramaten 1973* (Stockholm, 1973).
25. Bergman as quoted ibid., p. 192.
26. Törnqvist, in *Theatre Quarterly*, iii, no. 2, p. 8.
27. Bergman as quoted in Törnqvist, *Bergman och Strindberg*, p. 102.
28. Ibid., p. 226.
29. Ibid., p. 108.

Chapter 5   Choosing the Medium: Pinter's *The Homecoming* (1965)

1. According to Richard Hornby in *Script into Performance: A Structuralist View of Play Production* (Austin, Tex., 1977) p. 205, Pinter has published several versions of *The Homecoming*, 'which differ slightly from each other'. The following analysis is based on the 1965 Methuen edition.
2. Hugh Nelson, '*The Homecoming*: Kith and Kin', in John Russell Brown (ed.), *Modern British Dramatists* (Englewood Cliffs, 1968) p. 107.
3. Quoted from Anita R. Osherow, 'Mother and Whore: The Role of Woman in *The Homecoming*', *Modern Drama*, xvii, no. 4 (1974) 430.
4. Nelson, in Brown, *Modern British Dramatists*, p. 149.
5. Martin Esslin, *Pinter: The Playwright*, 4th edn (London, 1984) p. 160.
6. Quoted from Enoch Brater, 'Pinter's *Homecoming* on Celluloid', *Modern Drama*, xvii, no. 4 (1974) 443.
7. Jacoba Maria Bordewijk-Knotter, *Pinter Appeal: A Comparative Study of Responses to 'The Homecoming'* (Amsterdam, 1988) p. 255.
8. Peter Hall in John Lahr (ed.), *A Casebook on Harold Pinter's 'The Homecoming'* (New York, 1971) p. 20.
9. Bordewijk-Knotter, *Pinter Appeal*, p. 229.
10. Cf. C. Carpenter, '"Victims of Duty?": The Critics, Absurdity and *The Homecoming*', *Modern Drama*, xxv, no. 10 (1982) 489–95.
11. Bordewijk-Knotter, *Pinter Appeal* pp. 228–9.
12. Lahr, *Casebook*, p. 10.
13. Katherine Burkman, *The Dramatic World of Harold Pinter: Its Basis in Ritual* (Columbus, Ohio, 1971) p. 109.
14. Austin E. Quigley, *The Pinter Problem* (Princeton, NJ, 1975) p. 189.
15. Lahr, *Casebook*, p. 12.
16. Ibid., pp. 32–3.
17. Brater, in *Modern Drama*, xvii, no. 4, p. 444.
18. Jac Heijer, in *NRC Handelsblad*, 17 Sep 1984.
19. Ruud Gortzak, in *De Volkskrant*, 17 Sep 1984.
20. Willem van Toorn, in *Vrij Nederland*, 6 Oct 1984.
21. Lahr, *Casebook*, pp. 31–2.
22. Ibid., p. 11.
23. Quigley, *The Pinter Problem*, p. 179.
24. Esslin, *Pinter: The Playwright*, p. 264.
25. *Vrij Nederland*, 6 Oct 1984. Quoted from Bordewijk-Knotter, *Pinter Appeal*, p. 236.
26. Osherow, in *Modern Drama*, xvii, no. 4, p. 426.
27. Lahr, *Casebook*, p. 12.
28. Quigley, *The Pinter Problem*, p. 225.
29. Hornby, *Script into Performance*, p. 185.
30. Quigley, *The Pinter Problem*, p. 224.

Chapter 6   Medium and Vision

1. Cf. Szondi, *Theorie des modernen Dramas*, p. 96.
2. Chatman, *Story and Discourse*, p. 159.
3. Ibid., p. 160.
4. Rudolf Arnheim, *Film as Art*, 9th edn (Berkeley, Calif., 1974) p. 216.
5. Quoted from Clas Zilliacus, *Beckett and Broadcasting: A Study of the Works of Samuel Beckett for and in Radio and Television* (Åbo, 1976) p. 3.
6. Bazin, *What is Cinema?*, I, 123.

Productions

Macbeth

STAGE

12 March 1948, Göteborgs stadsteater. Translators: Carl August Hagberg and Per Hallström. Director Ingmar Bergman, designer Carl Johan Ström, music by Roman Maciejewski. *Macbeth* Anders Ek, *Lady Macbeth* Karin Kavli.

9 September 1976, Royal Shakespeare Company, The Other Place, Stratford. Director Trevor Nunn, designer John Napier. *Macbeth* Ian McKellen, *Lady Macbeth* Judi Dench.

TELEVISION

4 January 1979, Thames Television, London. Director Trevor Nunn, TV designer Mike Hall, TV director Philip Casson. Cast as for 1976 production.

5 November 1982, BBC2. Director Jack Gold, designer Gerry Scott, music by Carl Davis. *Macbeth* Nicol Williamson, *Lady Macbeth* Jane Lapotaire, *Banquo* Ian Hogg, *Ross* Gavin Granger.

FILM

1948, Republic Studios, Hollywood, USA. Screenplay by Orson Welles, director Orson Welles. *Macbeth* Orson Welles, *Lady Macbeth* Jeanette Nolan.

1972, Playboy Productions. Screenplay by Roman Polanski and Kenneth Tynan, director Roman Polanski. *Macbeth* Jon Finch, *Lady Macbeth* Francesca Annis, *Banquo* Martin Shaw, *Ross* John Stride.

Et Dukkehjem/*A Doll's House*
STAGE

30 April 1981, Residenztheater, Munich [title: *Nora*]. Translator Heinz Gimmler, director Ingmar Bergman, designer Gunilla Palmstierna-Weiss, music by Rudolf G. Knabl. *Torvald Helmer* Robert Atzorn, *Nora* Rita Russek.

14 October 1985, Göteborgs stadsteater. Translator Ernst Schönaich, director Anu Saari, designer Elisabeth Åström, music by Rainer Böhm. *Torvald Helmer* Jan Koldenius, *Nora* Mariann Rudberg.

RADIO

14 December 1944, Sveriges Radio. Translator Ernst Schönaich, adapter-director Ernst Eklund. *Torvald Helmer* Björn Berglund, *Nora* Alice Eklund.

4 December 1947, Sveriges Radio. Translator Ernst Schönaich, adapter Gunnar Ollén, director Alf Sjöberg. *Torvald Helmer* Ulf Palme, *Nora* Inga Tidblad.

29 January 1953, Sveriges Radio. Translator Ernst Schönaich, adapter-director Lars-Levi Læstadius. *Torvald Helmer* Nils Fritz, *Nora* Gertrud Fridh.

12 and 19 January 1986, Televisie en Radio Omroep Stichting (TROS), the Netherlands. Translator–adapter Nelly Nagel, director Bert Dijkstra, music by Piet Daalhuisen. *Torvald Helmer* Paul van der Lek, *Nora* Teuntje de Klerk.

TELEVISION

21 December 1958, Sveriges TV. Translator Herbert Grevenius, director Åke Falck. *Torvald Helmer* Herman Ahlsell, *Nora* Gun Arvidsson.

27 December 1970, Sveriges TV. Translator–director–adapter Per Sjöstrand, designer Bibi Lindström. *Torvald Helmer* Olof Bergström, *Nora* Solveig Ternström.

3 February 1974, Saarländisches Rundfunk, West German TV [title: *Nora Helmer*]. Translator Bernhard Schulze, director–adapter Rainer Werner Fassbinder. *Torvald Helmer* Joachim Hansen, *Nora* Margit Carstensen.

19 April 1975, Norsk Rikskringkasting. Director Arild Brinckman, designer Christian Egemar. *Torvald Helmer* Knut Risan, *Nora* Lise Fjeldstad.

FILM

1973, Elkins Productions and Freeward Films, England [Eastmancolor, wide screen]. Screenplay by Christopher Hampton, director Patrick Garland. *Torvald Helmer* Anthony Hopkins, *Nora* Claire Bloom.

1973, World Film Services, England, and Les Films la Boétie, France [Eastmancolor, wide screen]. Translator Michael Meyer, screenplay by David Mercer, director Joseph Losey. *Torvald Helmer* David Warner, *Nora* Jane Fonda.

Spöksonaten/The Ghost Sonata

STAGE

13 January 1973, Dramaten, Stockholm. Director Ingmar Bergman, designer Marik Vos, music by Daniel Bell. *Old Man* Toivo Pawlo, *Student* Mathias Henrikson, *Mummy* Gertrud Fridh, *Young Lady* Gertrud Fridh, *Milkmaid* Kari Sylwan.

RADIO

6 May 1962, Sveriges Radio. Director–adapter Per Verner-Carlsson, music by Bengt Hambræus. *Old Man* Allan Edwall, *Student* Lars Lind, *Mummy* Margareta Krook, *Young Lady* Christina Schollin.

TELEVISION

30 October 1972, Sveriges TV2. Director Johan Bergenstråhle, designer Bo Lindgren, music by Kåre Kollberg. *Old Man* Allan Edwall, *Student* Stefan Ekman, *Mummy* Ulla Sjöblom, *Young Lady* Marie Göranzon, *Milkmaid* Lilian Johansson.

23 March 1980, BBC. Translator Michael Meyer, director Philip Saville, designer Barrie Dobbins, music by Peter Howell. *Old Man* Donald Pleasance, *Mummy* Lily Kedrova, *Student* Clive Arrindell, *Young Lady* Nina Zuckerman, *Milkmaid* Debbie Linden.

The Homecoming

STAGE

3 June 1965, Royal Shakespeare Company, Aldwych Theatre, London. Director Peter Hall, designer John Bury. *Max* Paul Rogers, *Lenny* Ian Holm, *Sam* John Normington, *Joey* Terence Rigby, *Teddy* Michael Bryant, *Ruth* Vivien Merchant.

15 September 1984, Appeltheater, Scheveningen [title: *De thuiskomst*]. Translator Walter Kous, director Erik Vos, designer Caroline Elliott. *Max* Peter van de Linden, *Lenny* Aus Greidanus, *Sam* Willem Wagter, *Joey* Rein Edzard, *Teddy* Robert Prager, *Ruth* Trudy Labij.

TELEVISION

29 March 1972, Sveriges Radio/TV, Malmö [title: *Hemkomsten*]. Translator Olof Jonason, director Håkan Ersgård, designer Lennart Olofsson-Leo. *Max* Georg Rydeberg, *Lenny* Stig Törnblom, *Sam* Roland Söderberg, *Joey* Tomas von Brömssen, *Teddy* Bo Brundin, *Ruth* Yvonne Ingdahl.

FILM

1973, England. Screenplay by Harold Pinter, director Peter Hall. *Max* Paul Rogers, *Lenny* Ian Holm, *Sam* Cyril Cusack, *Joey* Terence Rigby, *Teddy* Michael Jayston, *Ruth* Vivien Merchant.

Bibliography

General

Arnheim, Rudolf, *Film as Art*, 9th edn (Berkeley, Calif., 1974).
Ash, William, *The Way to Write Radio Drama* (London, 1985).
Bazin, André, *What is Cinema?*, tr. Hugh Gray, 2 vols (Berkeley, Calif., 1967).
Bentley, Eric, *The Life of the Drama* (London, 1965).
Bordwell, David, and Thompson, Kristin, *Film Art: An Introduction*, 2nd edn (New York, 1986).
Brandt, George W. (ed.), *British Television Drama* (Cambridge, 1981).
Bussell, Jan, *The Art of Television* (London, 1952).
Chatman, Seymour, *Story and Discourse: Narrative Structure in Fiction and Film* (Ithaca, NY, 1978).
Eisenstein, Sergei, *Film Form* and *The Film Sense*, ed. and tr. Jay Leyda (New York, 1957).
Elam Keir, *The Semiotics of Theatre and Drama* (London, 1980).
Elghazali, S. A., *Literatur als Fernsehspiel* (Hamburg, 1966).
Erenstein, Robert L. (ed.), *Theatre and Television* (Amsterdam, 1988).
Esslin, Martin, *Mediations: Essays on Brecht, Beckett and the Media* (London, 1980).
Fischer-Lichte, Erika, *Semiotik des Theaters*, 3 vols (Tübingen, 1983).
Fiske, John, and Hartley, John, *Reading Television* (London, 1978).
Hallingberg, Gunnar, *Radio och TV-dramatik* (Lund, 1973).
Hilton, Julian, *Performance* (London, 1987).
Hogendoorn, Wiebe, *Lezen en zien spelen: een studie over simultaneïteit in het drama*, with a summary in French (Leiden, 1976).
Hornby, Richard, *Script into Performance: A Structuralist View of Play Production* (Austin, Tex., 1977).
Horton, Andrew S., and Magretta, Joan (eds), *Modern European Filmmakers and the Art of Adaptation* (New York, 1981).
Ingarden, Roman, *Das literarische Kunstwerk*, 2nd edn (Tübingen, 1960).
Jensen, Th. Borup, *Roman og drama bli'r til film* (Copenhagen, 1975).
McLuhan, Marshall, *The Medium is the Message* (London, 1967).
Pavis, Patrice, *Languages of the Stage: Essays in the Semiology of the Theatre*, tr. Susan Melrose *et al.* (New York, 1982).
Pfister, Manfred, *Das Drama* (Munich, 1977), tr. John Halliday as *The*

Theory and Analysis of Drama (Cambridge, 1988).

Reynolds, Peter, *Drama: Text into Performance* (Harmondsworth, 1986).

Schneider, Irmela (ed.), *Dramaturgie des Fernsehspiels* (Munich, 1980).

Strindberg, August, *Letters to the Intimate Theatre*, tr. Walter Johnson (London, 1967).

Szondi, Peter, *Theorie des modernen Dramas (1880–1950)*, 7th edn (Frankfurt, 1970), tr. Michael Hays as *Theory of the Modern Drama* (Cambridge, 1987).

Ubersfeld, Anne, *Lire le théâtre*, 4th edn (Paris, 1977).

Waldmann, Werner, and Rose, *Einführung in die Analyse von Fernsehspielen* (Tübingen, 1980).

Wells, Stanley, *Literature as Drama* (London, 1970).

Zilliacus, Clas, *Beckett and Broadcasting: A Study of the Works of Samuel Beckett for and in Radio and Television* (Åbo, 1976).

Zuber, O. (ed.), *The Languages of Theatre: Problems in the Translation and Transposition of Drama* (Oxford, 1980).

Macbeth

Shakespeare, William, *Macbeth*, Arden edn, ed. Kenneth Muir (London, 1986).

Bradley, A. C., *Shakespearean Tragedy*, 2nd edn (London, 1963).

Brown, John Russell (ed.), *Focus on 'Macbeth'* (London, 1982).

Clemen, Wolfgang, *The Development of Shakespeare's Imagery* (Cambridge, Mass., 1951).

Fridén, Ann, *'Macbeth' in the Swedish Theatre 1838–1986* (Malmö, 1986).

Jorgens, Jack J., *Shakespeare on Film* (Bloomington, Ind., 1977).

Manvell, Roger, *Shakespeare and the Film* (London, 1971).

Mullin, Michael, 'Stage and Screen: the Trevor Nunn *Macbeth*', in Robert L. Erenstein (ed.), *Theatre and Television* (Amsterdam, 1988).

Nagler, A. M., *Shakespeare's Stage* (New Haven, Conn., 1958).

Rosenberg, Marvin, *The Masks of Macbeth* (Berkeley, Calif., 1978).

Williams, Gordon, *'Macbeth': Text and Performance* (London, 1985).

Et Dukkehjem/A Doll's House

Ibsen, Henrik, *Et Dukkehjem*, in *Samlede Verker*, Hundreårsutgave, ed. Francis Bull *et al.*, vɪɪɪ (Oslo, 1933).

——, *A Doll's House*, tr. James W. McFarlane, in *The Oxford Ibsen*, v (London, 1961).

——, *A Doll House*, in *The Complete Major Prose Plays*, tr. Rolf Fjelde (New York, 1965).

——, *A Doll's House*, in *Plays: Two*, tr. Michael Meyer (London, 1965).

——, *A Doll's House*, in *A Doll's House and Other Plays*, tr. Peter Watts (Harmondsworth, 1965).

Haugen, Einar, *Ibsen's Drama: Author to Audience* (Minneapolis, 1979).
Hirsch, Foster, *Joseph Losey* (Boston, Mass., 1980).
Marker, Frederick J. and Lise-Lone, *Ingmar Bergman: A Project for the Theatre* (New York, 1983).
Meyer, Michael, *Ibsen: A Biography* (London, 1971).
Northam, John, *Ibsen's Dramatic Method* (London, 1953).
Quigley, Austin E., *The Modern Stage and Other Worlds* (New York, 1985).
Styan, J. L., 'The Opening Moments of *A Doll House*: For Performance and Analysis in Class', in Yvonne Shafer (ed.), *Approaches to Teaching Ibsen's 'A Doll House'* (New York, 1985).
Thomsen, C. Braad, '*Et Dukkehjem*. R. W. Fassbinder: Nora Helmer', in Ulla Strømberg and Jytte Wiingaard (eds), *Den levende Ibsen: analyser af udvalgte Ibsen-forestillinger 1973–78* (Copenhagen, 1978).

Spöksonaten/The Ghost Sonata

Strindberg, August, *Spöksonaten*, in *Samlade Skrifter*, XLV, ed. John Landquist (Stockholm, 1917).
——, *The Ghost Sonata*, in *Easter and Other Plays*, tr. Erik Palmstierna and James Bernard Fagan (London, 1929).
——, *The Ghost Sonata*, in *Six Plays of Strindberg*, tr. Elizabeth Sprigge (New York, 1955).
——, *The Ghost Sonata*, in *The Chamber Plays*, trans. Evert Sprinchorn *et al.* (New York, 1962).
——, *The Ghost Sonata*, in *Plays: One* tr. Michael Meyer (London, 1964).
——, *The Ghost Sonata*, in *Eight Expressionist Plays*, tr. Arvid Paulson (New York, 1965).
——, *The Ghost Sonata*, tr. Carl Richard Mueller (San Francisco, 1966).
——, *The Ghost Sonata*, in *A Dream Play and Four Chamber Plays*, tr. Walter Johnson (Seattle, 1973).
——, *The Ghost Sonata*, in *Five Plays*, tr. Harry Carlson (Berkeley, Calif., 1981).

Bryant-Bertail, Sarah, 'The Tower of Babel: Space and Movement in *The Ghost Sonata*', in Göran Stockenström (ed.), *Strindberg's Dramaturgy* (Minneapolis, 1988).
Falck, August, *Fem år med Strindberg* (Stockholm, 1935).
Marker, Lise-Lone and Frederick, J., *Ingmar Bergman: Four Decades in the Theater* (Cambridge, 1982).
Northam, John, 'Strindberg's *Spook Sonata*', in Carl Reinhold Smedmark (ed.), *Essays on Strindberg* (Stockholm, 1966).
Rokem, Freddie, *Theatrical Space in Ibsen, Chekhov and Strindberg: Public Forms of Privacy* (Ann Arbor, Mich., 1986).
Törnqvist, Egil, 'Ingmar Bergman Directs Strindberg's *Ghost Sonata*', *Theatre Quarterly*, III, no. 2, 1973.
——, *Bergman och Strindberg: 'Spöksonaten' – drama och iscensättning*.

Dramaten 1973 (Stockholm, 1973).
——, *Strindbergian Drama: Themes and Structure* (Stockholm, 1982).
Törnqvist, Egil, and Jacobs, Barry, *Strindberg's 'Miss Julie': A Play and its Transpositions* (Norwich, 1988).

The Homecoming

Pinter, Harold, *The Homecoming* (London, 1965).

Brater, Enoch, 'Pinter's *Homecoming* on Celluloid', *Modern Drama*, xvii, no. 4 (1974).
Brown, John Russell, *Theatre Language: A Study of Arden, Osborne, Pinter and Wesker* (London, 1972).
Bordewijk-Knotter, Jacoba Maria, *Pinter Appeal: A Comparative Study of Responses to 'The Homecoming'* (Amsterdam, 1988).
Burkman, Katherine, *The Dramatic World of Harold Pinter: Its Basis in Ritual* (Columbus, Ohio, 1971).
Carpenter, C., ' "Victims of Duty?": The Critics, Absurdity and *The Homecoming*', *Modern Drama*, xxv, no. 10 (1982).
Esslin, Martin, *Pinter: The Playwright*, 4th edn (London, 1984).
Hollis, James R., *Harold Pinter: The Poetics of Silence* (Carbondale, Ill., 1970).
Jiji, Vera M., 'Pinter's Four-Dimensional House: *The Homecoming*', *Modern Drama*, xvii, no. 4 (1974).
Lahr, John (ed.), *A Casebook on Harold Pinter's 'The Homecoming'* (New York, 1971).
Nelson, Hugh, '*The Homecoming*: Kith and Kin', in John Russell Brown (ed.), *Modern British Dramatists* (Englewood Cliffs, NJ, 1968).
Osherow, Anita R., 'Mother and Whore: The Role of Woman in *The Homecoming*', *Modern Drama*, xvii, no. 4 (1974).
Quigley, Austin E., *The Pinter Problem* (Princeton, NJ, 1975).

Index